How

XML

Titles by John Shelley

Other Titles of Interest

How to use XML

by

John Shelley

BERNARD BABANI (publishing) LTD
THE GRAMPIANS
SHEPHERDS BUSH ROAD
LONDON W6 7NF
ENGLAND

www.babanibooks.com

PLEASE NOTE

Although every care has been taken with the production of this book to ensure that any projects, designs, modifications and/or programs, etc., contained herewith, operate in a correct and safe manner and also that any components specified are normally available in Great Britain, the Publishers and Author(s) do not accept responsibility in any way for the failure (including fault in design) of any project, design, modification or program to work correctly or to cause damage to any equipment that it may be connected to or used in conjunction with, or in respect of any other damage or injury that may be so caused, nor do the Publishers accept responsibility in any way for the failure to obtain specified components.

Notice is also given that if equipment that is still under warranty is modified in any way or used or connected with home-built equipment then that warranty may be void.

© 2002 BERNARD BABANI (publishing) LTD

First Published – November 2002

British Library Cataloguing in Publication Data

A catalogue record for this book is available from the British Library

ISBN 0 85934 532 7

Cover Design by Gregor Arthur
Printed and Bound in Great Britain by Cox and Wyman Ltd

Preface

The Internet has proved successful, at least to those using it to provide information. It is a fast, efficient and world-wide means for transmitting e-mails, newsgroup discussions and web pages. Commercial activities have not fared so well. If it is such a fast and efficient way of sending and receiving information, why not send data over the Internet?

The problem with data is that it has to be created by proprietary programs, such as Excel for spreadsheets, Word for text documents, Photoshop for improving images. These programs are seldom set up to handle data created in other application programs.

Now, imagine that data, any sort of data - music, videos, text documents, spreadsheet data, could be prepared in a standard and common format such that *any* program could open the data and display it, incorporate it into a company database, or whatever. That is the promise of XML. It allows data of any kind to be structured in a simple way and in a common format. Any program which can read an XML structured file will be able to handle its data with ease.

Are there such programs? Internet Explorer 5 (IE5) is already XML compliant. Many of our common application programs are being made XML compliant. True, in some cases, special programs have to be written in order to manipulate the XML document data for tailor-made applications. But such programs can be written more quickly and efficiently if the data has been structured in a simple and clear format. Whereas, programs written to manipulate data formatted according to proprietary applications are much more difficult to write.

Today, there are many programs in existence which XML authors have access to which can handle their XML documents and, therefore, without the need to write their own special programs.

XML documents can easily be displayed by web browsers and formatted according to the cascading style sheet (CSS) language or XSL, the Extensible Stylesheet Language. This language is capable of selecting just those parts of an XML document which are relevant to some particular instance.

Many larger organisations have already converted their old data into an XML format. In time, many organisations will create their data in nothing other than XML.

So XML is here. One of its main objectives is to enable data to be structured in a simple way for transmission over the Internet, and for any program to be able to open and read the data with ease. Soon, many of our everyday application programs will be XML compliant.

In this book, we examine how to create XML documents. That is the simple part. But is the data typed into an XML document correct? Has the typist made some silly typing error? That has always been a problem, but now an XML document can have its data checked for validity before being entered into a database. This is done in one of two ways, by document type definitions (DTDs) or by the much more rigorous methods employed by XML Schemas.

XML, DTDs and XML Schemas are examined in detail in this book.

I would like to thank Roger Costello for his material on XML Schemas. His site can be found in Appendix A.

All examples have been validated using XML Spy.

About the Author

John Shelley took his Masters degree in Computing at Imperial College, London, where he has worked as a lecturer in the Centre for Computing Services for some thirty years.

He has written over a dozen other books on computing. He hopes this text will prove useful to those who want to learn XML at a human level.

Trademarks

Microsoft, MS-DOS, Microsoft Windows, Internet Assistant, Internet Explorer, FrontPage, Outlook, Word are registered trademarks of Microsoft Corporation.

Unix is a registered trademark of AT&T.

The World Wide Web Consortium (W3C) is responsible for creating Web standards.

References to the various URLs on the Internet are acknowledged here.

All other trademarks are the registered and legally protected trademarks of the companies who make the products. There is no intent to use the trademarks generically and readers should investigate ownership of a trademark before using it for any purpose.

Contents

x

ONE

Why XML?

What is XML?
XML stands for Extensible Mark-up Language. Essentially, XML was devised to allow for the transmission of information of all kinds in a common and standard format over the Internet.

Information
We have always needed information. Today, we have graphs (tabular columns of data), memos, letters, images, music, sound, TV, films, books, brochures, magazines, news programmes, documentaries, newspapers, web pages, etc.

Computers can display text, e-mails, text messages, images, sound (spoken and music), graphs, web pages.

Problem
With computer data (information, if you prefer), we require a separate program for each type of media we create. A word processor, such as Word, is used for creating text files. Excel is used for creating spreadsheets. Although it is possible, we would not use Excel to open a Word document and vice versa.

The Lotus spreadsheet program cannot really display a spreadsheet created in Excel. Only web browsers can display HTML web pages. Indeed, early versions of

1: Why XML?

browsers cannot fully display web pages containing cascading style sheets (CSS). Only the later versions were designed to recognise CSS. Browsers can only display images saved in one of three image formats (.jpg, .gif or .png). They cannot display .pcx or .tiff images. You can think of more examples.

Generally speaking, when information of whatever kind is created, it is only the program application which was used to create it which can open and display that file of information correctly. In short, we cannot easily share information between different program applications. That is why we have to *attach* spreadsheets, images or music files to e-mail messages and then the recipient of those e-mails needs to have the appropriate program (and version) in order to open such attachments.

Would it not be nice if a standard data format could be agreed upon to share and display information regardless of its kind and regardless of what application program we choose to use? Well, that is precisely what XML attempts to do and why it was introduced. XML allows information of all kinds to be shared, or as the reference books prefer to say: *XML allows for a common, standard data interchange format.*

Data Transmission
Over the millennia, mankind has displayed and transmitted information in a variety of ways: speech, on stone, papyrus, paper, smoke signals, flags, telegraph, telephone, celluloid, computers and more recently via local area computer networks (LANs) which eventually led to the Internet.

The Internet is used to transmit e-mails and web pages. Web pages are created using HTML, the hypertext mark-up language. However, it was not designed to cope with multi-media nor with the many newer devices for accessing the Internet, such as palm-top computers, TV set-top boxes, talking car phones, mobile phones, etc. With the increasing demand for transmitting data over the Internet, a new web language is required. XML has helped us here via XHTML, the new web language. But it is also a means for sharing data. In this text, we concentrate on how XML helps us to share data in a common, standard format.

Where XML came from
In the late 1960s, IBM used computers to manage their technical documentation. They developed a language for this purpose called a General Mark-up Language (GML). To cut a long story short[1], it was adopted and adapted by the International Organization for Standardization, ISO 8879: *Information processing -- Text and office systems -- Standard Generalized Mark-up Language (SGML)*, ([Geneva]: ISO, 1986).

SGML is a language for creating other, specialised languages and is technically called a *meta-language*. For example, it was used to create TEI – the Text Encoding Initiative:

"Initially launched in 1987, the TEI is an international and interdisciplinary standard that helps libraries, museums, publishers, and individual scholars represent all kinds of literary and linguistic texts for online research and teaching, using an encoding scheme that is maximally expressive and minimally obsolescent."

SGML was also used to create the HTML web language. What has this to do with XML? If we return to the need for sharing information, it was decided that a new language

---

[1] See Appendix A for a reference to a longer discussion.

1: Why XML?

should be created in order to allow data to be shared. Although SGML is a perfect vehicle for creating new languages, it is also the mother of all complexity. So it was decided to create a new but simplified version of SGML, namely XML. Consequently, XML is a descendent of SGML with 80% of its functionality but with only 20% of its complexity, making it an ideal language for the Internet.

Like SGML, XML is also a meta language, that is a language which is used to create other languages. SGML spawned many new and specialised languages and so does XML. One of the new XML languages is XHTML which has been developed to replace HTML. XHTML is a specialised language for creating web pages but is based on XML, unlike HTML which was based on SGML. Fortunately, many of the elements used in HTML are included in XHTML.

We are not going to be concerned about creating web pages using XHTML[2], but as we progress through the text, we shall encounter some of the other languages created using XML and of which we shall need to be aware. For the moment, we only need to know that XML is really a simplified version of SGML and as such is used to create other languages.

An XML document

In order to understand just what is meant by sharing information via XML, let us take this simple example. We need to stock a new library with books for the 3rd form. We intend to ask teachers, school governors and members of the Parents/Teachers Association to nominate one book each (our funds are limited). Shakespeare and the Bible are to be included by default.

---

[2] See: XHTML & CSS explained, by John Shelley, Babani books.

When creating an XML file, the first and perhaps the most important part is to make a list of all the details required. Thus, we would need at least the following five pieces of information:

the name of the nominee
the book title
the author's name
the ISBN - if known, it will aid the ordering process, otherwise to be left blank
the cost - if known, otherwise to be left blank

At a later stage, we would compile the complete list into a database. But, initially, we simply want to gather all the information in an XML format and will use the following structure to get all the pertinent data from each person in the group.

```
<NOMINEE>Enter your name </NOMINEE>
<TITLE>Enter title of book </TITLE>
<AUTHOR>Enter the name of the author</AUTHOR>
<ISBN>if known, otherwise delete this text
and leave blank </ISBN>
<COST>if known, otherwise delete this text
and leave blank</COST>
```

Note how our five pieces of data look like HTML elements. There is a starting tag enclosed in angle brackets, e.g.: `<NOMINEE>`
This is followed by text, here the name of the Nominee.
Finally, there is a closing tag: `</NOMINEE>`

Each member of the group could be sent the above via an e-mail. They would type their text between each of the opening and closing tags and simply return the e-mail to the co-ordinator. If they do not know the ISBN and/or the cost, they would delete the contained text to leave it blank, but would not remove the tag names. What could be more simple? The co-ordinator would need to fill in any blank

1: <u>Why XML?</u>

ISBN and cost elements, once the information was found, and simply add each return to the final list.

In the next Chapter, we shall do precisely this and add three more lines to complete our XML document. For the moment, we shall just summarise what we have done and point out some characteristics of an XML document which makes it so useful.

The first thing to note is that our very simple structure is just plain text. Here is one example of what could have been returned:

```
<NOMINEE>Samatha Jones </NOMINEE>
<TITLE>The   Adventures   of   Huckleberry   Finn
</TITLE>
<AUTHOR>Mark Twain</AUTHOR>
<ISBN>0140390-464 </ISBN>
<COST>$5.35</COST>
```

Because it is simple, plain text, it can be sent and returned by e-mail. It could even have been typed into any text editor or word processor and saved as a text file. It can be read by any text editor such as Notepad or opened in any word processor. In other words, no special application program is required when we create an XML file or by anyone wanting to read it. That was a conscious decision made by the developers of XML. Anyone can *create* an XML document without requiring any proprietary program. Anyone can *read* an XML document without the need for any special program. Think about that. It is one of the reasons which make XML so appealing and attractive.

Because it is a simple text file, it is comparatively small in file size and it can travel over the Internet quickly.

Of course, few of us would like to read the raw XML format as it stands. But by using cascading style sheets, CSS, we could display the document more attractively and 'remove' the tags. Just for the moment we need to concentrate on how to create a simple XML document.

Another point of interest, is that we made up our own tag names so that they described what was contained within them. XML was designed so that tag names could be 'invented' by the author to describe the data. That is something new. In HTML, tag names are used to format text. So we have an <H1>Heading</H1> element, but it does not describe what the heading is. It could be a chapter title, the name of a book, the name of a person.

XML does not format its text, it simply describes what the text represents. We have to use other languages in order to format our text, such as CSS or XSL, the Extensible Stylesheet Language. But, we are going too quickly.

Let us note that an XML file looks like a database. It has column headings or field names and the content is the actual data:

Nominee	Title	Author	ISBN	Cost
Samatha Jones	The Adventures of Huckleberry Finn	Mark Twain	0140390-464	$5.35
Henry Smith	Silas Marner	George Eliot		

We began by saying that XML was developed in response to the need to share information more easily. We extended this to mean that XML provides for a common, standard data interchange format. Finally, we can extend this even further and say that XML allows for data to be structured. XML is a set of rules (we shall meet them in the next Chapter) for designing structured data.

1: Why XML?

In my example, you may not have liked my tag names and you may have thought of other pieces of information which could have been included, such as the publisher, whether the book is a hard-back or soft-back. Well, the beauty of XML is that you could include all your own tag names when you were making a list of the details *you* want.

Just one final point. We said that XML is used to create other languages. Is the XML document we created earlier XML or a separate language? We shall leave the answer until the next Chapter. But you might like to think about it now.

Summary

XML is a simplified version of SGML

XML describes its data, unlike HTML

XML shows the structure of its data

XML is pure text so that no special program is required to create or read an XML document

We can create our own tag names, the reason why it was called an extensible mark-up language

XML files are comparatively small in size and can travel over the Internet quickly

In the worst case, anyone can open an XML document and work out what it is all about by reading the descriptive tag names

XML looks a bit like HTML

Test 1:

1. Where did XML come from?
2. Which language was used to create HTML?
3. Which language was used to create XHTML?
4. What does the term eXtensible mean in XML?
5. When creating an XML document, what is the first thing you need to consider?

TWO

Creating a Well-formed XML Document

Fortunately, the rules or syntax for creating XML documents are simple. In fact there is only one, that it must be *well-formed*. So let us see what this involves.

Well-formed
In a well-formed XML document:

there must be a *root element*
all tags must be *closed*
case is significant
elements must be properly *nested*
names must be *valid*

We shall look at these now and then turn our individual book records into a complete XML document. But first, the terms *element* and *tag* need further explanation. Consider this example:

`<NOMINEE>Samantha Jones</NOMINEE>`

The entire code is formally called an *element*.

This element consists of:

an *opening* or *start* tag: `<NOMINEE>`
a *closing* or *end* tag: `</NOMINEE>`
a tag *identifier:*   `NOMINEE`

The text between the opening and closing tags is called the *content* or sometimes the *contained text*.

The Root Element
Every XML document must contain what is called a root element, a pair of tags which encases all the other elements in the XML document.

Document or File

We keep calling our XML file a *document*. This is simply because the XML specification states that the content taken in its entirety has to be considered as a document. When the document is saved on to a hard disc, it is, of course, a file and will be saved with an xml extension: `filename.xml`

So, we can call it a file or a document.

We shall make up the name BOOKLIST for our root element.

```
<BOOKLIST>
… entire list of books …
</BOOKLIST>
```

The root element must be unique and can appear only once. It is used to mark the beginning and the end of the complete XML document.

All elements must be closed
If you know HTML, then you will understand what this means. The opening tag has a name enclosed in angle brackets < >. But there must also be a matching closing tag which has a forward slash in front of the tag name and again enclosed in angle brackets.

```
<FORM>   … content … </FORM>
```

We shall see a variation of this later, in Chapter 3.

Case is significant
Unlike HTML, case is significant. If the opening tag name is in uppercase, then the closing tag name *must be* in uppercase, otherwise it will not be recognised. Thus: the following are three completely different names in XML:

```
<NOMINEE>   <nominee>   <Nominee>
```

It is easy, even for experienced XML authors, to muddle up their case. One word of advice is to make a decision at the start of your XML voyage to always use uppercase (or lowercase) or initial-capitals for your tag names. Some people dislike uppercase since it can become difficult to read when long names are used. Others advocate the use of interCapping.

Correct nesting – no overlapping
When using tags, correct nesting is essential. Tags must not overlap. This makes more sense once we have introduced the parent-child concept on page 16 where we shall make the point more forcefully. However, for the moment, we must appreciate that a closing tag of one element cannot overlap the closing tag of another element. For example, this is correct nesting:

```
<AUTHOR>Mark Twain</AUTHOR>
<ISBN>0140390-464 </ISBN>
<COST>$5.35</COST>
```

But this is *incorrect*:

```
<AUTHOR>Mark Twain
<ISBN>0140390-464 </AUTHOR>
<COST>$5.35</ISBN></COST>
```

For those of you who know HTML, the above incorrect nesting of tag names would be tolerated (despite being illegal according to strict HTML). Most browsers would still display the web page. But you cannot get away with it in XML (nor in

2: Well-formed XML

XHTML since the rules of well-formed elements are rigorously enforced).

Rules for creating tag names

Because XML is a standard, it defines how names are to be constructed.

- names must *begin* with a letter or an underscore
- names cannot begin with a digit
- names may have one or more valid characters
- the valid characters are letters a to z or A to Z, period (full stop), underscore, hyphen and digits. (Colons may be used but have a special purpose)
- spaces or tabs are not allowed
- names cannot begin with `xml` (or any case variation of these three letters) since these are reserved for special features of XML which may be implemented in a future version

The following shows valid and invalid names, the angle brackets have been left off:

valid names	invalid names
`_p`	`p name`
`name5`	`5name`
`stock.number`	`stock*number`
`main_book`	`!invoice`
`Para3`	`xmlelement`
`this.is.a.long.name`	`this-is-a-long-name`
`INVOICE`	
`_` (correct but hardly sensible)	

Creating our XML book list document

We are now in a position to create our first complete XML document.

```
<?xml version="1.0" ?>
<BOOKLIST>
<BOOK>
<NOMINEE>Samantha Jones </NOMINEE>
<TITLE>The Adventures of Huckleberry Finn
</TITLE>
<AUTHOR>Mark Twain</AUTHOR>
<ISBN>0140390-464 </ISBN>
<COST>$5.35</COST>
</BOOK>
<BOOK>
<NOMINEE>Henry James </NOMINEE>
<TITLE>Silas Marner </TITLE>
<AUTHOR>George Eliot</AUTHOR>
<ISBN>055321229X </ISBN>
<COST>$3.35</COST>
</BOOK>
<BOOK>
<NOMINEE>G. Brown </NOMINEE>
<TITLE> Nicholas Nickleby </TITLE>
<AUTHOR>Charles Dickens</AUTHOR>
<ISBN>0987632155 </ISBN>
<COST>$5.65</COST>
</BOOK>
</BOOKLIST> <!-- Ex2-1.xml -->
```

Each member of the group, three for the sake of simplicity, has supplied us with their book suggestion. Here is the one sent to us by e-mail, for example, by George Brown:

```
<NOMINEE>G. Brown </NOMINEE>
<TITLE> Nicholas Nickleby </TITLE>
<AUTHOR>Charles Dickens</AUTHOR>
<ISBN>0987632155 </ISBN>
<COST>$5.65</COST>
```

In the above, we have added three extra elements to the raw items sent in by each member of the group in order to turn the items into a complete XML document:

2: Well-formed XML

```
<?xml version="1.0" ?>
<BOOKLIST> ... </BOOKLIST>
<BOOK> ... </BOOK>
```

The XML Declaration

```
<!xml version="1.0" ?>
```

This line appears at the start of the document as the first line. Here we are stating that the document is an XML document and includes a version attribute. At the time of writing, there is only version 1.0. The attribute in the XML declaration takes the following format:

```
attribute-name = "a value"
```

The attribute name must be in *lowercase* followed by an equals symbol and the version number enclosed in quotes, either single or double, but not a mixture.

Two other attributes are frequently used within the XML declaration and these are discussed later on page 32.

Note also the strange `<? ... ?>`.

This is actually part of the SGML syntax. Remember that XML is derived from SGML and sometimes it needs to use some of the SGML syntax.

The Root Element - <BOOKLIST>

All XML documents must have a root element as we discussed earlier. We have chosen the name BOOKLIST in uppercase.

The <BOOK> Element

Somehow or other we need to separate each submission. A simple approach could be to keep each one in a pair of <BOOK> tags so that we can easily see the beginning and end of each submission.

The above additions are all we need to create our complete XML document. We simply need to save it as a text only file and append an `.xml` extension to it. Any program capable of reading a text file would be able to display our document. Try opening it in IE5. It will be displayed just as it stands:

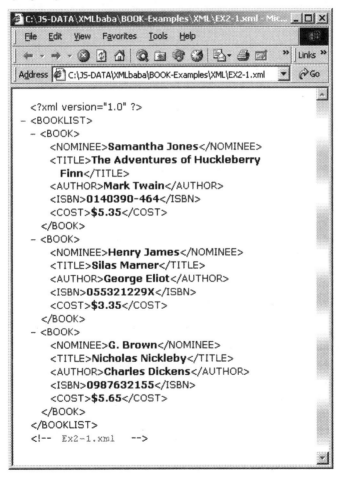

2: Well-formed XML

You will notice that IE5 indents some of the lines and that a minus (hyphen) sign shows against the opening <BOOKLIST> and the <BOOK> tags. If you click the minus sign, the contents are collapsed and it is replaced by a plus sign as shown below. Clicking a plus sign will expand the contents of that tag.

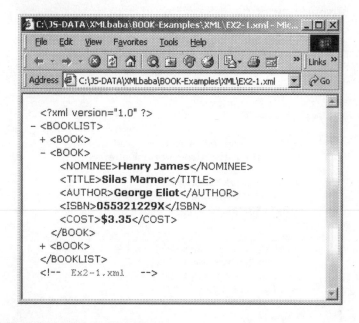

Parent-Child Relationships

In XML, some elements may contain other elements. The *root element* for example contains all the other elements in the XML document. It is known as a *parent* element, although, in the case of the root parent element, it also serves as the container for all the document's elements. IE5 indents all the contained elements to make it easier to see which elements are parents and which are children.

In the above, <BOOK> is also a parent and the elements it contains are all indented. These are known as *child elements*, their parent being the <BOOK> element. One child element could also become a parent and have child elements of its own. We have none in the above example but we shall soon meet some. When an element has no children of its own, there will no plus or minus sign attached. What is so important about that?

Well, we shall need to look at some other features of XML before being able to answer that in detail, but briefly, it helps XML authors to understand the structure of their XML documents. When changes to a document are required, it is vital to appreciate the parent-child structure.

Formatting an XML Document
Our XML document does not look very pretty, but if you know CSS, you could easily get IE5 to present it as follows:

2: Well-formed XML

We do not discuss CSS in detail here (see XHTML and CSS explained, in this Babani Books series). For those who may be interested, here is the style sheet code in CSS.

```
BOOK      {display:block; font-size:12pt;
           color:rgb(102,51,0);}
NOMINEE  {display:block; font-size:18pt;
           color:red;
COST      {display:in-line; font-size:12pt;
           font-family:verdana, sans-serif;}
ISBN      {display:in-line; font-size:12pt;
           font-family:verdana, sans-serif;
           color:rgb(132,12,34);}
TITLE     {display:block;
           font-family:verdana, sans-serif;}
AUTHOR   {display:block;
           font-family:verdana, sans-serif;
           font-size:12pt; font-style:italic;}
HR        {display:block;  margin-top:1em;}
```

There is also XSL which is another style sheet language used to format XML documents. It is more difficult to learn than CSS and is the subject of another book. For the time being, we are simply learning how to create XML documents and to understand the jargon terms being used.

Is it really an XML document or a new Language?
Yes and No. If you recall we said that XML is used to create other languages. So what is our file? Is it XML or a new language? It is actually a new language, it is unique. It is mine, all mine! It was created by me, no one else, using the rules or syntax of XML. The XML authors decide what names to give their elements. This implies that each time XML is used to create such documents, each one is a new language and consequently there are millions of them in existence, rather like using HTML to create a unique

web page. So, it is a new language and it is an XML document since it conforms to the syntax of a well-formed XML document.

Creating & Reading XML documents

To create an XML file you simply require any text editor or word processor, such as Notepad, Word or even `vi` or `emacs` on a Unix system. The only thing to remember is that you must save the file as text only and change the `.txt` to an `.xml` extension.

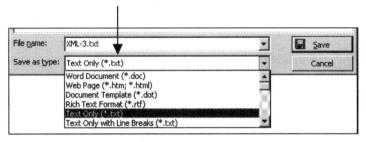

File Extensions

All saved files have an extension after the filename and a period to separate the two: `fred.xml` Here the filename is called `fred` and the extension is `xml` to signify an XML document. The extension lets the operating system know which application was used to create the file in the first place. Thus, if you were to *double-click* a file name in any folder, the operating system knows which application to call up to open it.

Application	File extension
Word	doc
Excel	xls
PowerPoint	ppt

2: Well-formed XML

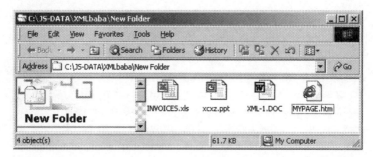

Thus, a file with an `xls` extension would be opened in Excel. A file with an `htm` extension would be opened in your default browser. So what about a file with an `xml` extension?

Any program which can read simple text files can open an XML document. Recall that an XML document is saved as pure text. Thus, any e-mail, word processor, text editor can open and display an XML document. Try it in Excel 2000 if you do not believe me. It would not look very exciting as yet, but perhaps in the future an Xp version of Excel may be able to do something more with it. However, if you double-click an XML file in a folder and you have Internet Explorer 5 on your machine, then IE5 will be the program used by the operating system to open it. That is because, IE5 is XML compliant. In addition to the text, IE5 will add plus and minus signs, as explained on page 16 and will indent children elements.

Summary

We have seen that all XML documents must be well-formed. All XML documents must have a root element which contains all the other elements in the document.

Element names are invented by the XML author, hence the term *extensible* in XML, but the names must follow the rules for creating valid XML names. Such names are formally known as identifiers.

All XML documents must have the XML declaration.

Elements which contain other elements are said to be the parent element and the elements which they contain are known as child elements.

Every time a new XML document is created, it is a new language which is based on the syntax of XML.

All XML documents are saved as text-only files and given an `xml` extension.

Test 2:
1. What purpose does the root element serve in an XML document?

2. How significant is case in XML?

3. Every XML document is a new language. True or false?

4. Parent elements cannot contain grandchildren elements. True or false?

2: <u>Well-formed XML</u>

THREE

Introducing Attributes

Attributes can provide additional information inside an element's opening tag. For example, in our previous document, we had the following:

```
<NOMINEE>Henry James</NOMINEE>
```

But is the person called Henry James or James Henry? We did not specify any order for first and last names; we simply asked the nominees to enter their name and people will always do different things. But, we could have made the issue clearer by adding the following two elements:

```
<NOMINEE>
  <FIRSTNAME>  ... </FIRSTNAME>
  <LASTNAME>   ... </LASTNAME>
</NOMINEE>
```

However, there is a shorter way of doing this by employing *attributes* and asking the nominees to enter their names as *values* of the attributes:

```
<NOMINEE first="Henry" last="James" />
```

The first thing to notice is that we have added two attributes within the element NOMINEE, namely, first and `last`. Again, these names were chosen by the XML author. Each is followed by an equals symbol and, in quotes, a name ("Henry" and "James"). These last two are called the *values* of the two attributes.

When entering attributes, the attribute name (`first` or `last` in the above) is separated from its value by the equals symbol and the value must always be in quotes, either single or double, but never a mixture.

The second thing to notice is that we have a forward-slash before the closing angle bracket. That has nothing to do with attributes. It is simply that the `NOMINEE` element no longer requires any content. The 'content' has been supplied by the attributes' values.

Empty Elements
Some elements which we create may not need to contain any content, in which case they are called *empty* elements. However, the XML syntax requires that all elements must be closed. That is easy for elements which contain content, because the closing tag has a forward-slash inserted before the element name:

`<TITLE>Silas Marner </TITLE>`

Empty tags, however, do not have a closing tag, so the syntax requires that the forward-slash is placed at the end of the single tag and just before its closing bracket.

Another Example
We could add an attribute to the `<BOOK>` element which specifies the `ISBN`[1] and thus avoid using an entire element for the information.

---

[1] All published books must have a unique International Standard Book Number. The ISBN for this book is0 85934 532 7.

```
<BOOK ISBN="1234567890">
  ... etc.
</BOOK>
```

Note that the BOOK element has content (albeit child elements) as well as an attribute.

Revised Booklist using attributes

```
<?xml version="1.0" ?>
<BOOKLIST>
<BOOK ISBN="0140390-464">
<NOMINEE first="Samantha" last="Jones" />
<TITLE>The Adventures of Huckleberry Finn
</TITLE>
<AUTHOR>Mark Twain</AUTHOR>
<COST>$5.35</COST>
</BOOK>
<BOOK ISBN="055321229X">
<NOMINEE first="Henry" last="James" />
<TITLE>Silas Marner </TITLE>
<AUTHOR>George Eliot</AUTHOR>
<COST>$3.35</COST>
</BOOK>
<BOOK ISBN="0987632155">
<NOMINEE first="G" last="Brown" />
<TITLE> Nicholas Nickleby </TITLE>
<AUTHOR>Charles Dickens</AUTHOR>
<COST>$5.65</COST>
</BOOK>
</BOOKLIST>  <!-- Ex3-1.xml -->
```

Rules for Creating Attributes
XML imposes rules for creating attributes.

1. An attribute must take the following form:
```
<element attribute-name="attribute-value">
```

3: **Attributes**

2. The attribute name follows the same conventions as those for creating valid XML element names, as given on page 12.

3. All attributes must take a value enclosed in matching quotes (either double or single).

4. An attribute may appear just once in an element. That is not to say that elements can take only one attribute, they can have many, but each one can appear once.

5. Case is significant in attribute names, thus: first FIRST First would result in three different attribute names.

When to use Attributes

In the following we have not used any attributes at all:

```
<?xml version="1.0" ?>
<BOOKLIST>
 <BOOK>
  <NOMINEE>
   <FIRSTNAME>Samantha</FIRSTNAME>
   <LASTNAME>Jones </LASTNAME>
  </NOMINEE>
  <TITLE>The Adventures of Huckleberry Finn
  </TITLE>
  <AUTHOR>Mark Twain</AUTHOR>
  <ISBN>0140390-464 </ISBN>
  <COST>$5.35</COST>
 </BOOK>
 <BOOK>
  <NOMINEE>
   <FIRSTNAME> Henry </FIRSTNAME>
   <LASTNAME> James </LASTNAME>
  </NOMINEE>
  <TITLE>Silas Marner </TITLE>
  <AUTHOR>George Eliot</AUTHOR>
  <ISBN>055321229X </ISBN>
  <COST>$3.35</COST>
```

```
  </BOOK>
  <BOOK>
   <NOMINEE>
    <FIRSTNAME>G.</FIRSTNAME>
    <LASTNAME>Brown </LASTNAME>
   </NOMINEE>
   <TITLE> Nicholas Nickleby </TITLE>
   <AUTHOR>Charles Dickens</AUTHOR>
   <ISBN>0987632155 </ISBN>
   <COST>$5.65</COST>
  </BOOK>
 </BOOKLIST> <!-- Ex3-2.xml -->
```

Whereas in the following we have:

```
<?xml version="1.0" ?>
<BOOKLIST>
 <BOOK ISBN="0140390-464">
  <NOMINEE FIRST="Samantha" LAST="Jones"/>
  <TITLE>The Adventures of Huckleberry Finn
  </TITLE>
  <AUTHOR>Mark Twain</AUTHOR>
  <COST>$5.35</COST>
 </BOOK>
 <BOOK ISBN="055321229X">
  <NOMINEE FIRST="G" LAST="Brown"/>
  <TITLE>Silas Marner </TITLE>
  <AUTHOR>George Eliot</AUTHOR>
  <COST>$3.35</COST>
 </BOOK>
 <BOOK ISBN="0987632155">
  <NOMINEE FIRST="G" LAST="Brown"/>
  <TITLE> Nicholas Nickleby </TITLE>
  <AUTHOR>Charles Dickens</AUTHOR>
  <COST>$5.65</COST>
 </BOOK>
</BOOKLIST> <!-- Ex3-3.xml -->
```

3: <u>Attributes</u>

Which is 'better'? Both are valid but which one is better will depend upon how you want to use the file. That comes from experience. Here are some things you would have to consider before you begin to construct your XML document.

If the file was just for my own use and I simply wanted to display the books on the Web, then I would go for the first construction because via CSS I could display all the information content of the elements. The second construction would be no good if I wanted the information in the attribute values to be displayed. CSS does not allow the display of attribute values.

In which case, why not create a simple HTML document rather than an XML document? There would be more work for *me* if I wrote my own HTML document. I would have to re-type all the information garnered from the nominees.

By getting others to fill in the element content, each member of the group is doing much of the hard work and, furthermore, I can make sure that just the information I need and in the correct order will be supplied. However, XML documents are seldom created for personal use.

Typically, XML documents are created and interrogated by programs held on servers. These programs may need to search and sort the information and to store the data in databases. Server programmers will create programs to specifically handle our XML documents. In which case, we may be told to use attributes since sorting and searching information can be done by looking at the values of attributes. In our example, a program may need to search for an ISBN for a given book and then to display just its title, author and cost.

A search is not restricted just to attribute values. We could have a ISBN element and search on the *content* of the

ISBN element. However, when documents become more complex, searching on attributes can reduce the amount of programming complexity. But, there are no hard and fast rules. Entering information as an element content or as an attribute value is a matter of personal choice.

The main aim of this book is to explain how to create and validate XML documents. Exactly how those files will be used and interrogated is another matter.

Comments

Comments may be added to your XML documents as follows.

< ! - - here is the comment which can spread over several lines if necessary - - >

All comments begin with < ! - - (no spaces!) and end with - - >

This is pure SGML and is another of the SGML syntax which has been retained in XML. (For those familiar with HTML, the above is how comments are entered into HTML documents, simply because HTML was developed from SGML.)

Summary

We have seen how to add attributes to elements. They comprise an attribute name and a value separated by an equals symbol.

Empty elements must be closed, and because they have no content, they are frequently given attributes.

There are no hard and fast rules about using attributes over elements. It is often a matter of personal choice.

3: __Attributes__

FOUR

Further XML Basics

In this Chapter we shall look at some more of the basics of XML, namely:

- the XML Prolog
- the XML parser
- entities
- parsed character data
- vocabularies versus applications

The XML Prolog
Every XML document can take a document Prolog which consists of two types of declarations:

XML PROLOG

├────── the XML *declaration*

├────── the document type *declaration*

We shall discuss the document type declaration in the next Chapter.

The XML *declaration*
We have discussed this earlier but used just one declaration, namely, the version of XML being used. In fact, there are three possible declarations:

4: Further XML Basics

```
<?xml version="1.0"
     encoding="UTF-8"
     standalone="yes" ?>
```

Notice that everything, apart from UTF, is, and *must be*, in lowercase and that question marks are used at the start and end. Angle brackets are used to enclose the entire declaration. Actually, the above prolog is optional but everyone is encouraged to include it. Although they look like *attribute-value* pairs and the whole thing looks like an *element* they are *declarations* and form part of the SGML syntax.

version: this declaration is always required when the XML declaration is used. It simply specifies which version of XML to use. There is only one at the time of writing but others will emerge. This is one reason for encouraging the use of the declaration in all your XML documents. The values of a declaration must be surrounded by double or single quotes (but not a mixture!).

```
version="1.0" or version='1.0'
```

encoding: this optional declaration specifies which character encoding set to use for your document. By default it will be UTF-8 (Unicode Transformation Format) suitable for most Western languages, but no good for languages such as Chinese, Urdu, Arabic, and so on. These languages require different encoding sets, see the reference section, Appendix A. By changing the value of the encoding declaration, XML provides world-wide access to any known language.

```
encoding="UTF-8"
```

standalone: this declaration may take one of two values: "yes" or "no"

```
standalone="no" or standalone="yes"
```

If the value is *yes*, then it specifies that the document is completely self-contained. If the value is *no*, then some external document is required before the XML document can be used, such as a document type definition (a DTD). The default is "yes".

We have yet to discuss DTDs, so we shall return to this declaration later.

The declarations above are case sensitive and must occur in the order shown. When the XML declaration is used, the version declaration must always be used and must be the first in the list. The other two are optional, but when both are included, they must occur in the order shown below.

You are strongly advised to always include the XML declaration and to provide all three declarations as shown:

```
<?xml version="1.0" encoding="UTF-8"
     standalone="yes" ?>
```

It will then make it easier to change the version number, convert to another language by changing the value of the encoding declaration and to specify whether an external DTD is to be used or not (even if it is available). This will become clearer, once we have discussed the document type declaration in the next Chapter,

The minimum XML declaration is therefore:

```
<?xml version="1.0" ?>
```

and since it is optional the following is a perfectly well-formed XML document, but quite useless:

```
<fred> </fred>
```

4: <u>Further XML Basics</u>

XML Parsers

How does IE5 (but not Netscape 4) read XML documents? It has a built-in program which is capable of reading XML files. It is called a *parser*. When an XML compliant program (that simply means it has the XML parser built in to the program) opens an XML document, it will read the file according to the rules of a well-formed XML document. If the document contains syntax error, the parser *must generate* an error and *not display* the document. This is not like HTML browsers which will frequently tolerate any errors and display the web page as best it can. An example will illustrate what we mean.

An Example

Suppose I want an XML element to contain the following company name.

```
<COMPANY>Dreag & Thols, Solicitors </COMPANY>
```

Well, we cannot because the ampersand (&) would generate an error.

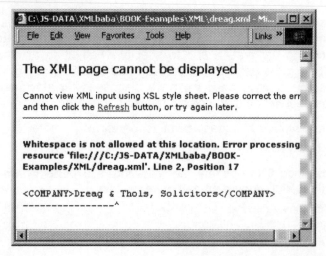

Instead of:

```
<?xml version="1.0" ?>
<COMPANY>Dreag & Thols, Solicitors</COMPANY>
```

Likewise, putting the word *Solicitors* in angle brackets would generate an error. I know it would look silly to have angle brackets around the word *Solicitors* and we would not do so in practice, but we need to know why the symbols < and & cause problems. What is so special about them? They help the parser to read XML documents correctly.

What is a Parser?

Any formal language has a parser. The Concise Oxford Dictionary gives the following meaning for the verb *parse*, (the italics are mine):

> "resolve (sentence *or XML document*) into its components parts and describe them *according to the syntax (grammar) of the language*."

Let us see what a parser would do with the following which has the ampersand removed:

```
<COMPANY>Dreag and Thols, <Solicitors>
</COMPANY>
```

When a document with an xml extension is opened in IE5, the XML browser calls up the XML *parser* to check whether the document is correct, i.e. well-formed. If it meets an error, the parser is bound to report the error to the browser and stop further processing. The browser will display an error message complaining that an end tag does not match a start tag:

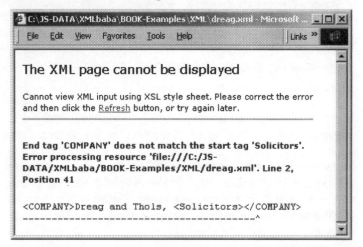

How does it detect such errors? It does so by examining the characters. The parser would meet the < of <COMPANY> and because the next character is not a forward slash (/), the parser assumes that this has to be an opening tag. The < is called a mark-up symbol. So far, so good. It reads the rest of the characters until a > symbol is met. (The combination of />, would indicate an empty element.) The characters between the < and > would form the tag name – COMPANY is our example.

It now expects to find a corresponding closing tag somewhere: </COMPANY>. So it keeps looking for another <, but it meets <Solicitors>. This is actually quite valid, because it could be a child element of <COMPANY>. However, when it now meets the closing </COMPANY> tag the game is up:

> either <Solicitors> is not a child element
> or it could be an incorrectly nested child

or it could be an empty child with the / missing
or it is an invalid use of angle brackets

Any of the four are possible errors and the parser will be forced to generate a message and stop processing the rest of the XML document. It does not know (and could not care less) which error has occurred, so it simply says:

The end tag of `<COMPANY>` does not match start tag of `<Solicitors>` and leave you to work out which error you have committed. Your XML document will not be displayed.

So how can you tell the browser that `<Solicitors>` is actually something you want to have displayed complete with open and closing angle brackets and that it is not an opening tag? You simply use a *character entity*.

Character Entities
HTML authors will be familiar with this term. A character entity tells a parser to display a character and *not attempt* to interpret it as a mark-up symbol. So we need to dress up the `<` and the `>` as character entities so that they will be displayed rather than be taken as mark-up.

A character entity take the following form: `&entity;`

It begins with an ampersand, then has the special name of the character and ends with a semi-colon. The special name for an opening angle bracket is: "`lt`" standing for *less than*, which is the mathematical term for the symbol. The special name for the closing angle bracket is "`gt`" standing for *greater than*. Thus, if we now change our code to:

```
<COMPANY>Dreag and Thols, &lt;Solicitors&gt;
</COMPANY>
```

the parser would be happy to continue with our document and would display the following in IE5:

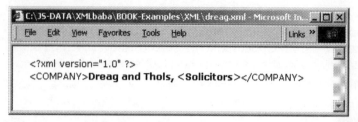

We do not really want the word Solicitors to appear with angle brackets, but we would like to display the ampersand: *Dreag & Thols*.

But we cannot just put in an ampersand, why not? Because the parser would think it was the beginning of a character entity. The text after the ampersand would be taken to refer to a special entity name and, furthermore, it would expect to find a semi-colon somewhere to complete the character entity. The parser would become distraught and throw up an error message.

So, we need to convert the ampersand into a character entity, as follows: `&amp;` where `amp` is the special name for ampersand. Our final code looks like the following, where we have also removed the somewhat ugly angle brackets surrounding Solicitors :

```
<COMPANY>Dreag &amp; Thols,
Solicitors</COMPANY>
```

Now, the ampersand can be displayed by the browser, because we have correctly informed the parser how to interpret and handle the ampersand.

XML has five built-in character entities as shown in the table below. But we must not get too ahead of ourselves because we need to know how to create other character entities, for example, the ½ or ê.

Character Entity	Meaning
&amp;	generates the & - ampersand
&apos;	generates the ' – apostrophe
&gt;	generates the > - greater than
&lt;	generates the < - less than
&quot;	generates the " – double quote

Parsed character data

An XML document contains characters. That is obvious, but some of those characters will represent data and some will be mark-up.

```
<COMPANY>Dreag &amp; Thols,
Solicitors</COMPANY>
```

All text in an XML document, therefore, has to be parsed to find out whether it is pure text or mark-up. (There is one exception to this which we shall meet in the next Chapter.)

There are two characters which will trigger the parser into believing that what follows is mark-up. The < is used to mark the beginning of an opening or closing tag and the & to indicate the beginning of an entity. Other characters help the parser to know when a tag has been closed; a semi-colon to mark the end of an entity; and quotes (either double or single) to mark the start and end of an attribute's value.

4: **Further XML Basics**

As characters are being parsed, these special characters help the parser to identify whether a document is well-formed. Any misuse of these characters will generate an error. This is one reason why XML has its own five built-in entities. We can use those when we need them to appear as part of our real data rather than as mark-up symbols. It is recommended, especially for < > and &, that we use entities when they form part of our data. The / ; and quotes are not so important.

However, when quotes form part of an attribute's value, the other type of quote or entity should be used, thus:

```
<gangster name="Al 'Scarface' Capone">
or
<gangster
      name="Al &apos;Scarface&apos; Capone" >
```

Vocabularies versus Applications

XML has to formalise certain jargon terms in order to ensure that everyone keeps to the same standard. The following are some of the jargon terms we have already met: element, opening tag, well-formed, and so on. Here is another example. Some references call an XML document a *vocabulary*, others call it an *application*. Do they mean the same thing? Well they do. So let us try to explain these terms.

XML is a meta language which means that we can create other languages but we do so by using the XML syntax. Our <BOOKLIST> example could be called our BkListML, standing for our Booklist Markup Language. It is a language which we have created to enable us to create a list of books for the 3rd Year library for their Literature subject. We had to create our own tags:

`<BOOKLIST>` (the root), `<NOMINEE>`, `<AUTHOR>`, `<ISBN>`, etc. These are the words or vocabulary we are using in our `BkListML` language.

They are the tag names we can use. We actually had to invent them because XML does not have any tags. (Well, it does have the xml in the XML declaration, but it is not really a tag name.) That is why XML is called the *Extensible* Markup Language, because we can extend it by creating our own tags provided we follow the rules for well-formed XML documents.

Another way of looking at it is to think of XML as providing the alphabet and the grammar while we create the words. So when we decided to create our `BKListML`, we created our own words which suited our particular application.

In another example, we shall create an Audio CD List Language for which we shall have to make up our own vocabulary. Consequently, we could call our new language a vocabulary. However, the W3C Recommendation uses the word *application* instead or even *document*.

In this text, we prefer to use the term *vocabulary* or *document* rather than application, so that there is no confusion over the more common meaning of *application* such as Word, Excel or PowerPoint.

Other Vocabularies
So far, we have created our own XML documents or vocabularies. There is no reason why someone else could not borrow our BkListML vocabulary or better still buy it. It would save them the effort of having to create their own and somewhat similar vocabulary and they could simply insert the books and other information for their 4th Year library. If they wanted to use our language, they would have to remain faithful to our tag names and attributes.

They could add some elements of their own, but then it would no longer be our language.

Many bodies and organisations often collaborate with others in their field to come up with a suitable vocabulary. Two examples are in the fields of Mathematics and Chemistry.

Chemical Markup Language (CML)

CML is designed to enable Chemists to describe and exchange chemical information. It consists of an agreed vocabulary. The CML site is given in Appendix A. The following is taken from their home page:

> *"CML (Chemical Markup Language) is a new approach to managing molecular information. It has a large scope as it covers disciplines from macromolecular sequences to inorganic molecules and quantum chemistry. CML is new in bringing the power of XML to the management of chemical information. In simple terms it is "HTML for Molecules", but there is a great deal more to it than that. CML and associated tools allows for the conversion of current files without semantic loss into structured documents, including chemical publications, and provides for the precise location of information within files."*

Mathematical Markup Language (MathML)

In the following taken from the W3C's home page for MathML, see Appendix A. Note the use of the term application where some would prefer the term vocabulary.

> *"MathML is cast as an application of XML. As such, with adequate style sheet support, it will ultimately be possible for browsers to natively render mathematical expressions. For the immediate future, several vendors offer applets and plug-ins which can render MathML in place in a browser. Translators and equation editors which can generate HTML pages*

where the math expressions are represented directly in MathML will be available soon."

There are literally hundreds of organisations getting together to define new XML languages or applications. Appendix A gives a number of useful references where you can find out whether some group in your particular field has already started on an XML based language.

The main aim of such groups is to provide a mark-up language which adequately describes the data issues in their field of work. If your field is in dentistry, medicine, in travel, banking, estate agents, publishing, teaching, libraries, manufacturing, etc., there may be some XML language which you could make use of or amend for your own particular requirements.

XML has also been used to create vocabularies for scaleable vector graphics (SVG), multimedia (Synchronized Multimedia Integration Language – SMIL, pronounced 'smile'), as well as the eXtensible HTML (XHTML) language which will replace the old HTML language for the web. These are just a few.

However, before we can go much further we shall need to discuss an important part of many of these vocabularies, namely their document type definition. We look at DTDs in the next chapter. To prepare for that we shall create another document. It will be a simple one which allows us to describe data relating to the contents of audio CDs.

Audio CD example
A good place to begin when creating a new XML document is with a list of what the document should contain. We know that we shall need a root element, so `<CD-list>` may be sensible.

4: Further XML Basics

Each CD will need the following. They have been entered into a table and a meaningful tag name supplied:

Description	Element name
the root name	`<CD-list>`
data for one complete CD	`<CD>`
a title field	`<TITLE>`
name of artist	`<ARTIST>`
track name, (many)	`<TRACK>`
price of CD	`<PRICE>`
internal code number	`<INT-CODE>`

Now we can begin to build up the document for each CD. To keep the file small for this book, we shall have just two CDs and limit the number of tracks to under five.

```
<?xml version="1.0" encoding="UTF-8"
      standalone="yes" ?>
<CD-list>
 <CD>
  <TITLE>Seasons</TITLE>
  <ARTIST>James Galway</ARTIST>
  <TRACK>Over the Sea to Skye </TRACK>
  <TRACK>Suo Gan</TRACK>
  <TRACK>The Rowan Tree</TRACK>
  <PRICE>10.99</PRICE>
  <INTCODE>JG001 </INTCODE>
 </CD>

 <CD>
  <TITLE>Seasons</TITLE>
  <ARTIST>James Galway</ARTIST>
  <TRACK>Over the Sea to Skye </TRACK>
  <TRACK>Suo Gan</TRACK>
  <TRACK>The Rowan Tree</TRACK>
  <TRACK>Suo Gan</TRACK>
  <PRICE>10.99</PRICE>
  <INTCODE>JG001 </INTCODE>
 </CD> </CD-list> <!-- Ex4-1.xml -->
```

You may have other pieces of information you would include, perhaps as attributes. Well, there is no reason why you could not use this as the basis for your own XML document.

Suo Gân

The correct title for the Welsh lullaby is Suo Gân. Now that you know how to create character entities, you can find the ASCII code for 'â' from Appendix B. This will be one of the test exercises below.

Summary

All XML documents should contain a Prolog which consists of an XML declaration and a document type declaration.

XML documents are checked by parsers to ensure that they are well-formed. If not, they must generate an error and stop further processing. IE5 has an XML parser which can check any file with an `xml` extension.

Mark-up symbols inform parsers when to expect elements and attributes. However, the five basic mark-up symbols must be entered as character entities. These must be used when they form part of element content rather than mark-up.

There are five mark-up symbols built into the XML parser as character entities when we need to use them as part of element content.

Each XML document is a new language with its own vocabulary set as determined by the author.

Test 4:

1. How would you enter Suo Gân in an XML document?

2. Can any program open an XML file?

4: **Further XML Basics**

3. What does a parser do?

4. How does a parser recognise a character entity?

5. Why do we need character entities?

6. What two characters must not appear in parsed character data?

7. When an XML document is created, all the element and attribute names are known as a vocabulary. True or False?

Document Type Definition - DTD

In this Chapter we shall look at:

- what are DTDs and why they are needed
- the difference between well-formed and valid XML documents
- how to define element declarations in a DTD containing only other elements or only text
- the use of the plus occurrence symbol
- #PCDATA
- how to create internal and external DTDs

In the previous chapter, we created a CD List document, `EX4-1.xml`. But now, we may want others to add to our list. For example, one person could be responsible for all the melody CDs, someone else for the classics, another person for the jazz CDs and so on. We want to delegate the labour. There is no reason why this cannot be done. But each person would need to know the tag names and which are parents and which are child elements, as follows:

5: DTD

All Element Names	Description
`<CD-list>`	the root name
`<CD>`	one complete data set for a CD
`<TITLE>`	a title field
`<ARTIST>`	name of artist
`<TRACK>`	track name, (many)
`<PRICE>`	price of CD
`<INTCODE>`	internal code number

Relationship		Contents
`<CD-list>` root		`all the CD elements`
`<CD>` parent of:		`TITLE, ARTIST, TRACK, PRICE, INTCODE`
`<TITLE>`	child	text only
`<ARTIST>`	child	text only
`<TRACK>`	child	text only
`<PRICE>`	child	text only
`<INTCODE>`	child	text only

Once the individual XML documents have been created by each member of the group (melody, classics and jazz), they can be combined into the final version. But suppose one of the group mis-types a tag name, forgets to add attributes (although we have none in this example), or adds in some extra elements of their own. The final XML document would contain errors. So how can you check and track down errors? You would create a separate document type definition (DTD) for your original XML document and validate the work of each group member against that DTD.

Why have DTDs?

An XML document must be *well-formed*, that is it must abide by the XML syntax. But XML documents can also be *valid*. All our examples so far have consisted of well-formed documents, but we have not checked to see whether they are *valid* XML documents.

To ensure that our final XML document is valid, it would have to be validated against a DTD by the parser. Parsers are also called *XML processors*, but some parsers are *non-validating* parsers. They can handle an XML document and see whether it is well-formed but not validate it against a DTD. Others, called *validating parsers*, can compare an XML document against a DTD to ensure that it is valid *and* well-formed. IE5 is an example of a non-validating parser. It only checks for well-formed documents.

To validate a document, we need to create a separate document, the DTD. Briefly, a DTD contains the structure which an XML document must adhere to in order to be valid. The DTD contains all the element names, lists any children they may have, any attributes, user defined entities (that is any which is not part of the five built-in entities – see Chapter 9), and a few other weird looking things. In this chapter we shall look at some of the basics for constructing DTDs and how to link an XML document to its relevant DTD.

Although XML documents do not need to be associated with any DTD, in practice it makes sense to do so, especially for those vocabularies of the more complex XML languages such as CML and XHTML. The DTDs for such languages will have been drawn up by those responsible. Anyone wishing to use the language would then have to abide very strictly to those DTDs. Hence the need for XML authors to know about DTDs in the first place so that they can read them and understand how to construct their own XML documents on which they are based.

We can summarise the usefulness of a DTD as follows.

By checking an XML document against its DTD:

- the XML document can be declared valid
- if it contains an error, the area where the error occurred can be indicated by the validating parser
- DTD authors can define their own character entities, see Chapter 9
- a DTD will enforce a structure on an XML document and thereby ensure the integrity of its data
- it helps to manage large documents especially when others are collaborating

DTDs versus XML Schemas

Just in case some of you may have heard about schemas we shall briefly mention them here. A *schema* is a term used to define an information model. An XML document contains information and can have a schema which describes its construction. *(A simple analogy may help. A memo, letter, poem or book written in English can be checked to see whether it conforms to the rules of English Grammar. If it does, then the document can be considered correct or valid. The poem, memo, etc., could be the equivalent of an XML document. The English Grammar is the schema against which the document is compared for validity. Fortunately, the rules (syntax) of a DTD are less complicated than those for English.)*

A DTD is a schema but it is only one type of schema. One problem with the DTD is that it is based on SGML syntax and is not an XML document. That means that we have to learn the syntax for two languages, XML and DTD. It is also the reason why some parsers are non-validating. They just deal with the XML syntax, whereas a validating parser also needs to have the DTD syntax built into it.

Some feel that any schema should be based on XML so that we would need to learn but one syntax. Good thinking! However, the DTD got in first and many XML documents are based on DTDs. For example, XHTML has three types of DTDs, one of which has to be specified at the start of every XHTML document. So if you need to use some of the XML vocabularies, such as SVG, MathML, or XHTML, you may need to know how to read its DTD.

The W3C has produced another type of schema called an *XML Schema* which provides certain useful features not supported by DTDs. But the problem is that it is not yet widespread. (Although this is changing rapidly and is expected to supplant the earlier DTDs.) The XML Schema is discussed fully from Chapter 13 onwards, but for the present, we shall concentrate on the DTD, especially since all *validating* parsers are required to support DTDs according to the XML 1 Specification, but not necessarily XML Schema.

Creating a DTD for `Ex4-1.xml`

Here is our `EX4-1.xml` document from Chapter 4 displayed in IE6.

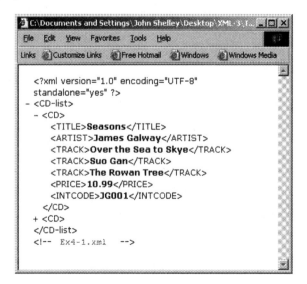

5: <u>DTD</u>

We have:

- a root element, CD-list which contains all the other elements
- a CD parent element which contains other elements, but no text

there are five child elements, whose parent is CD, containing text only and have no children of their own

We shall have to list all this information in our DTD, using any text editor or word processor to type it in.

The Element declaration

When an element simply contains other elements it is said to have *element content*. That is it cannot contain text. CD is such an example.

Those elements which have text only as their content and no child elements must be defined as containing only text. They are known as text content elements, such as TITLE, TRACK.

There is a third type called mixed content which we shall discuss later in Chapter 6. Such elements contain both text and child elements. But we need to be wary about their use.

Relationship		Contents
<CD-list>	root	CD
<CD>	parent of:	TITLE, ARTIST, TRACK, PRICE, INTCODE
<TITLE>	child	text only
<ARTIST>	child	text only
<TRACK>	child	text only
<PRICE>	child	text only
<INTCODE>	child	text only

The Root element declaration

Here is the first line of the DTD code which will specify the name of the root element and exactly what it should contain, namely at least one CD element and, perhaps, many:

```
<!ELEMENT CD-list (CD+)>
```

All elements listed in the DTD begin with the `<!ELEMENT`
The `<!` is part of SGML and indicates the beginning of a declaration. There must be no space between the `!` and the keyword `ELEMENT`. Case is important, it must be in uppercase. The keyword `ELEMENT` specifies that an XML element is about to be declared. We shall see how to specify entities and attributes later.

Next comes the name of the element: `CD-list` in our example. It is also the root element. Naturally, in the XML document the same name and case must be used.

Next, and in round brackets, we list all the main elements which it contains. In other words, which child elements it is the parent of. There is only one in our example, namely, `CD`. All the other elements are the children of `CD`. Grandchildren are never mentioned, just parents and their children. Therefore, `CD-list` can mention just its own one child element *(This is where the use of plus and minus signs can help when viewing your XML documents in IE5.)*

So what is the plus sign doing inside the round brackets? It tells the an XML author that there must be at least one occurrence of a `CD` element and perhaps many other occurrences. It is called an *occurrence indicator*. If we had not used any occurrence indicator, then the XML document could contain one and only one `CD` element.

The general syntax for element declarations then is:

5: DTD

```
<!ELEMENT name-of-element (type-of-content) >
```

<!	a DTD declaration
ELEMENT	an element declaration
name of element	CD-List for example
(content)	what the element can contain, other elements or text
occurrence indicator	for example a +

Every element used in the XML document must be declared in the DTD, otherwise, an error would occur when the XML document is validated. In other words, each element in the XML document is compared against the elements listed in the DTD. If it is not present in the DTD, an error must be generated and the XML document declared as invalid.

The CD element declaration
```
<!ELEMENT CD
    (TITLE, ARTIST, TRACK+, PRICE, INTCODE) >
```

The CD element is the parent of the five other elements. The order is important. A CD element must begin with a TITLE element. The comma after TITLE means "is followed by". Because there is no occurrence indicator, there must be *one and only one* occurrence of each element, except for TRACK which does have an occurrence indicator. We must have at least one track (nobody would buy the CD otherwise!) and we shall doubtless have more than one. The plus (+) occurrence indicator tells any validating program that one or more TRACKs are allowed *between* the ARTIST element and the PRICE element.

Note how our DTD forces anyone who wishes to create a valid XML document based on our DTD to adopt the same structure. When an XML document based on this DTD is read by a validating XML parser, it will try to match the

XML elements against this model. Any deviation in the XML document will force the processor to report an error and halt further processing.

The remaining elements

All that is left are the five child elements of CD. Each one has to be declared:

```
<!ELEMENT TITLE    (#PCDATA)>
<!ELEMENT ARTIST   (#PCDATA)>
<!ELEMENT TRACK    (#PCDATA)>
<!ELEMENT PRICE    (#PCDATA)>
<!ELEMENT INTCODE  (#PCDATA)>
```

None of them have any child elements and they all contain text. The odd looking #PCDATA is how we say that the elements are to contain text.

#PCDATA

Elements which contain text are *not allowed* to include an opening angle bracket nor an ampersand (&) as part of their textual content. The reason being is that a parser would not be able to tell whether the angle bracket was part of the text or part of mark-up indicating the beginning of a child element or the beginning of the ending tag enclosing the text. PCDATA (parsed character data) gets around this problem. It states that any text content except < and & may be included.

```
<!ELEMENT TITLE (#PCDATA)  >
```

The TITLE element can contain only parsed text. The element content (the character text) within the two tags must be parsed so that the parser can detect:

- the closing tag
- perhaps an opening tag of a child element
- a character entity

Why is there a hash symbol (#)? The hash symbol is simply a device for avoiding possible confusion. Since

5: <u>DTD</u>

names are *not allowed* to begin with a hash symbol, an XML parser would have no problems with the following:

```
<!ELEMENT TITLE (#PCDATA) >
```

Without the hash it would mean that the TITLE element would contain a child element called PCDATA but no text.

```
<!ELEMENT TITLE (PCDATA) >
```

The hash symbol makes it clear that the special PCDATA keyword is being used rather than an element name.

(Using PCDATA as an element name would not be a sensible choice.)

Saving the DTD document
We now have all the declarations which our XML document can use. So, we simply save all of the following as a text only file with a .dtd extension, for example: Ex5-1.dtd

```
<!ELEMENT CD-list (CD+)>
<!ELEMENT CD
    (TITLE, ARTIST, TRACK+, PRICE, INTCODE) >
<!ELEMENT TITLE    (#PCDATA)>
<!ELEMENT ARTIST   (#PCDATA)>
<!ELEMENT TRACK    (#PCDATA)>
<!ELEMENT PRICE    (#PCDATA)>
<!ELEMENT INTCODE  (#PCDATA)>
<!-- external DTD:  Ex5-1.dtd -->
```

Linking the DTD to an XML document
How do we link the XML document to our DTD document? There are two ways. The first is to copy and paste it into the XML document, in which case it becomes an internal DTD; the second is to add some extra code which will link the XML document to an external (separate) DTD file. The previously saved file Ex5-1.dtd is an example of an external DTD.

The Internal DTD

All we need is a *document type declaration* which must be placed after the XML declaration:

```
<?xml version="1.0" ?>
<!DOCTYPE root-element-name [
    ...   copy & paste your Ex5-1.dtd file here   ...
] >
<root-name>
...  the rest of the XML document goes here  ...
</root-name>
```

the < ! denotes a declaration

the DOCTYPE (must be uppercase) specifies that a document type is to follow

the name of the root element in the XML document must also be given

[ ] square brackets enclose your entire internal DTD. Simply paste it between the two brackets

> do not forget to add the closing angle bracket to complete the DOCTYPE declaration, *a common mistake!*

Figure 5.1 shows the final XML document with its internal DTD.

The External DTD

When an external DTD is referenced in an XML document the DTD must be a separate file. The DOCTYPE declaration in the XML document provides the link to the external DTD document. (To save a DTD as an external document, follow the procedure on page 56.) Here is the general syntax for the declaration:

```
<!DOCTYPE   root-name   SYSTEM "uri">
```

5: DTD

```xml
<?xml version="1.0" encoding="UTF-8"
      standalone="yes" ?>
<!-- the internal DTD follows -->
<!DOCTYPE CD-list[
 <!ELEMENT CD-list (CD+)>
 <!ELEMENT CD
   (TITLE, ARTIST, TRACK+, PRICE, INTCODE) >
 <!ELEMENT TITLE   (#PCDATA)>
 <!ELEMENT ARTIST  (#PCDATA)>
 <!ELEMENT TRACK   (#PCDATA)>
 <!ELEMENT PRICE   (#PCDATA)>
 <!ELEMENT INTCODE (#PCDATA)>
]>
<!-- the XML document follows -->
<CD-list>
 <CD>
  <TITLE>Seasons</TITLE>
  <ARTIST>James Galway</ARTIST>
  <TRACK>Over the Sea to Skye </TRACK>
  <TRACK>Suo Gan</TRACK>
  <TRACK>The Rowan Tree</TRACK>
  <PRICE>&#163;10.99</PRICE>
  <INTCODE>JG001 </INTCODE>
 </CD>
 <CD>
  <TITLE>Classics</TITLE>
  <ARTIST>James Galway</ARTIST>
  <TRACK>Over the Sea to Skye </TRACK>
  <TRACK>Suo Gan</TRACK>
  <TRACK>The Rowan Tree</TRACK>
  <PRICE>&#163;10.99</PRICE>
  <INTCODE>JG001 </INTCODE>
 </CD>
</CD-list> <!-- An internal DTD: Ex5-1.xml -->
```

Figure 5.1 The Internal DTD in Ex5-1.xml

```
<!DOCTYPE CD-list
```

is the same as before when used with an internal DTD. It states that it is a document type declaration and provides the name of the root element used in the XML document.

The new bit is SYSTEM "uri" which replaces the square brackets. SYSTEM (must be uppercase) is a keyword which specifies that an external resource is being referenced

uri is the actual name and address of where that resource can be located. For our purposes it is the same as the older term URL.

This is what we would type for our declaration:

```
<!DOCTYPE   CD-list
            SYSTEM "DTDdocs/Ex5-1.dtd">
```

I decided to call the DTD Ex5-1.dtd and place it in a sub-directory (DTDdocs) of the directory where my XML documents are stored. It is, therefore, a *partial* (also known as a *relative*) address. If the DTD has been stored elsewhere, perhaps on another server, then a full URL would have to be provided:

```
SYSTEM "http://www.ab.com/xmldocs/Ex5-1.dtd"
```

Important: *Make sure that the* uri *after the SYSTEM keyword is enclosed in quotes.*

URI - Uniform Resource Identifier

This is the new way of referring to what were called URLs (Uniform Resource Locators).

A URI includes a URL and a URN (Uniform Resource Name) which is a recent W3C specification and is becoming a more common way of referring to external resources and is technically more precise. For most purposes, a URI is equivalent to a URL.

5: DTD

> URLs were intended for network (Internet) use.
>
> When partial URIs are given, the processor assumes that the resource is in the same location as the document it is currently reading:
>
> ```
> SYSTEM "fred.dtd"
> ```
>
> or is in a sub-folder (sub-directory) of where it found the document it is currently reading:
>
> ```
> SYSTEM "subdirectory/fred.dtd"
> ```

Here, then, is what we would need to do in order to link to an external DTD. We have replaced

`[..internal DTD..]` with

`SYSTEM "DTDdocs/Ex5-1.dtd"`

and changed the value of `standalone` to `"no"`.

```
<?xml version="1.0" encoding="UTF-8"
                   standalone="no" ?>
<!-- the external DTD reference follows -->
<!DOCTYPE CD-list
         SYSTEM "DTDdocs/Ex5-1.dtd">
<!-- the rest of the XML document follows -->
<CD-list>
 <CD>
  <TITLE>Seasons</TITLE>
  <ARTIST>James Galway</ARTIST>
  <TRACK>Over the Sea to Skye </TRACK>
  <TRACK>Suo G&#226;n</TRACK>
  <TRACK>The Rowan Tree</TRACK>
  <PRICE>&#163;10.99</PRICE>
  <INTCODE>JG001 </INTCODE>
 </CD>

 <CD>
  <TITLE>Classics</TITLE>
  <ARTIST>James Galway</ARTIST>
  <TRACK>Morning</TRACK>
```

```
<TRACK>Concerto in G Minor</TRACK>
<TRACK>Clair de lune</TRACK>
<PRICE>&#163;9.99</PRICE>
<INTCODE>JG002 </INTCODE>
</CD>
</CD-list>   <!-- An external DTD: Ex5-2.xml -->
```

Validating your XML documents

It is clearly important to be able to check that your XML document is valid. IE5 is a non-validating parser, so you can check that your XML document is *well-formed* but not whether it is valid. Now that we have begun to include DTDs some of you may like to check the validity of your XML documents. See Chapter 8.

Summary:

We have seen how to create a DTD and discussed some of the reasons why DTDs are useful.

Every element in an XML document must be declared in the corresponding DTD. This is done via element declarations: `<!ELEMENT name ..`

Furthermore, the DTD must specify whether the element contains child elements (and, if so, what their names are) or whether they simply contain text.

Elements containing text must not use < or & in the text. If these characters are required then they must be inserted as character entities.

#PCDATA tells a validator that the text content must be parsed. A parser will now look for < and & so that it can recognise any possible child elements, character entities or the start of a closing tag.

We have seen how to create both internal and external DTDs and how to link an XML document to a DTD via the `<!DOCTYPE ...>` declaration

5: <u>DTD</u>

Validating and non-validating parsers were discussed as well as well-formed and valid XML documents.

We looked at the purpose of the + occurrence indicator.

Jargon Terms
DTD
validating parsers & non-validating parsers
occurrence indicator
PCDATA
schemas & XML Schema
URI
valid XML documents v. well-formed XML documents

Test 5:
1. How is a well-formed XML document checked for validity?

2. If an XML document is not linked to an external DTD, it can still be validated. True or false?

3. An XML document can be validated only against its DTD. True or false?

4. How is the XML root element declared in an external DTD?

5. How is the XML root element declared in an internal DTD?

6. How is a text-only element declared as such in a DTD?

7. A DTD is written in the XML language. True or false?

8. What does the following declaration mean?
`<!ELEMENT MOMMA (john, mary+, susan)>`

9. Why is there a hash in front of #PCDATA?

10. How is an XML document linked to an external DTD?

SIX

Further Element Declarations

In this Chapter we shall look at:

- elements with mixed content and how to declare them
- how to declare child elements who have their own child elements
- the * and the ? occurrence indicators
- the content model keywords EMPTY and ANY
- the use of the OR symbol - | (the bar symbol)

Mixed Content

An element containing only child elements looks like this:

```
<book>
<title>Watership Down</title>
<author>Richard Adams</author>
</book>
```

book contains two child elements, title and author. It would have the following DTD declaration:

```
<!ELEMENT book (title, author) >
```

According to the declaration, book cannot contain any text and it must contain just one occurrence of title and author and in that prescribed order.

6: Further Element Declarations

Whereas, an element with just text as its content would look like this:

```
<title>Watership Down</title>
```

and its DTD declaration would look like:

```
<!ELEMENT title (#PCDATA) >
```

However, the following is quite valid. `<book>` now contains both text and a child element. This is called *mixed content*.

```
<book>Watership Down
<author>Richard Adams</author>
</book>
```

A DTD declaration would need to be written as follows:

```
<?xml version="1.0"?>
<!DOCTYPE book [
 <!ELEMENT book (#PCDATA|author)*>
]
```

Within the round brackets, the `#PCDATA` *must come first*. Any child elements follow each separated by the bar (|) symbol which indicates OR. After the closing round bracket, we type an asterisk. It *must be* an asterisk and it must be present. It is an occurrence indicator meaning that what it refers to may appear many times or not even once.

The mixed content model requires extra care. There is no order imposed in the actual XML document. Thus the following are all valid according to this DTD:

```
<?xml version="1.0"?>
<!DOCTYPE book [
 <!ELEMENT book (#PCDATA|author|title)*>
 <!ELEMENT author (#PCDATA) >
 <!ELEMENT title (#PCDATA) >
] >
```

```
<!-- author, text, no title -->
<book>
<author>Richard Adams</author>
Watership Down
</book>
```

```
<!-- text, title, more text, no author -->
<book>Text here
<title>Richard Adams</title> Watership Down
</book>
```

```
<!-- text, but no title, no author -->
<book>
Watership Down
</book>
```

```
<!-- text, author, text, no title -->
<book>Text here
<author>Richard Adams</author>
Watership Down
</book>
```

Even this:

```
<?xml version="1.0"?>
<!DOCTYPE book [
 <!ELEMENT book (#PCDATA|author|title)*>
 <!ELEMENT author (#PCDATA)>
 <!ELEMENT title (#PCDATA)>
]>
<book>
<title>Something Silly</title>
Fred sat down
<author>Fred</author>
Fred sat down again
<title> Something Sillier</title>
</book>
<!-- mixed-content: Ex6-1.xml -->
```

6: Further Element Declarations

Although #PCDATA must appear first in the declaration, order in the XML document is not imposed. Sometimes you need to use *mixed* content but you should note that you have less control over the structure of XML documents which have to be validated against the corresponding DTD declaration.

> *Important*: *In an element declaration, there must be a space after the element name and before the opening bracket of the content model. However, when a bar is used, a space can be absent or present.*

Invalid:
```
<!ELEMENT book(#PCDATA|author|title)*>
```

Valid:
```
<!ELEMENT book (#PCDATA |author| title)*>
```

The Occurrence Indicators
There are three occurrence indicators used with elements in a DTD.

Indicator	Meaning
+	an element must appear at least once and possibly many times
*	an element may appear many times or not at all
?	zero or one occurrence
no indicator	must occur once and only once

Here are some examples which will help you to understand how to use the indicators. We have an element called message which can contain to, from, subject and content child elements:

```
<!ELEMENT message
          (to, from, subject, date, content) >
```

As it stands, message must contain all the child elements, once only and in the given order.

```
<?xml version="1.0" ?>
<!DOCTYPE message [
<!ELEMENT message
         (to, from, subject, date, content)>
<!ELEMENT to      (#PCDATA) >
<!ELEMENT from    (#PCDATA)>
<!ELEMENT subject (#PCDATA)>
<!ELEMENT date    (#PCDATA)>
<!ELEMENT content (#PCDATA)>
]>
<message>
<to>John Doe</to>
<from>M. Smith</from>
<subject>ASP Meeting</subject>
<date>12th Feb. 2003</date>
<content>Please turn up.</content>
</message> <!-- Ex6-2.xml -->
```

By adding a ? indicator to, say the `subject` and the `date` elements, we could make them optional so that they could occur once or not at all:

```
<!ELEMENT message
         (to, from, subject?, date?, content) >
```

```
<message>
<to>John Doe</to>
<from>M. Smith</from>
<subject>ASP Meeting</subject>
<date>12th Feb. 2003</date>
<content>Please turn up.</content>
</message>
```

As it stands, the root element, `message`, can appear once only. If we wanted to enable more than one message, say all the messages belonging to one person, we would need to create some other root element and make message a child of this other root, thus:

6: Further Element Declarations

```
<?xml version="1.0" ?>
<!DOCTYPE JDmail[
<!ELEMENT JDmail (message+)>
<!ELEMENT message (to, from, subject, date,
content)>
<!ELEMENT to      (#PCDATA) >
<!ELEMENT from    (#PCDATA)>
<!ELEMENT subject (#PCDATA)>
<!ELEMENT date    (#PCDATA)>
<!ELEMENT content (#PCDATA)>
]>
<JDmail>
<message>
<to>John Doe</to>
<from>M. Smith</from>
<subject>ASP Meeting</subject>
<date>12th Feb. 2003</date>
<content>Please turn up.</content>
</message>

<message>
<to>John Doe</to>
<from>F.Bloggs</from>
<subject>Term Dates</subject>
<date>19th Feb. 2003</date>
<content>Please see attachment.</content>
</message>
</JDmail> <!-- Ex6-3.xml -->
```

Now JDmail becomes the root and message becomes a child of root. By including the + indicator after the child element message, we can now have multiple messages, otherwise it would be allowed to occur only once!

```
<!ELEMENT JDmail (message+)>
```

Declaring EMPTY elements
An empty element is one which contains neither child elements nor any character data. However, we need to specify this in the DTD as follows:

`<!ELEMENT fred EMPTY>`

This would be represented in an XML document as:

`<fred />` or as `<fred></fred>`

Note how the uppercase EMPTY keyword is used without any brackets. Previously, any content-model had to be enclosed in parentheses.

As it stands, the empty element does not serve any practical purpose. When used, the element would usually contain one or more attributes, the subject of the next Chapter. However, it could be useful when developing your application. You may have an element which you intend to use but have not quite decided how. For example, it may contain an attribute which has yet to be agreed upon. You would still like it to be present in the XML document and consequently in the DTD.

Sometimes, empty elements are used as some kind of flag or marker within an XML document. A special program, for example, may have been written which needs to find a particular place within an XML document. In which case an empty flag element with no attributes could prove useful.

The ANY keyword
There is another keyword which can be used, namely ANY, and again the case is significant. It means that the element can contain any combination of text and elements. In this sense it is the opposite of an empty element, it is unrestricted. It can contain any element

which is declared elsewhere in the DTD, but you cannot impose the order in which they appear.

```
<!ELEMENT fred ANY>
```

You will seldom see this used in real working DTDs because the author would lose control over the structure of the resulting XML document. But it could be used during the development of a DTD, so you may well come across its use during this stage.

Here is a silly example which illustrates its use. date can take any of the other declared elements with the exception of the root.

```
<?xml version="1.0" ?>
<!DOCTYPE JDmail [
        <!ELEMENT JDmail (message+)>
        <!ELEMENT message (to, from,
                    subject, date, content)>
        <!ELEMENT to       (#PCDATA)>
        <!ELEMENT from     (#PCDATA)>
        <!ELEMENT subject (#PCDATA)>
        <!ELEMENT date ANY>
        <!ELEMENT content (#PCDATA)>
]>
<JDmail>
<message>
<to>John Doe</to>
<from>F.Bloggs</from>
<subject>Term Dates</subject>
<date>
  <content>Something daft is going on
  </content>
</date>
<content>Please see attachment.</content>
</message>
</JDmail>
        <!-- Using ANY:  Ex6-4 -->
```

6: <u>Further Element Declarations</u>

We can now see that elements are declared in one of two ways. Either with a content model enclosed in brackets, specifying that it can contain PCDATA and/or other elements:

```
<!ELEMENT fred (content model)>
```

or:

```
<!ELEMENT fred category-keyword>
```

where the category-keywords are: EMPTY or ANY.

The connector symbols
When an element is allowed child elements, the children may be separated by either a comma or a vertical bar.

The comma connector
The comma means that each one must appear in the order given:

```
<!ELEMENT message
    (to, from, subject?, date?, content) >
```

Each element can be further refined by including an occurrence indicator.

Quite complex examples can be built up:

```
<!ELEMENT details (name, address+,
            dateofbirth, email*, nickname?)>
```

- This would say that the `details` element must contain one `name` element
- at least one and possibly more than one `address` elements
- one and only one `dateofbirth` element
- zero or more `email` elements
- and a zero or one `nickname` element

Furthermore, they must appear in the order given when present.

6: Further Element Declarations

The OR connector

The vertical bar is called the OR connector.

```
<!ELEMENT flour (selfRaising | plain)>
```

Here, the element `flour` may contain either one occurrence of `selfRaising` or `plain`, but not both.

```
<!ELEMENT flour (brand, colour,
                (selfRaising | plain))>
```

Here, `flour` must contain one occurrence of `brand`, followed by one occurrence of `colour`, followed by either `selfRaising` or `plain`. A possible XML document with an internal DTD could be:

```
<?xml version="1.0" ?>
<!-- Home Made Bread -->
<!DOCTYPE bread [
<!ELEMENT bread (flour)>
<!ELEMENT flour (brand, colour,
                (selfRaising | plain))>
<!ELEMENT brand      (#PCDATA)>
<!ELEMENT colour     (#PCDATA)>
<!ELEMENT selfRaising (#PCDATA)>
<!ELEMENT plain      (#PCDATA)>
]>
<bread>
 <flour>
  <brand>Mac Duff</brand>
  <colour>brown</colour>
  <selfRaising>12ozs</selfRaising>
 </flour>
</bread> <!-- Ex6-5.xml -->
```

Note the matching parentheses for the content model of the `flour` element.

Warning about Mixed Content

Recall that mixed content may have text as well as other elements. Thus, according to the following DTD declaration:

```
<!ELEMENT flour (#PCDATA | brand | colour
                   | selfRaising | plain)*>
```

the `flour` element can contain text and any or none of the other child elements. When using the mixed content model each possible content:

- must be separated by the OR connector
- all must be enclosed in parentheses
- the #PCDATA must come first
- and the * indicator coming after the closing round bracket. No other indicator is permitted

Now you have lost all control over any order as well as being unable to specify the occurrences of individual elements! Any one of them can appear zero or more times in any order. Consequently, the following XML document would be valid, even down to having both self raising and plain flour.

```
<?xml version="1.0" ?>
<!-- Home Made Bread -->
<!DOCTYPE bread [
<!ELEMENT bread (flour)>
<!ELEMENT flour  (#PCDATA | brand | colour
                    | selfRaising | plain)*>
<!ELEMENT brand  (#PCDATA)>
<!ELEMENT colour (#PCDATA)>
<!ELEMENT selfRaising (#PCDATA)>
<!ELEMENT plain  (#PCDATA)>
]>
<bread>
 <flour>some text
   <colour>brown</colour>
    <selfRaising>12ozs</selfRaising>
```

```
   <brand>Mac Duff</brand>
more text
<plain>23ozs</plain>
 </flour>
</bread>   <!-- Ex6-6.xml -->
```

Mixed content must be declared as above. It is incorrect to do any of the following:

```
<!ELEMENT flour (#PCDATA | brand? | colour
                 | selfRaising+ | plain)*>
```
Error: mixed model content cannot contain occurrence indicators.

```
<!ELEMENT flour (#PCDATA , brand , colour
                (selfRaising | plain))*>
```
Error: mixed model content cannot contain comma connectors.

```
<!ELEMENT flour (#PCDATA | brand? | colour
                 | selfRaising+ | plain)+>
```
Error: mixed model content must contain a closing * indicator not a + or ?.

Summary
We have seen how to create mixed content type elements whereby both text and child element are allowed.

When mixed content is used, the DTD author loses all control over the order of text and child elements, indeed whether any of the child elements actually appear in the XML document.

We saw how the three *occurrence* indicators are used.

Elements which have no content are created by using the EMPTY keyword, whereas an element declared with the

ANY keyword can take text and/or any element which has been declared in the DTD.

When child elements are allowed, one of two *connectors* can be used, either the comma or the OR (denoted by the bar symbol). Each work differently. The comma connector allows each child element to be given an occurrence indicator. The OR connector prohibits such use.

Test 6:

1. How is a mixed content element declared?

2. What is the problem with mixed content elements?

3. What must appear immediately after an element name in a declaration?

4. If no occurrence indicator is given, how many times can the element appear?

5. How is an empty element declared?

6. How many and what are the connector symbols?

7. What is the difference between the following two declarations?

Note that one has the asterisk and the other does not.

```
<!ELEMENT flour (selfRaising | plain)*>
<!ELEMENT flour (selfRaising | plain)>
```

6: Further Element Declarations

SEVEN

Declaring Attributes

In this Chapter we shall:

- revise XML attributes
- learn how to declare them in a DTD
- discuss when they should be used
- examine the CDATA & enumeration types
- learn how and when to use various default keywords

Attributes in XML

Let us examine this piece of XML.

```
<JDmail>
<message>
<to>John Doe</to>
<from>M. Smith</from>
<subject>ASP Meeting</subject>
<date>12th Feb. 2003</date>
<content>Please turn up.</content>
</message>

<message>
  etc ...
</message>
</JDmail>
```

7: <u>Declaring Attributes</u>

Data can be stored in child elements or in attributes. Thus we could store the date-information in an attribute of the `message` element, rather than as a separate child element, thus:

```
<message date="23/02/2002">
```

`date` is the attribute name with a value enclosed in quotes. The same amount of information is still contained. But should it be an *attribute* or a *separate element*? It is really a matter of taste. Some would prefer to make it a child element of `message` rather than an attribute. Better still, according to some, make the `date` contain child elements for `day`, `month`, `year` as follows:

```
<message>
<date>
 <day>23</day>
 <month>02<month>
 <year>2003<year>
</date>
```

All three methods provide the same information.

When to use Attributes
Here are some problems when using attributes:

- elements can contain several attributes, but each attribute can take only one value
- attributes cannot describe structure, whereas child elements do
- attribute values are more difficult to test against a DTD
- attributes are more difficult to read and maintain

Attributes should be used only to provide information that is not relevant to the data. I came across one excellent of what this means from the `W3Schools.com` web site. A reference can be found in Appendix A and I would recommend a visit especially to see some examples of other XML documents. Here is the quote:

"The ID in these examples is just a counter, or a unique identifier, to identify the different notes in the XML file, and not a part of the note data.

What I am trying to say here is that metadata (data about data) should be stored as attributes, and that data itself should be stored as elements."

```
<messages>
 <note ID="501">
    <to>Tove</to>
    <from>Jani</from>
    <heading>Reminder</heading>
    <body>Don't forget me this weekend!</body>
 </note>
  <note ID="502">
    <to>Jani</to>
    <from>Tove</from>
    <heading>Re: Reminder</heading>
    <body>I will not!</body>
  </note>
</messages>
```

Deciding when to use attributes comes from experience. You begin to get a feel for what information is better stated as an attribute or as a child element.

What we now need is to see how we can declare attributes in a DTD.

Declaring Attributes in the DTD
Taking the above example, we first need to declare the root messages element as containing at least one and possibly more note elements and then declare the child elements for note, thus:

```
<!ELEMENT messages (note+)>
```

7: Declaring Attributes

```
<!ELEMENT note (to, from, heading, body)>
<!ATTLIST note ID CDATA "001">
```

There are five parts to an attribute declaration. The `<!ATTLIST` starts off the attribute list declaration. We have just one attribute to declare but elements may have more than one attribute, hence the reason for the *list*. The second part of the declaration specifies which element has the attribute. Because attribute declarations can be placed anywhere, there must be a link back to the element itself.

Next comes the name of the attribute, `ID` in our example.

Two more parts make up the attribute declaration. First, the *type* of attribute (there are in fact 10). `CDATA` is the attribute type in our example. Secondly, an optional default value which the attribute can take, in our case, the value "001" enclosed in quotes.

Here is the general syntax for the five components of an attribute declaration:

```
<!ATTLIST element-name attribute-name
          attribute-type default>
```

Types of attributes	Defaults
CDATA	"a string value"
enumeration	#IMPLIED
NOTATION	#REQUIRED
ENTITY	#FIXED
ENTITIES	
ID	
IDREF	
IDREFS	
NMTOKEN	
NMTOKENS	

We shall look at the four defaults and the first two types since these are the most common.

White Space in Attributes

In XML, tabs, carriage returns and extra spaces between words are collectively known as *white space*. When these appear within the value of attributes they are stripped out and replaced with a single space by the program.

```
<!ATTLIST fred bark CDATA "madness">
```
... the DTD

Thus, for the above declaration in a DTD, all the following XML documents

```
<fred bark="the cat sat
            on the    mat">
<fred bark="the   cat   sat   on the    mat">
```

would be collapsed by the XML parser as follows:

```
<fred bark="the cat sat on the mat">
```

The formal term for stripping out white space is *normalisation*.

CDATA

This is the easiest and most common attribute *type* in a DTD. It stands for *character data*. It indicates that an attribute value may consist of character data that will not be interpreted as mark-up. The parser has to parse the value's text to find the closing quote and perhaps any entities which may be included. In other words, we cannot use any form of mark-up symbols, < > & " *or* ' in the attribute's value. (In this respect, it is similar to #PCDATA.)

If any of these characters *are required*, they must appear as character entities, as discussed on page 37: `&lt;` `&quot;`, etc. Make sure you read the next Chapter on *Character Data* to clarify the differences between CDATA, PCDATA and CDATA *sections*.

7: Declaring Attributes

Attribute default values

We have seen one default value already, namely a string value.

String default value

```
<!ELEMENT fred EMPTY>
<!ATTLIST fred
     john CDATA "Something will appear.">
```

Here, the element `fred` takes a `john` attribute whose type is CDATA. The purpose of the default value of "Something will appear" is to provide something if an XML author did not include an attribute. For example:

```
<?xml version="1.0" ?>
<!-- BOOKATT.xml -->
<!DOCTYPE ATT-TEST [
<!ELEMENT ATT-TEST (fred) >
<!ELEMENT fred EMPTY>
<!ATTLIST fred
  john CDATA "Something will appear.">
]>
<ATT-TEST>
 <fred john="My own value inserted." />
</ATT-TEST> <!-- Empty: Ex7-1.xml -->
```

The EMPTY element `fred` takes an attribute called `john`. The XML author has decided to put in his/her own value: `"My own value inserted."`

IE5 will display what is shown in Figure 7.1.

Suppose another author types the following:

```
<ATT-TEST>
   <fred />
</ATT-TEST>
```

Here, the element `fred` has not been given an attribute. The XML parser is required *"to behave as though the attribute were present with the declared default value."*[1] Consequently, IE5 will display what is shown in Figure 7.2:

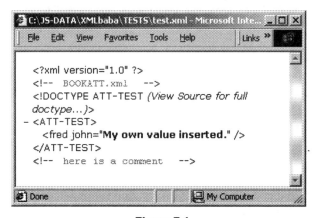

Figure 7.1

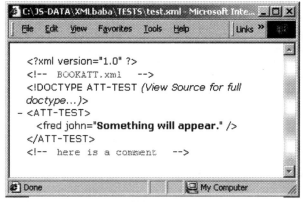

Figure 7.2

---

[1] Taken from the W3C Recommendation for XML 1.0.

7: Declaring Attributes

Leaving out attributes and expecting default values to be inserted by the parser is not to be recommended.

> **Warning:** *a non-validating parser will not read a DTD and therefore cannot supply default values. Having said that, IE5 does supply default values in the display window. XML Spy does not display the value but will 'supply' it in 'theory'.*

#IMPLIED attribute keyword

The IMPLIED keyword can be used if you do not wish to force the XML author to include an attribute and you have no default value. For example:

```
<?xml version="1.0" ?>
<!-- implied.xml -->
<!DOCTYPE PERSON [
<!ELEMENT PERSON (contact) >
<!ELEMENT contact EMPTY>
<!ATTLIST contact
  fax CDATA #IMPLIED>
]>
<PERSON>
 <contact />
</PERSON> <!-- IMPLIED: Ex7-2.xml -->
```

However, if someone does have a fax number and wishes to include it, then they can do so:

```
<PERSON >
 <contact fax="123-3456"/>
</PERSON >
```

#REQUIRED attribute keyword

When you need to enforce the use of an attribute then use the #REQUIRED keyword. Attributes with this keyword *must be specified* in the element. The value will be given by the author. In the following, each member of staff must be given their id-number:

```
<?xml version="1.0" ?>
<!-- required.xml -->
<!DOCTYPE STAFF [
<!ELEMENT STAFF (member+) >
<!ELEMENT member EMPTY>
<!ATTLIST member
  id-number CDATA #REQUIRED>
]>
<STAFF>
 <member id-number="234567" />
</STAFF> <!-- REQUIRED: EX7-3.xml -->
```

#FIXED attribute keyword

Use the #FIXED keyword when you want an attribute's value to be fixed thereby preventing an XML author from entering some other value. If the author does provide some other value, the parser will generate an error. The value that you want to supply must be given in the declaration. For example, we may wish a document to have a fixed version number, say 1.3:

```
<?xml version="1.0" ?>
<!DOCTYPE document [
<!ELEMENT document (author, editorName,
                   draftVersion) >
<!ELEMENT author (#PCDATA)>
<!ELEMENT editorName (#PCDATA)>
<!ELEMENT draftVersion EMPTY>
<!ATTLIST draftVersion number
        CDATA #FIXED "1.3">
]>

<document>
 <author>Helena Buttons</author>
 <editorName>George Murphy</editorName>
 <draftVersion number="1.3"/>
</document>
          <!-- FIXED:  EX7-4.xml -->
```

7: Declaring Attributes

The general syntax for an attribute with a `FIXED` value is:

```
<!ATTLIST elementname attributename
     CDATA #FIXED "theFixedValue">
```

Again, if the XML author does not include the attribute, the parser is bound to include it. So, using the above internal DTD where the XML document contains this line but without the attribute:

```
<draftVersion />
```

the parser would add it in, just as though the line of code had been written as:

```
<draftVersion number="1.3"/>
```

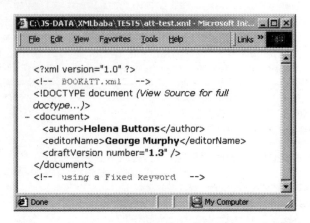

```
<?xml version="1.0" ?>
<!-- BOOKATT.xml  -->
<!DOCTYPE document (View Source for full
doctype...)>
- <document>
    <author>Helena Buttons</author>
    <editorName>George Murphy</editorName>
    <draftVersion number="1.3" />
  </document>
<!-- using a Fixed keyword  -->
```

If an XML author entered some other version number, such as "1.2", a validating parser will throw up an error message:

Errors:
```
line 13 C:\JS-DATA\XMLbaba\TESTS\att-test.xml:
error (1200): attribute value doesn't match
fixed default: number="1.2" (default "1.3")
```

The above was taken from the Brown University, Scholarly Technology Group (see Appendix A). Notice how the line number is a hypertext link which will take the user to the offending line of code. A very thoughtful extra from this web site.

IE5 on the other hand, did not validate the XML document, it simply checked for well-formedness. Consequently, the 'erroneous' version number was displayed. This provides one instance of why it is sometimes necessary to go to the trouble of creating a DTD so that such errors can be prevented.

Another way of preventing errors is make use of the `enumerated` attribute type

`enumerated` Attribute type

This is used when you want to force the XML author to choose an attribute's value from a set of possible values. For example, a payment element could be given an attribute which specifies the method of payment, by cheque, by Visa or by cash.

There is no formal keyword for enumerated types. The fact that it is an enumeration is given by enclosing the possible values within round parentheses and each possible value separated by the bar symbol:

```
<!ELEMENT payment (#PCDATA)>
<!ATTLIST payment method
  (cheque | visa | cash)  "visa">
```

In the above DTD declaration, the element `payment` takes a `method` attribute. The only possible values are given in parentheses each separated by the bar symbol. It is also given a default value, "visa" in the above.

XML authors wishing to validate their documents against the DTD, must use one of those three values. If they leave off the attribute, the default value will be supplied by the parser.

```
<?xml version="1.0" ?>
<!DOCTYPE item [
<!ELEMENT item (payment) >
<!ELEMENT payment EMPTY>
<!ATTLIST payment method
 (cheque | visa | cash)  "visa">
]>
<item>
 <payment method="cash"/>
</item>
<!-- using the Enumeration attribute type
            EX7-5.xml -->
```

If the XML document is checked by a *non-validating* parser, then the XML author can put in any value. Again, this may reinforce why attributes and DTDs are used.

Given that someone wants to validate their XML document against a DTD, but they need to enter a value which is not one of the choices, can it be done? Strictly speaking No! However, because this is not an unusual situation there is a way around the problem. The creator of the DTD must allow other choices to be made apart from the ones specified. Look at the following:

```
<!ELEMENT payment EMPTY>
<!ATTLIST payment  method
(cheque | visa | cash | other)  #REQUIRED
           method.other CDATA #IMPLIED>
```

There are thee additions:

- we have added 'other' as an additional choice
- we have changed the default value to #REQUIRED

- we have added `'method.other'` as an
  `#IMPLIED` and therefore optional *second* attribute

The `'other'` value allows the XML author to make a choice which is not one of the main three, cheque, Visa or cash. Because the method attribute is *required*, one of the four options is allowed and *must be chosen*. In our scenario, it makes sense to choose only the `'other'` value.

Finally, we have added the `method.other` attribute and made it a CDATA type with an #IMPLIED keyword. This keyword allows the author to include it (or not) with any chosen value. Here is a valid entry by an XML author:

```
<?xml version="1.0" ?>
<!DOCTYPE item [
<!ELEMENT item (payment) >
<!ELEMENT payment EMPTY>
<!ATTLIST payment  method
(cheque | visa | cash | other)  #REQUIRED
            method.other CDATA #IMPLIED>
]>
<item>
 <payment method="other"
          method.other="purchase order"/>
</item>
<!-- allowing extra choices for the
     Enumeration attribute type EX7-6.xml-->
```

`method="other"` *must be present* because it has been made required. It is only `method.other` which is optional. `method.other` could be any valid XML name, even `Fred` but it would not be in the spirit of what we are trying to achieve. Compare the following with the above and I hope you agree that poor old Fred does not have the same clarity or impact:

7: **Declaring Attributes**

```
<?xml version="1.0" ?>
<!-- enum2.xml -->
<!DOCTYPE item [
<!ELEMENT item (payment) >
<!ELEMENT payment EMPTY>
<!ATTLIST payment   method
(cheque | visa | cash | other)   #REQUIRED
 fred CDATA #IMPLIED>
]>
<item>
 <payment method="other"
          fred="purchase order"/>
</item>
<!-- allowing extra choices for the
     Enumeration attribute type -->
```

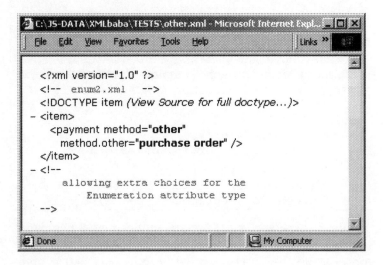

Summary
Attributes can be added to elements via the `<!ATTLIST` declaration. We looked at two types of attributes, CDATA and enumeration.

CDATA is similar to #PCDATA in that any character may appear as the value except < or &. Enumeration is used when you wish to limit the values an attribute is allowed.

Attributes may take one of four defaults. Validating parsers will supply any given default value, if the XML author leaves off the attribute.

Test 7:
1. Where can CDATA and #PCDATA be used?

2. How many types can an attribute take?

3. How many default values can an attribute take? 1 of 4

4. If an attribute has been given a default value and an XML author omits the attribute, what action is taken by a parser?

7: <u>Declaring Attributes</u>

EIGHT

Character Data, PCDATA & CDATA

In the preceding Chapters, we have mentioned mark-up, character data, PCDATA and CDATA. It can all become a little confusing. In this Chapter, we shall take time out to make sure that we understand when and how to use them. We shall also discuss the CDATA section and mention a web site where you can validate your XML documents against internal DTDs for free.

Character Data
An XML document will obviously contain information. That is its main purpose, to share data. But it will also contain mark-up. But, we need to be careful, because a parser has to look for both types. We want it to ignore our information but to react to mark-up. This is what is known as *parsed character data*, really text which can be parsed. There is another type of data which is not parsed, it is totally ignored by a parser even if it does contain what might otherwise be mark-up. It is called a *CDATA section*. But more of that later. So far, all our XML documents contain parsed character data (PCDATA).

8: Character Data, PCDATA & CDATA

Character data is all the text in a document which is not mark-up. On the other hand, mark-up consists of any of the following:

start tags `<company>`
end tags `</company>`
empty element tags `<department id="123" />`
entity references (see Chapter 9)
five built in character references, such as `&amp;`
comments `<!-- a comment -->`
CDATA section delimiters (see below)

To detect mark-up, the parser will look for any opening tag markers (`<`) and any opening entity markers (`&`). Consequently, neither of these two symbols can form part of regular data. For example, we cannot simply type this into an XML document:

`<company>John Doe & Sons</company>`

or this:

`<caution> salary < 2000 </caution>`

Either would generate an error. The `<` symbol would make the parser think that an element was about to follow. To avoid the error, and make the *less than* symbol form part of our data, we would have to use an entity reference:

`<caution> if salary &lt; 2000 </caution>`

Now, the parser would treat the symbol as regular text by *expanding* it (the technical term) as a character. Likewise, we cannot use the & by itself, otherwise a parser would think that we are using an entity reference. Hence the need to rewrite the company name as:

`<company>John Doe &amp; Sons</company>`

Both elements, `company` and `caution`, contain parsed character data; data which will be parsed by the parser, i.e. looking for opening tag and entity reference markers.

```
<company> For the year 2003
 <name>John Doe &amp; Sons</name>
 <type>Electrical retailer</type>
 <turnover>annual &lt; 100000 </turnover >
</company>
```

In the above, the `company` element contains three child elements. The < markers contain well-formed XML elements. But the parser can only detect them by searching for mark-up.

#PCDATA

If we wanted to make our well-formed XML document *valid*, we would add a DTD to include the following:

```
<!ELEMENT company  (name, type, turnover)>
<!ELEMENT name     (#PCDATA)>
<!ELEMENT type     (#PCDATA)>
<!ELEMENT turnover (#PCDATA)>
```

The PCDATA tells the parser that the content of the three child elements contains parsed character data and any occurrence of < or & is to be taken as mark-up.

PCDATA can appear only in *element* declarations and must be preceded by the # symbol so that it cannot be confused with an element name, see page 56.

The CDATA Attribute type

Attribute values may also contain character data. But they must not contain either of the special markers or if they do they must be entered as character entities.

Incorrect

```
<company name="John Doe & Sons"/>
<income salary = "< 30000"/>
```

8: Character Data, PCDATA & CDATA

Correct

```
<company name="John Doe &amp; Sons"/>
<income salary = "&lt; 30000"/>
```

CDATA can appear only as an attribute type:

```
<!ELEMENT company EMPTY>
<!ELEMENT income EMPTY>
```

```
<!ATTLIST company name CDATA #REQUIRED>
<!ATTLIST income salary CDATA #REQUIRED>
```

Whereas, #PCDATA can appear only as an element content type.

The CDATA Section

A CDATA section is a section or block which is marked up in a special way so that it will be ignored by the parser. You may have a large section of data which contains any number of mark-up characters. An example could be writing a tutorial about XML. Here is the XML document.

```
<TAGS>
XML elements have a starting tag, <tagname>
enclosed in angle brackets and a closing tag
</tagname>. Some elements may be empty, e.g.
<emptytag />. Entities are delimited by an &
and a ;
</TAGS>
```

The contents of the TAGS element will be parsed and of course all the XML mark-up tags will throw the parser into confusion. We do not want to go to the trouble of using entities, there are too many: `&lt;tagname&gt;`

XML has considered this problem and allowed the use of a CDATA section. It is merely a convenience for enclosing a block of text which contains mark-up characters but we do not want to use entity references all the time. The block is simply enclosed within the following and will be ignored by the parser, i.e. it will not be parsed:

```
<! [CDATA[  the block of text ]]>
```

So we can re-write the above as:

```
<?xml version="1.0"?>
<TAGS> <![CDATA[
XML elements have a starting tag, <tagname>
enclosed in angle brackets and a closing tag
</tagname>. Some elements may be empty, e.g.
<emptytag />. Entities are delimited by an &
and a ;
]]> </TAGS>   <!-- Ex8-1.xml -->
```

The one set of characters which must not appear within the block is, of course,]] >, otherwise the parser will think it has come to the end of the CDATA section.

However, should you want to include it within a DTD, then make the element empty. Here is an example:

```
<?xml version="1.0" ?>
<!DOCTYPE Tutorial-xml [
<!ELEMENT Tutorial-xml (lang, date, content)>
<!ELEMENT lang (#PCDATA)>
<!ELEMENT date (#PCDATA)>
<!ELEMENT content (TAGS+)>
<!ELEMENT TAGS EMPTY>
]>
<Tutorial-xml>
 <lang>ASP Meeting</lang>
 <date>12th Feb. 2003</date>
 <content>
<TAGS>
<![CDATA[
XML elements have a starting tag, <tagname>
enclosed in angle brackets and a closing tag
</tagname>. Some elements may be empty, e.g.
 <emptytag />. Entities are delimited by an &
and a ;
```

```
]]>
</TAGS>
</content>
</Tutorial-xml>
                <!-- Ex8-2.xml -->
```

How to validate your XML documents

We can use IE5 to check whether our XML documents are well-formed. But if we want to validate them against a DTD (and/or schema) then we either have to buy proprietary programs, such as XMLPro, or XML Spy or use the site mentioned below (current at the time of writing). It works very quickly even via a modem.

Brown University, Scholarly Technology Group

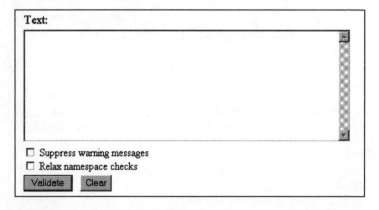

You can paste your XML document complete with its internal DTD into a text box and click the validate button. However, the text area is cleared after validation. You can re-paste and edit inside the text box, as shown above.

It allows you to enter a URI for document held on a server:

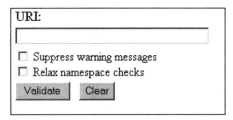

Very few of us can 'practice' our XML on servers, so if, like me, everything is done on a PC, you can click on the Browse button in the illustration below, find your document on your hard disc and have it uploaded. That is a very thoughtful addition.

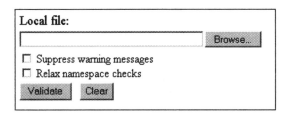

Another useful feature is the error messages. Line numbers are included along with links to the particular line, as shown over page.

However, if you need to validate against an external DTD held on your hard disc, then the site cannot help. In which case, you could buy a proprietary program such as XML Spy. The latter is very good (about $399 at the time of writing). You can validate DTDs and XML Schema and even create such documents using the editor. A great deal of typing effort is done automatically by the editor. See Appendix A for the web site.

8: <u>Character Data, PCDATA & CDATA</u>

Errors:

<u>line 13</u>, [user-supplied text]:
    error (1200): **attribute value doesn't match fixed default**: number="1.2" (default "1.3")

Original Document:

<u>line 11</u>: <author>Helena Buttons</author>
<u>line 12</u>: <editorName>George Murphy</editorName>
<u>line 13</u>: <draftVersion number="1.2"/>
<u>line 14</u>: </document>
<u>line 15</u>:
etc.

NINE

General Entities

We have already looked briefly at character entities in Chapter 4. Appendix B provides a complete list. In this Chapter we shall look at:

- predefined entities
- general entities
- character entities (AKA character references)
- external and internal entities

Predefined Entities

XML has five predefined entities as discussed in Chapter 4. Here is the list again:

Character Entity	Meaning
&amp;	generates the & - ampersand
&apos;	generates the ' – apostrophe
&gt;	generates the > - greater than
&lt;	generates the < - less than
&quot;	generates the " – double quote

They are built into the XML parser and are instantly recognised. However, if other characters are required, such as é or ½, then they will have to be explicitly declared in a DTD before they can be used in an XML document. We look at what is involved later, under character entities. For the moment, we shall discuss general entities.

General Entities

For want of a better name, we shall distinguish *character entities* from shorthand entities by calling the latter *general entities*. These are used to reduce the amount of typing in an XML document. For example, let us say we have a list of books each contained within a book element. <book> will have a child element for the publisher. We have several publishers but they all have long names. In the following, we shall just mention one publisher to see how it works. Assume that we have 25 books in our XML document which come from "Bernard Babani (publishing) Ltd". That will entail quite a lot of typing, but we can reduce the amount by using a general entity.

The important point is that our entity must be declared in a DTD before it can be used it in our XML document.

The General Entity Declaration

The syntax is as follows:

```
<!ENTITY entityname "what it represents">
```

We shall use the name BB for the Babani publisher, and include it in an internal DTD, thus:

```
<!ENTITY BB "Bernard Babani (publishing)
Ltd">
```

We can now use the entity name BB enclosed between an ampersand and a semi-colon wherever we need the full text in our XML document.

```
<?xml version="1.0" ?>
<!DOCTYPE bookList[
```

```
<!ENTITY BB
        "Bernard Babani (publishing) Ltd">
<!ELEMENT bookList  (book+)>
<!ELEMENT book (publisher | author| title)* >
<!ELEMENT publisher (#PCDATA)>
<!ELEMENT author     (#PCDATA)>
<!ELEMENT title      (#PCDATA)>
]>
<bookList>
  <book>
  <publisher>&BB;</publisher>
  <author>John Shelley</author>
  <title>XHTML &amp; CSS explained</title>
  </book>
</bookList>   <!-- EX9-1.xml -->
```

When displayed in IE5 or XML Spy, the parser will replace the general entity with its full text. XML Spy has a browser view window for displaying entities and what they represent.

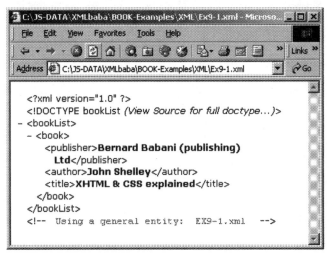

9: <u>General Entities</u>

There are several things you must appreciate with these general entities. First, when you create your own entities you will need to declare them in a DTD, otherwise how could the parser know what to replace the entity name with? Entities can be placed within an internal DTD (as illustrated above) or in an external DTD which we shall look at shortly.

Using General Entities within an Internal DTD

You do not have to create a full-blown DTD in order to create and use your own entities, as we see in the following. However, this implies that you do not want to *validate* your document. Non-validating parsers will be happy to display the well-formed XML document. But, if you try to validate the document, validating parsers will generate errors because no declarations will have been made for the XML elements, such as bookList, book, publisher, etc.

In the following, we have included two general entity declarations, BB and JW. Nothing else has been declared, implying that we shall not require the XML document to be validated.

```
<?xml version="1.0" ?>
<!DOCTYPE bookList [
<!ENTITY BB "Bernard Babani (publishing)
                                Ltd">
<!ENTITY JW "John Wiley Ltd">
] >
<bookList>
 <book>
  <publisher>&BB;</publisher>
  <author>John Shelley</author>
  <title>XHTML &amp; CSS explained</title>
 </book>
```

```
<book>
 <publisher>&JW;</publisher>
 <author>John Smith</author>
 <title>XHTML2 &amp; CSS explained</title>
 </book>
</bookList>
              <!-- EX9-2.xml -->
```

When a non-validating parser meets the &BB; and &JW;
entities, it will replace them in the XML document with the
text in the declaration.

Using General Entities within an External DTD
If we declare entities in an external DTD, we need to put a
link in the XML document to the external DTD. In the
following we have an external DTD called EX9-3.dtd:

```
<!ENTITY BB "Bernard Babani (publishing)
                                Ltd">
<!ENTITY JW "John Wiley Ltd (USA) ">
<!ELEMENT bookList (book+)>
<!ELEMENT book (publisher | author| title)* >
<!ELEMENT publisher (#PCDATA)>
<!ELEMENT author    (#PCDATA)>
<!ELEMENT title     (#PCDATA)>
              <!-- EX9-3.dtd -->
```

In our XML document, we add a link to this external DTD
via the SYSTEM keyword:

```
<?xml version="1.0" standalone="no" ?>
<!DOCTYPE bookList SYSTEM "EX9-3.dtd">
<bookList>
<book> ... etc ... </book>
</bookList>
              <!-- EX9-3.xml -->
```

Note the inclusion of the standalone="no".

9: General Entities

```
Ex9-3.xml *

<?xml version="1.0" standalone="no" ?>
<!DOCTYPE bookList (View Source for full doctype...)>
- <bookList>
 - <book>
    <publisher>Bernard Babani (publishing) Ltd</publisher>
    <author>John Shelley</author>
    <title>XHTML & CSS explained</title>
   </book>
 - <book>
    <publisher>John Wiley Ltd (USA)</publisher>
    <author>John Smith</author>
    <title>XHTML2 & CSS explained</title>
   </book>
 </bookList>
 <!-- EX9-3.xml   -->
```

We have linked our XML document to an external DTD
which includes not just the entity declarations but also all
the element declarations used in the XML document.
Therefore, we could now validate our XML document if we
so desired against this complete DTD.

Overriding external entities
It is also possible to include some extra entities of your
own which are not in an external DTD. For example, in the
above DTD, John Wiley is the USA company. But suppose
we wanted to use this DTD but need to be able to refer to
our own UK branch: 'John Wiley (UK Division)' in our XML
document. We can do so by declaring our own entity
within an internal DTD.

We may also need an entity for *MaCarthur's & Daughters
Inc* for one particular publisher who is not in the original
DTD. If we have no authority to change the external DTD,
because it is used in its original form by others in the
organisation, then we could include our own entities

internally within our XML document. Here is the XML document which will do it.

```
<?xml version="1.0" ?>
<!DOCTYPE bookList SYSTEM "EX9-3.dtd"
[
<!ENTITY JW "John Wiley Ltd (UK Division)">
<!ENTITY Mac "MaCarthur's &amp; Daughters
Inc">
]>
<bookList>
<book>
<publisher>&BB;</publisher>
<author>John Shelley</author>
<title>XHTML &amp; CSS explained</title>
</book>

<book>
<publisher>&JW;</publisher>
<author>Susan Heron</author>
<title>JavaScript explained</title>
</book>

<book>
<publisher>&Mac;</publisher>
<author>Jim Smith</author>
<title>XML for beginners</title>
</book>
</bookList>
                    <!-- Ex9-4.xml -->
```

Note how we are still linking it to the EX9-3.dtd external DTD via the SYSTEM keyword in the DOCTYPE declaration and that we have included our own entity declaration for MaCarthur's. It does not exist in the external DTD.

However, in the case of the JW entity, one already exists in the external DTD and another (with exactly the same name) now appears in our internal DTD. Which one takes effect?

```
<!ENTITY JW "John Wiley Ltd (UK Division)">
   <!-- our internal entity declaration -->
```

```
<!ENTITY JW "John Wiley Ltd (USA)">
   <!-- the external entity declaration -->
```

```
C:\JS-DATA\XMLbaba\BOOK-Examples\XML\Ex9-4.xml - Microsoft ...  _ □ X
 File  Edit  View  Favorites  Tools  Help                    Links »

  <?xml version="1.0" ?>
  <!DOCTYPE bookList (View Source for full doctype...)>
 - <bookList>
 - <book>
     <publisher>Bernard Babani (publishing)
       Ltd</publisher>
     <author>John Shelley</author>
     <title>XHTML & CSS explained</title>
   </book>
 - <book>
     <publisher>John Wiley Ltd (UK Division)
       </publisher>
     <author>Susan Heron</author>
     <title>JavaScript explained</title>
   </book>
 - <book>
     <publisher>MaCarthur's & Daughters
       Inc</publisher>
     <author>Jim Smith</author>
     <title>XML for beginners</title>
   </book>
 </bookList>
 <!-- Ex9-4.xml   -->
```

Because entity declarations do not have to be unique there may be two or more with the same name, one in an external DTD and one in an internal DTD.

The rule is that whichever declaration is met *first* is the one which will be used (*binding* is the technical term). It so happens, that an internal DTD is considered to be read *before* an external DTD. Therefore, our internal entity declaration will become binding.

General entities are for use *within the XML document itself*, given that they have been previously declared in a DTD. There is another type of entity which is for use within the DTD itself and *not* within the body of an XML document. We shall discuss that type, the so-called *parameter entity*, in the next Chapter.

Why Use general Entities
General entities can have a highly practical purpose other than simply being a means of reducing the amount of typing. Suppose one of the publishers changed its name. If an entity had been used, it would need just *one* change to the entity declaration rather than in each occurrence of the publisher's name. It is worth thinking about this because general entities could prove useful in many similar situations.

Using numbers in Character References
Let us now turn our attention to character references, also known as character entities. This type is used when we want to use specific characters such as â or © rather than just any (general) piece of text which is when the general entity is used. Character references may be written in one of three ways: by name, by its decimal number or by its hexadecimal number. Suppose we need to use a double quote within the text content of an element (or attribute value). We shall see how to create the double quote in the three possible ways.

9: General Entities

Names
Very few characters have a names.[1] The double quote is
one of these few and has the name `quot`. When
surrounded by the & and closed with a semi-colon, it
becomes a character reference or entity, thus: `&quot;`

Decimal numbers
Character entities without names must be referenced via
their ASCII numbers. *(Those with names may also take
the numbered form.)* Thus, the decimal number for the
double quote is 34. However, when it is represented by
this number we need to prefix it with a hash symbol (#)
and, of course, enclose it within the & and ; `&#34;` From
the list in Appendix B, we can see that *acute e* (é) has a
decimal number of 233.

Thus: `ros&#233; wine` would yield *rosé wine*.

Hexadecimal numbers
XML may also have character entities referenced by their
hexadecimal values. Thus, decimal 34 is hexadecimal 22
and 233 is E9. *(Case is not significant with the letters A-F
as used in the hexadecimal number system.)*

To show that a hexadecimal number is being used, it is
necessary to add the letter x after the hash symbol, thus:

`&#x22; ros&#xE9; &#x22;` would result in: " rosé "

where `&#x22;` = double quote and `&#xE9;` = é

We could also use either of the following:

`&quot;ros&#xE9;&quot;` *or* `&#34;ros&#233;&#34;`

Since it is rare to see hexadecimal numbers, we shall only
use decimal numbers in this text.

---

[1] See Appendix B for a complete list as well as a discussion about the
ASCII character set.

Beware the following:
Of the five *predefined* entities, special care must be taken when using the numerical values for the < and & symbols. The following Table 9.1, shows the five entities with their decimal and hexadecimal values. But note the odd use of *double escaping* for the *less than* and *ampersand* symbols.

Character Entity	Meaning	Decimal	Hexadecimal
&amp;	&	&#38;	&#x26;
&apos;	'	&#39;	&#x27;
&gt;	>	&#62;	&#x3E;
&lt;	<	&#60;	&#x3C;
&quot;	"	&#34;	&#x22;

Table 9.1: Predefined Entities

You will have no problem if you stick to using names for & and <. But you may have problems with *some* parsers, (not IE5), if you use the numbers, either decimal or hexadecimal, for these two. Consider the following:

```
<!ENTITY Mac "MaCarthur's &#38; Daughters">
```

and in the XML document:

```
<publisher>&Mac;</publisher>
```

When the XML processor meets & in the ENTITY declaration, it will expand it into the & symbol. It will now expect to find a character reference code name or number and a closing semi-colon. It will not find them, instead it will find a space and immediately generate an error message saying that white space cannot follow an *ampersand* (or the *less than*) mark-up character.

So, we have to double up on the reference code, thus:

&#38;

9: **General Entities**

The bold part will effectively insert the ampersand symbol in front of the non-bold part thus making it a valid character reference. This is what is known as *double escaping*. The same process needs to be applied to the less than symbol. **&**#60; to make it **&**#60;

Thus, if you wanted to display the following using numbers, an incorrect and a correct version are shown:

```
MaCarthur's & Daughters or
MaCarthur's & <Daughters>
```

Incorrect:

```
<!ENTITY Mac "MaCarthur's &#38; Daughters">
<!ENTITY Mac "MaCarthur's &#60;Daughters&#62;">
```

Correct:

```
<!ENTITY Mac "MaCarthur's &#38;#38; Daughters">
<!ENTITY Mac "MaCarthur's
&#38;#60;Daughters&#62;">
```

Or, better still, you could simply use the names:

```
<!ENTITY Mac "MaCarthur's &amp; Daughters">
<!ENTITY Mac "MaCarthur's &lt;Daughters&gt;">
```

Internal Entities

In the above examples, the XML parser has been told exactly what the *general* entity has to be replaced with. The entity Mac has been defined within quotes. These are called *internal entities.* (Not to be confused with whether the declaration is made in an *internal* or *external* DTD.)

General entities are also parsed, which simply means that a parser would not expect to find mark-up within the definition. If mark-up characters are required as part of the text, such as the & symbol, then character entity references are required: &

This type of entity is an *internal* and *parsed* entity which implies that others may be unparsed and external entities. But more of that later.

Summary

We have seen how to cut down the amount of typing by using a general entity. These entities can be used within the XML document. They have to be enclosed within a leading ampersand and a closing semi-colon.

The entity itself must be declared in a DTD, either in an external DTD or within an internal DTD before it can be used in an XML document. If the same entity name appears in an external and an internal DTD, the internal reference becomes *binding* since an internal DTD is always read before an external DTD.

We made a distinction between a character entity (or character reference) and a general entity. The former is a notation for displaying special characters such as ½ é Ø, etc. Again they are enclosed within an ampersand and a closing semi-colon.

A few character entities have names, but the vast majority require to be referenced by numbers, either decimal or hexadecimal.

We also noted a warning about two of the pre-defined entities when their numerical representation is used rather than their name values. The less than and the ampersand character need to be *double escaped*.

Finally, the entities used so far are said to be *internal* entities (whether in an external or internal DTD) simply because their definition is included in the DTD.

Jargon

internal entity: one which is completely defined by an external or internal DTD

parsed entity: one which is parsed by the XML processor

character entity: also called a character reference, is an entity which defines a special character

9: General Entities

general entity: one which is used to replace text in the XML document, The parser will expand (replace) the entity with its replacement text

Test 9:

1. What are the five predefined entities built into an XML parser?

2. What is the main purpose for using general entities?

3. General entities are parsed, so what characters cannot appear as their content?

4. How is a general entity recognised by a parser?

5. How is a general entity declared?

6. How does a character entity differ from a general entity?

7. How would you link an XML document to a DTD document which contains some entities you wish to use?

8. Internal entities cannot appear in an external DTD. True or false?

9. In `Ex9-3.dtd`, we had the following declaration:

`<!ELEMENT book (publisher | author| title)* >`

What is it saying? Is it a good way to declare element `book`?

10. In the text, `EX9-3.xml` is shown in XML Spy. Why not use IE?

TEN

Parameter Entities

Parameter Entities

There is another type of entity called a *parameter entity*. It is designed to work within a DTD rather than an XML document because it would serve no useful purpose there.

It is important to clarify the distinction between *general* entities and *parameter* entities. The former are used to make replacements within the body of the XML document, whereas parameter entities are used to make replacements within the DTD. It may be worth reading that again!

Parameter entities came about because writing large DTDs can be complicated. They help to reduce the amount of typing as well as allowing *one* change to be reflected at many other points, just as we have seen with the general entity.

Let us suppose that we are creating an XML document to list certain details about the various departments within our organisation: human relations (HR), finance (FIN), research (RSCH), etc. Each one requires the following child elements:

10: Parameter Entities

```
<!ELEMENT HR    (location, manager, staff+)>
<!ELEMENT FIN   (location, manager, staff+)>
<!ELEMENT RSCH  (location, manager, staff+)>
<!ELEMENT location (#PCDATA)>
<!ELEMENT manager  (#PCDATA)>
<!ELEMENT staff    (#PCDATA)>
```

But we have 20 other departments to type in as well. We could use a parameter entity to reduce the amount of typing by turning (location, manager, staff+) into a parameter entity.

The general syntax for a parameter entity is:

```
<!ENTITY % parameterName  "the characters to
be replaced">
```

The % sign informs the parser that a parameter entity is being declared. There must be a space before and after it. Next comes the name we want to give to the entity and it must follow the naming conventions used in XML. Finally, we supply the replacement text enclosed in quotes which the entity will represent. It is similar to a general entity apart from the use of the % symbol and the fact that the 'text' to be replaced will obviously relate to what can be contained within a DTD.

In the following, the parameter entity LMS can now be used within an *external* DTD as follows:

```
<!ENTITY % LMS  "(location, manager, staff+)">
<!ELEMENT HR    %LMS;>
<!ELEMENT FIN   %LMS;>
<!ELEMENT RSCH  %LMS;>
```

Every time the parser meets LMS and provided it is enclosed within the % and a semi-colon, %LMS; the entity will be expanded (replaced) by the text within the declaration. Clearly, this reduces the amount of typing. We shall also see another practical use of parameter entities shortly.

An Example Use of parameter entities
Let us look at an example of an XML document before we had heard about parameter entities. We shall create a departmental staff list. Here is the XML document:

```
<?xml version="1.0" standalone="no" ?>
<!DOCTYPE PERSONNEL SYSTEM "Ex10-1.dtd">
<PERSONNEL>
<HR>
 <location>Room 484</location>
 <manager>Fred Smith</manager>
 <staff>Molly1</staff>
 <staff>Molly2</staff>
 <staff>Molly3</staff>
</HR>
<FIN>
 <location>Room 234</location>
 <manager>Danny Boy</manager>
 <staff>Boy1</staff>
 <staff>Boy2</staff>
</FIN>
<RSCH>
 <location>Room 567</location>
 <manager>Al Defoe</manager>
 <staff>Meg1</staff>
 <staff>Meg2</staff>
 <staff>Meg3</staff>
 <staff>Meg4</staff>
</RSCH>
</PERSONNEL>
                 <!-- Ex10-1.xml
         A departmental staff list -->
```

We have three departments HR (human resources), FIN (finance) and RSCH (research). Each requires the same three child elements: `location`, `manager`, `staff` (one or more). Here is a typical external DTD saved as: `Ex10-1.dtd` and it is referenced in our XML document, called: `Ex10-1.xml` via the following line:

```
<!DOCTYPE PERSONNEL SYSTEM "Ex10-1.dtd">
```

```
<!ELEMENT PERSONNEL (HR, FIN, RSCH)>
<!ELEMENT HR   (location, manager, staff+)>
<!ELEMENT FIN  (location, manager, staff+)>
<!ELEMENT RSCH (location, manager, staff+)>
<!ELEMENT location (#PCDATA)>
<!ELEMENT manager  (#PCDATA)>
<!ELEMENT staff    (#PCDATA)>
           <!-- Ex10-1.dtd -->
```

If we had 20 departments, then it could be a chore having to type:

```
<!ELEMENT DEPT (location, manager, staff+)>
```

and we would probably make a few typing errors.

So, why not use a parameter entity? We amend our external DTD as follows and call it `Ex10-2.dtd`:

```
<!ELEMENT PERSONNEL (HR, FIN, RSCH)>
<!ENTITY % LMS
           "(location, manager, staff+)">
<!ELEMENT HR   %LMS;>
<!ELEMENT FIN  %LMS;>
<!ELEMENT RSCH %LMS;>
<!ELEMENT location (#PCDATA)>
<!ELEMENT manager  (#PCDATA)>
<!ELEMENT staff    (#PCDATA)>
           <!-- Ex10-2.dtd -->
```

In the above, we have created a parameter entity for use within our DTD and called it LMS for (*location, manager, staff+*). The % sign makes it a parameter entity. Where ever we place our parameter entity (%LMS;), the XML processor will make the necessary replacement.

```
Ex10-2.xml                                              _ ☐ ×
<?xml version="1.0" standalone="no"?>
<!DOCTYPE PERSONNEL SYSTEM "DTDdocs/Ex10-2.dtd">
<PERSONNEL>
    <HR>
        <location>Room 484</location>
        <manager>Fred Smith</manager>
        <staff>Molly1</staff>
        <staff>Molly2</staff>
        <staff>Molly3</staff>
    </HR>
    <FIN>
        <location>Room 234</location>
        <manager>Danny Boy</manager>
        <staff>Boy1</staff>
        <staff>Boy2</staff>
    </FIN>
    <RSCH>
        <location>Room 567</location>
        <manager>Al Defoe</manager>
        <staff>Meg1</staff>
        <staff>Meg2</staff>
        <staff>Meg3</staff>
        <staff>Meg4</staff>
    </RSCH>
</PERSONNEL>
<!-- Ex10-2.xml
     A departmental staff list -->

This file is valid.                              OK
```

We have also amended our XML document to refer to this revised DTD:

```
<?xml version="1.0" standalone="no" ?>
<!-- Ex10-2.xml
     A departmental staff list -->
```

10: Parameter Entities

```
<!DOCTYPE PERSONNEL SYSTEM "Ex10-2.dtd">
<PERSONNEL>
<HR> ... etc ... </HR>
</PERSONNEL>
```

The only requirement is that the parameter entity must be declared before the parameter can be used. *(Pretty sensible when you think about it!)*

Furthermore, we must use the % symbol *before* and add a semi-colon *after* the parameter name. The name we give our parameter entity must follow the rules for creating XML names (see page 12).

Suppose we do not want to use an external DTD? Can we simply add the declarations as an internal DTD into our original XML document, as follows? No!

INCORRECT

```
<?xml version="1.0" standalone="yes" ?>
<!DOCTYPE PERSONNEL
[
<!ELEMENT PERSONNEL (HR, FIN, RSCH)>
<!ENTITY % LMS
  "(location, manager, staff+)">
<!ELEMENT HR     %LMS;>
<!ELEMENT FIN    %LMS;>
<!ELEMENT RSCH   %LMS;>
<!ELEMENT location (#PCDATA)>
<!ELEMENT manager  (#PCDATA)>
<!ELEMENT staff    (#PCDATA)>
]>
<PERSONNEL>
<HR>
 <location>Room 484 </location>
 <manager>Fred Smith</manager>
 <staff>Molly1</staff>
 <staff>Molly2</staff>
```

```
<staff>Molly3</staff>
</HR>
......
</PERSONNEL>
                    <!—XEx10-2.xml -->
```

As the following error from IE6 shows:

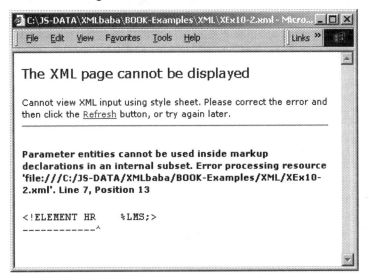

The error states that we cannot use parameter entities *inside mark-up declarations* in an internal subset. The term *internal subset* is a common one to refer to an internal DTD. It is not saying that parameter entities cannot be used in an internal DTD because they can. But note the following:

- In the internal DTD, parameter entities can only be used between other declarations:

```
<!ELEMENT HR (location, manager, staff+)>
%parameterEntity; <!—between -->
<!ELEMENT FIN (location, manager, staff+)>
```

10: Parameter Entities

- In an external DTD, a parameter entity can be used between other declarations as well as inside them.

Having said all of the above, XML Spy seemed quite happy to validate as correct the 'incorrect' example on page 120.

Using Parameter Entities in an Internal DTD

Here is an example of where we can use parameter entities in an internal DTD. Assume there is an external DTD which we would like to reference via an internal DTD. Our external DTD is the same one as that shown on page 118. However, here is a revised XML document called Ex10-3.xml:

```
<?xml version="1.0" standalone="no" ?>
<!DOCTYPE PERSONNEL [
<!ENTITY % Ex10-2dtd SYSTEM "Ex10-2.dtd">
%Ex10-2dtd;
]>
<PERSONNEL>
<HR>
 <location>Room 484</location>
 <manager>Fred Smith</manager>
 <staff>Molly1</staff>
 <staff>Molly2</staff>
 <staff>Molly3</staff>
</HR>
... etc ...
</PERSONNEL>
              <!-- Ex10-3.xml
        A departmental staff list -->
```

See how the internal DTD contains an entity *declaration* called Ex10-2dtd and uses the SYSTEM keyword to reference the external DTD called Ex10-2.dtd. The *declaration* is now followed by the *use* of the parameter entity enclosed between the % and the semi-colon.

```
[<!ENTITY % Ex10-2dtd SYSTEM "Ex10-2.dtd">
%Ex10-2dtd;]
```

By using the parameter entity in this way, we can refer to another external DTD.

But, we were also able to refer to an external DTD without using a parameter entity, simply via the following:

```
<!DOCTYPE PERSONNEL SYSTEM "Ex10-2.dtd">
```

So what is the difference?

To explain the difference, let us take a look at the following. We have an XML document, Ex10-4.xml **(A)** which refers to two DTDs: Ex10-4.dtd **(B)** and paramEnts.dtd **(C)**. Here is our XML document, Ex10-4.xml which makes a reference to both DTDs.

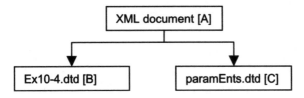

Here are the two external DTDs:

```
<!ELEMENT bookList (book+)>
<!ELEMENT book (publisher | author| title)* >
<!ELEMENT publisher (#PCDATA)>
<!ELEMENT author   (#PCDATA)>
<!ELEMENT title    (#PCDATA)>
          <!-- Ex10-4.dtd -->
```

```
<!ENTITY BB "Bernard Babani (publishing)
                              Ltd">
<!ENTITY JW "John Wiley Ltd (USA)">
          <!-- paramEnts.dtd -->
```

10: Parameter Entities

We are now using two DTDs, one with elements declared for use in an XML document, another with just parameter entities (only two in our example).

Here is the XML document displayed in XML Spy.

```
Ex10-4.xml                                            _ □ ×

   <?xml version="1.0" ?>
   <!DOCTYPE bookList (View Source for full doctype...)>
 - <bookList>
   - <book>
      <publisher>Bernard Babani (publishing)
        Ltd</publisher>
      <author>John Shelley</author>
      <title>XHTML & CSS explained</title>
    </book>
   - <book>
      <publisher>John Wiley Ltd (UK Division)
        </publisher>
      <author>Susan Heron</author>
      <title>JavaScript explained</title>
    </book>
   - <book>
      <publisher>MaCarthur's & Daughters
        Inc</publisher>
      <author>Jim Smith</author>
      <title>XML for beginners</title>
    </book>
   </bookList>
   <!-- Ex10-4.xml  -->
```

Here is the actual XML document:

```
<?xml version="1.0" ?>
<!DOCTYPE bookList SYSTEM "Ex10-4.dtd"
[
<!ENTITY JW "John Wiley Ltd (UK Division)">
<!ENTITY Mac "MaCarthur's &amp; Daughters
Inc">
<!ENTITY % myparams SYSTEM "paramEnts.dtd">
%myparams; ]>
```

```
<bookList>
<book>
<publisher>&BB;</publisher>
<author>John Shelley</author>
<title>XHTML &amp; CSS explained</title>
</book>

<book>
<publisher>&JW;</publisher>
<author>Susan Heron</author>
<title>JavaScript explained</title>
</book>

<book>
<publisher>&Mac;</publisher>
<author>Jim Smith</author>
<title>XML for beginners</title>
</book>
</bookList>
                 <!-- Ex10-4.xml -->
```

There are many examples of so-called public or common DTDs which simply contain a collection of various entities, currency, chemical symbols, or whatever. (See xFront site in Appendix A.) Typing them from scratch for your own use would be a chore. So why not link to one via a parameter entity? All you would need to do is to create your own DTD to declare those elements and attributes required for your particular XML document, DTD *[B]*. Then, simply link to the common DTD *[C]* via a parameter entity. This is what we are doing above, albeit with very simple examples.

Another important issue in the above is that the John Wiley is the UK Division, not the USA as specified in the external paramEnts.dtd. This is because of the position of the John Wiley UK entity. It comes *before* the external declaration. If we had this arrangement:

```
[<!ENTITY % myparams SYSTEM "paramEnts.dtd">
%myparams;
<!ENTITY JW "John Wiley Ltd (UK Division)">
<!ENTITY Mac "MaCarthur's &amp; Daughters
Inc">
]>
```

Then, because the USA reference is met first, the second John Wiley reference (UK Division) would be ignored.

Notice that the external `paramEnts.dtd` mentions John Wiley USA and Bernard Babani. We have added two in our internal document: MaCarthur and John Wiley UK. In other words, we can pick up entities created by others and over-ride external entities with out own internal entities provided that all the entities have been positioned correctly.

Summary of Entities
Let us discuss the four different types of entities we have discussed so far. Three of them come from the example just described.

1. We have used a parameter entity `%myparams;` in the *internal* DTD of `Ex10-4.xml` to refer to a complete external DTD called `paramEnts.dtd`. `%myparams;` is in an internal DTD, but when using such a parameter entity, there must be a declaration to the external DTD via the SYSTEM keyword to which it refers:

```
<!-- declaration to external DTD -->
[<!ENTITY % myparams SYSTEM " paramEnts.dtd
">
<!-- using the parameter -->
%myparams; <!—use between declarations -->
<!ENTITY JW "John Wiley Ltd (UK Division)">
<!ENTITY Mac "MaCarthur's &amp; Daughters
Inc">      ]>
```

2. Within the body of the XML document, we make use of two general entities JW and Mac. They follow next:

```
<!ENTITY JW "John Wiley Ltd (UK Division)">
<!ENTITY Mac  "MaCarthur's  &amp;  Daughters
Inc">
```

Here is their use within an XML document:

```
<publisher>&JW;</publisher>
. . .
<publisher>&Mac;</publisher>
```

3. In the definition for the Mac general entity, we have made use of a *character entity*: &

4. In an earlier external DTD called Ex10-2.dtd, we used a parameter entity *within* an existing declaration. This is allowed because we are using an external DTD.

```
<!-- Ex10-2.dtd -->
<!ENTITY % LMS
  "(location, manager, staff+)">
<!ELEMENT HR %LMS;> <!-- use within a declaration -->
<!ELEMENT FIN %LMS;>
```

Summary
We have seen how to use parameter entities and when and where they can be used. It is important to remember that internal DTDs can contain parameter entities between other declarations. Only external DTDs can have parameters within (inside) declarations.

Parameter entities were designed for use in a DTD and cannot be used within an XML document. Only general and character entities can be used as replacements within an XML document.

10: <u>Parameter Entities</u>

Parameter entities begin with the % symbol, whereas general entities begin with an ampersand. Both are concluded with a semi-colon. In the parameter entity *declaration*, the % symbol is also used but must have a space before and after it.

Parameter entities can also be used with attributes. But we shall leave that to the next Chapter

Test 10:
1. In what document is a general entity used?

2. In what document is a parameter entity used?

3. What symbol is used to denote that a parameter entity is being declared and not a general entity?

4. What symbol is used to denote that a general entity is being declared and not a parameter entity?

5. How does a parser recognise that a parameter entity is being referenced rather than a general entity?

6. What is the difference between a parameter entity used in an Internal DTD and one used in an external DTD?

ELEVEN

Parameter Entities and Attributes

Using parameter entities for attribute replacement

If many elements require the same attributes, parameter entities could again prove useful. However, because we are going to use them *within* a declaration, we shall need to create an external DTD. Let us take an example. We shall add two attributes to each of the following three departments in an organisation: Human Resources (HR), Finance (FIN) and Research (RSCH). The first attribute is *required* - the name of the security officer, the second is the telephone number. There is a default value if the XML author leaves off the telephone number Here is our external DTD saved as Ex11-1.dtd:

```
<!ENTITY % LMS
   "(location, manager, staff+)">
<!ENTITY % paramAttribs
    "securityOfficer CDATA #REQUIRED
    securityTel CDATA '9999' ">
<!ELEMENT PERSONNEL (HR, FIN, RSCH)>
<!ELEMENT HR    %LMS;>
<!ATTLIST HR    %paramAttribs;>
<!ELEMENT FIN   %LMS;>
<!ATTLIST FIN   %paramAttribs;>
<!ELEMENT RSCH %LMS;>
<!ATTLIST RSCH %paramAttribs;>
<!ELEMENT location (#PCDATA)>
```

11: Parameter Entities and Attributes

```
<!ELEMENT manager    (#PCDATA)>
<!ELEMENT staff      (#PCDATA)>
            <!-- Ex11-1.dtd -->
```

Here is the corresponding XML document: Ex11-1.xml

```
<?xml version="1.0" standalone="no" ?>
<!DOCTYPE PERSONNEL SYSTEM "Ex11-1.dtd">
<PERSONNEL>
<HR securityOfficer="A Cashmad"
    securityTel="1234">
 <location>Room 484</location>
 <manager>Fred Smith</manager>
 <staff>Molly1</staff>
 <staff>Molly2</staff>
 <staff>Molly3</staff>
</HR>
<FIN securityOfficer="A F Franks">
 <location>Room 234</location>
 <manager>G. Elliott</manager>
 <staff>Boy1</staff>
 <staff>Boy2</staff>
</FIN>
<RSCH securityOfficer="GK Chesterton ">
 <location>Room 567</location>
 <manager>S Boffin</manager>
 <staff>Meg1</staff>
 <staff>Meg2</staff>
 <staff>Meg3</staff>
 <staff>Meg4</staff>
</RSCH>
</PERSONNEL>
        <!-- a departmental staff list
               Ex11-1.xml   -->
```

11: Parameter Entities and Attributes

```
Ex11-1.xml *                                              _ □

  <?xml version="1.0" standalone="no" ?>
  <!DOCTYPE PERSONNEL (View Source for full doctype...)>
- <PERSONNEL>
  - <HR securityOfficer="A Cashmad" securityTel="1234">
      <location>Room 484</location>
      <manager>Fred Smith</manager>
      <staff>Molly1</staff>
      <staff>Molly2</staff>
      <staff>Molly3</staff>
    </HR>
  - <FIN securityOfficer="A F Franks" securityTel="9999">
      <location>Room 234</location>
      <manager>G. Elliott</manager>
      <staff>Boy1</staff>
      <staff>Boy2</staff>
    </FIN>
  - <RSCH securityOfficer="GK Chesterton"
      securityTel="9999">
      <location>Room 567</location>
      <manager>S Boffin</manager>
      <staff>Meg1</staff>
      <staff>Meg2</staff>
      <staff>Meg3</staff>
      <staff>Meg4</staff>
    </RSCH>
  </PERSONNEL>
- <!--
      a departmental staff list
      Ex11-1.xml
  -->
```

Examining the external DTD

```
1. <!-- Ex11-1.dtd   -->
   <!ENTITY % LMS
            "(location, manager, staff+)">
```

The above creates a parameter entity LMS. Below is how it
is used with the elements, for example with HR:

```
<!ELEMENT HR %LMS;>
```
it will be replaced by:
```
(location, manager, staff+)
```

11: Parameter Entities and Attributes

This now states that the HR element must have just one occurrence of location, followed by just one occurrence of manager and followed by at least one occurrence (or more) of staff.

Each of the three elements which form part of the LMS parameter entity needs to be declared. Each takes PCDATA.

```
<!ELEMENT location (#PCDATA)>
<!ELEMENT manager  (#PCDATA)>
<!ELEMENT staff    (#PCDATA)>
```

2. Here is the declaration for the attributes:

```
<!ENTITY % paramAttribs
    "securityOfficer CDATA #REQUIRED
    securityTel CDATA '9999' ">
```

Wherever the %paramAttribs; entity appears, it will be replaced by:

```
"securityOfficer CDATA #REQUIRED
    securityTel CDATA '9999' ">
```

Thus in: `<!ATTLIST HR %paramAttribs;>`

the parameter entity will be replaced by a *required* securityOfficer attribute followed by a securityTel attribute. If the second attribute is not included in the XML document, it will have the number 9999 as a default. Thus, although the XML author merely typed:

```
<FIN securityOfficer="A F Franks">
```

The browser will insert all of the following:
```
<FIN securityOfficer="A F Franks"
    securityTel="9999">
```

This can be verified by looking at the screen dump on the previous page.

3. `<!ELEMENT PERSONNEL (HR, FIN, RSCH)>`

The above states that PERSONNEL (the root element) will contain one and only one occurrence of the three departments in the order given. Each child element has to be declared. Here is the one for RSCH:

```
<!ELEMENT RSCH %LMS;>
<!ATTLIST RSCH %paramAttribs;>
```

In an Internal DTD
Without an external DTD, we would need to do the following. Note that we cannot use any parameter entities, because internal DTDs cannot have parameter entities within a declaration:

```
<?xml version="1.0" standalone="yes" ?>
<!DOCTYPE PERSONNEL [
<!ELEMENT PERSONNEL (HR, FIN, RSCH)>
<!ELEMENT HR (location, manager, staff+)>
<!ATTLIST HR securityOfficer CDATA  #REQUIRED
            securityTel CDATA #IMPLIED>
<!ELEMENT FIN (location, manager, staff+)>
<!ATTLIST FIN securityOfficer CDATA #REQUIRED
            securityTel CDATA '9999'>
<!ELEMENT RSCH (location, manager, staff+)>
<!ATTLIST RSCH securityOfficer CDATA
                               #REQUIRED
            securityTel CDATA '9999'>
<!ELEMENT location (#PCDATA)>
<!ELEMENT manager (#PCDATA)>
<!ELEMENT staff (#PCDATA)>
]>
<PERSONNEL>
<HR securityOfficer="A Cashmad"
    securityTel="1234">
 <location>Room 484</location>
 <manager>Fred Smith</manager>
 <staff>Molly1</staff>
```

```
 <staff>Molly2</staff>
 <staff>Molly3</staff>
</HR>
<FIN securityOfficer="A F Franks">
 <location>Room 234</location>
 <manager>G. Elliott</manager>
 <staff>Boy1</staff>
 <staff>Boy2</staff>
</FIN>
<RSCH securityOfficer="GK Chesterton ">
 <location>Room 567</location>
 <manager>S Boffin</manager>
 <staff>Meg1</staff>
 <staff>Meg2</staff>
 <staff>Meg3</staff>
 <staff>Meg4</staff>
</RSCH>
</PERSONNEL>
        <!-- Ex11-2.xml  a staff list -->
```

We might now begin to appreciate the usefulness of
parameter entities.

TWELVE

Further Attributes

We discussed attributes default, the CDATA and enumeration types in Chapter 7. We shall now take a look at some of the other attribute types.

Types of attributes	Defaults
CDATA	"a string value"
enumeration	#IMPLIED
NOTATION	#REQUIRED
ENTITY	#FIXED
ENTITIES	
ID	
IDREF	
IDREFS	
NMTOKEN	
NMTOKENS	

The ID Attribute type
The basic idea behind the ID type is to provide a means for *uniquely* identifying any element in an XML document. No two elements can have the same ID attribute value in the same document, otherwise it would not be unique. Parsers will generate an error, if the same ID attribute value is met more than once.

12: **Further Attributes**

The ID can be used by programs and scripting languages to process XML documents and to react when a certain ID has been encountered. Here is an example:

```
<?xml version = "1.0"
       encoding="UTF-8"
       standalone = "yes" ?>
<!DOCTYPE CONTACTS [
 <!ELEMENT CONTACTS (contact+)>
 <!ELEMENT contact (name, email)>
 <!ELEMENT name (#PCDATA)>
 <!ELEMENT email (#PCDATA)>
 <!ATTLIST contact contactNum ID #REQUIRED>
]>
<CONTACTS>

    <contact contactNum = "a1001">
    <name>Mary Smith</name>
    <email>m.smith@abc.com</email>
    </contact>

    <contact contactNum = "a1002">
    <name>Harry Forbes</name>
    <email>harry.f@abc.com</email>
    </contact>
</CONTACTS>
                    <!-- Ex12-1.xml -->
```

It would now be possible for a program to search for one of the contacts via its unique ID.

It is becoming conventional to use 'id' as the attribute *name* in addition to the ID type, so that it is more obvious that the element has an ID attribute. Hence a better way of writing the above would be:

```
<!ATTLIST contact id ID #REQUIRED>
```

and the following in the XML document:

```
<contact id = "a1001">
```

In our example, the attribute is #REQUIRED. We could have used #IMPLIED but it could never be #FIXED. If it were, then every element would have the same fixed value and, therefore, not be unique.

The value of the ID attribute must be a valid XML name. In other words it must begin with a letter and not a number. This could be a drawback when working with databases which may require numbers to identify records. In which case, you may have to resort to using a plain CDATA attribute type which can contain any character, thus:

```
<?xml version = "1.0"
        encoding="UTF-8"
        standalone = "yes" ?>
<!DOCTYPE CONTACTS [
 <!ELEMENT CONTACTS (contact+)>
 <!ELEMENT contact (name, email)>
 <!ELEMENT name (#PCDATA)>
 <!ELEMENT email (#PCDATA)>
 <!ATTLIST contact id CDATA #REQUIRED>
]>
<CONTACTS>
    <contact id = "1001">
    <name>Mary Smith</name>
    <email>m.smith@abc.com</email>
    </contact>

    <contact id = "1002">
    <name>Harry Forbes</name>
    <email>harry.f@abc.com</email>
    </contact>
</CONTACTS>
            <!-- Using CDATA as ID
            Ex12-2.xml -->
```

Despite the attribute name of id (not to be confused with the attribute *type* ID), it can still serve as an identifier but is no longer a true ID type. This could lead to potential confusion, indeed, even errors.

Rules for creating XML names

Because XML is a standard, it defines how names are to be constructed. We repeat it here for convenience.

- names must *begin* with a letter or an underscore
- names cannot begin with a digit
- names may have one or more valid characters
- the valid characters are letters a to z or A to Z, period (full stop), underscore, hyphen and digits. (Colons may be used but have a special meaning)
- spaces or tabs are not allowed
- names cannot begin with xml (or any case variation of these three letters) since these are reserved for special features of XML which may be implemented in a future version

IDREF & IDREFS

These attributes are used to refer to another element which has an ID attribute.

```
<?xml version = "1.0"
      encoding="UTF-8"
      standalone = "yes" ?>
<!DOCTYPE CONTACTS [
 <!ELEMENT CONTACTS (contact+)>
 <!ELEMENT contact (name, email)>
 <!ELEMENT name (#PCDATA)>
 <!ELEMENT email (#PCDATA)>
 <!ATTLIST contact id ID #REQUIRED
           idref IDREF #IMPLIED>
]>
<CONTACTS>

    <contact id="a1001">
    <name>Mary Smith</name>
    <email>m.smith@abc.com</email>
    </contact>
```

```
    <contact id="a1002" idref="a1001">
    <name>Harry Smith</name>
    <email>harry.f@abc.com</email>
    </contact>
</CONTACTS>
              <!-- Ex12-3.xml -->
```

We use 'idref' as the attribute name (although any other name could be used) so that it is quite clear that this is a reference to some unique ID. Note how easy it is to see that Harry Smith is referencing Mary Smith.

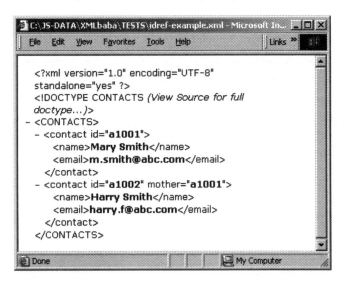

IDREFS

IDREFS refer to more than one ID, but each one must be separated by a single space (not commas!). It allows for grouping of certain elements and may be a useful means of organising data. One day you may have a need for this type of attribute, so here is a simple example:

12: Further Attributes

```xml
<?xml version = "1.0"
         encoding="UTF-8"
         standalone = "yes" ?>
<!DOCTYPE CONTACTS [
 <!ELEMENT CONTACTS (contact+)>
 <!ELEMENT contact (name, email)>
   <!ATTLIST contact id ID #REQUIRED
                 idref IDREF #IMPLIED
                 idrefs IDREFS #IMPLIED
                 relation CDATA #REQUIRED>
 <!ELEMENT name (#PCDATA)>
 <!ELEMENT email (#PCDATA)>
]>
<CONTACTS>
    <contact id = "a1001" relation="mother">
    <name>Mary Smith</name>
    <email>m.smith@abc.com</email>
    </contact>
    <contact id = "a1002" idref="a1003"
            relation="father">
    <name>Harry Smith</name>
    <email>h.smith@abc.com</email>
    </contact>
    <contact id = "a1003"
        idrefs="a1001 a1002" relation="son">
    <name>Harry Smith Jnr</name>
    <email>harry.son@abc.com</email>
    </contact>
</CONTACTS>
                <!-- Use of IDREF
                   Ex12-4.xml -->
```

As you can see, a program could work out who the parents are for Harry Smith Jnr. It is a somewhat contrived example but shows you how the process works.

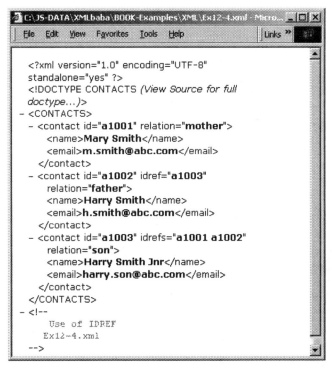

```
<?xml version="1.0" encoding="UTF-8"
standalone="yes" ?>
<!DOCTYPE CONTACTS (View Source for full
doctype...)>
- <CONTACTS>
  - <contact id="a1001" relation="mother">
      <name>Mary Smith</name>
      <email>m.smith@abc.com</email>
    </contact>
  - <contact id="a1002" idref="a1003"
    relation="father">
      <name>Harry Smith</name>
      <email>h.smith@abc.com</email>
    </contact>
  - <contact id="a1003" idrefs="a1001 a1002"
    relation="son">
      <name>Harry Smith Jnr</name>
      <email>harry.son@abc.com</email>
    </contact>
  </CONTACTS>
- <!--
     Use of IDREF
     Ex12-4.xml
  -->
```

As mentioned earlier, IDs and IDREFs really come into their own when the XML documents need to be processed by specially written programs or by style sheets. The same applies to the following attribute type: NMTOKEN and NMTOKENS.

NMTOKEN and NMTOKENS
An attribute of type NMTOKEN (name token) can only take as its value any valid character *that can appear in a valid XML name*, nothing else. If an element has such an attribute type, then a program or database can be certain how the name is constructed.

12: **Further Attributes**

Note that we are not saying that a NMTOKEN value must be a valid *XML name*, just that it must be a *valid name character*.

(See the following web site for the definition of XML names and name characters as taken from the W3C Recommendation. It will also introduce you to the syntax used in the Recommendation:

http://www.w3.org/TR/2000/WD-xml-2e-20000814#dt-name.)

A NMTOKEN value, then, unlike the ID type, can begin with a digit.

ID type must be an XML name and therefore cannot have a leading zero.

NMTOKEN type must consist of XML name characters and, therefore, can have a leading zero.

Great Heavens! Then why not use a NMTOKEN instead of an ID? Simply because a NMTOKEN could have one or more identical values, in which case it would not be unique. A validating parser would accept identical NMTOKEN values, but not identical ID values.

NMTOKENS are used when there are two or more possible values for the attribute. It is quite rare to see this variation. However, you must separate each value by a space, not a comma.

```
<?xml version="1.0" standalone="yes"?>
<!DOCTYPE server [
<!ELEMENT server (administrator,
                  authorised_users)>
<!ELEMENT administrator EMPTY>
<!ATTLIST administrator
          person NMTOKEN #REQUIRED >
<!ELEMENT authorised_users EMPTY>
```

```
<!ATTLIST authorised_users
         names NMTOKENS #IMPLIED >
]>
<server>
<administrator person="FredBloggs" />
<authorised_users names="Igg1 Biggi2 Cfred3"
/>
</server> <!-- nmtoken Ex12-5.xml-->
```

The following attributes and elements are not seen very often and are included here more for the sake of completeness than anything else. It is one of the least clear parts of XML. Most XML authors can safely leave them alone until it becomes essential to use them. So feel free to ignore this part or just glance through it to get some idea of how they may be useful to you in the future.

NOTATION attribute type

The English word *notation* simply means a note, a comment or an explanation. It provides a means for an XML parser reading the XML document to pass additional information to a program. For example, suppose an XML document has to contain a piece of programming code. A NOTATION attribute could provide additional information about which language is actually being used.

```
<?xml version="1.0" standalone="yes" ?>
<!DOCTYPE codefrag [
 <!NOTATION c_code SYSTEM "C source code">
 <!NOTATION java_code SYSTEM "Java source
code">
<!ELEMENT codefrag (#PCDATA)>
<!ATTLIST codefrag
      codelang NOTATION (java_code | c_code)
                                #REQUIRED >
]>
<codefrag codelang="c_code">
```

```
<!-- the actual code would go here probably
as a CDATA Section (see page 144)-->
</codefrag>
 <!-- using a notation type attribute:  Ex12-6.xml-->
```

In the above, our code could be one of two languages, either C or Java. This information is provided in the NOTATION attribute called codelang within the XML document.

```
<codefrag codelang="c_code">
```

However, in the DTD (internal in our case), two declarations are required. The first is:

```
<!ATTLIST codefrag
     codelang NOTATION (java_code | c_code)
                                #REQUIRED >
```

This informs the parser that codelang is an attribute of the codefrag element and is of type NOTATION. We have specified that the attribute is REQUIRED and that its value must be either java_code or c_code.

The second thing that must be declared are NOTATION declarations for each of the two values. Even though this instance of the XML document may only contain the C code, both values must have their separate NOTATION declarations as follows, and, they must come *before* the attribute list declaration as shown in the original listing:

```
<!NOTATION c_code SYSTEM "C source code">
<!NOTATION java_code SYSTEM "Java source
```

A program written to handle this XML file would need to 'capture' the particular value of the NOTATION attribute within the document's body and handle it appropriately.

```
<?xml version="1.0" standalone="yes"?>
<!DOCTYPE codefrag [
 <!NOTATION c_code SYSTEM "C source code">
```

```
<!NOTATION java_code SYSTEM "Java source
code">
<!ELEMENT codefrag EMPTY>
<!ATTLIST codefrag
  codelang NOTATION (java_code | c_code)
                              #REQUIRED>
]>
<codefrag codelang="c_code">
<![CDATA[ gdsf87y874b<ocde> !!! ANYTHING
GOES HERE &&&&&</ocde>fufs7]]>
</codefrag>
```

In the above, we make codefrag EMPTY and include a
CDATA section as content. It will be ignored by the parser.

ENTITY attribute type with NDATA
We could write the above XML document using the
NDATA (notation data declaration). Here is the document
followed by an explanation:

```
<?xml version="1.0" standalone="yes" ?>
<!DOCTYPE codefrag [
<!NOTATION c_code SYSTEM "C source code">
<!NOTATION java_code
                SYSTEM "Java source code">
<!ENTITY ccode SYSTEM "C.cc" NDATA c_code>
<!ENTITY javacode SYSTEM "J.jj"
                    NDATA java_code>
<!ELEMENT codefrag (#PCDATA)>
<!ATTLIST codefrag
        codelang ENTITY #REQUIRED >
]>
<codefrag codelang="javacode" >
<!-- Java code would go here -->
</codefrag> <!-- Example 12.7 -->
```

There is actually a little more to type. First look at the XML
document:

12: Further Attributes

```
<codefrag codelang="javacode" >
```

Here is the DTD declaration. We have a codelang attribute as before but note how this is of type *ENTITY* rather of type NOTATION.

```
<!ATTLIST codefrag
          codelang ENTITY #REQUIRED >
```

There must now be an ENTITY declaration for the attribute's value 'javacode'. Since we may also wish to choose a value of 'ccode' instead of 'javacode', we need to supply an ENTITY declaration for that as well.

```
<!ENTITY ccode SYSTEM "C.cc" NDATA c_code>
<!ENTITY javacode SYSTEM "J.jj"
                  NDATA java_code>
```

What is new here, is the NDATA keyword. This informs the parser that the ENTITY refers to a NOTATION declaration. Consequently, after the NDATA keyword is the name of the NOTATION declaration. There must be one for each of the attribute's possible values.

```
<!NOTATION c_code SYSTEM "C source code">
<!NOTATION java_code
                  SYSTEM "Java source code">
```

Summary
Both CDATA and enumeration are the most widely used types for attributes. The others are used for more special occasions.

ID type is useful for uniquely identifying an attribute. A program could then check the XML document for the unique field.

NMTOKEN is useful when you need to ensure that the attribute's value comprises only valid XML name characters.

THIRTEEN

XML Schemas

XML Schemas are an alternative method for validating XML documents. In this sense, there is no difference between a DTD and an XML Schema, both are used for ensuring that an XML document has been written 'correctly', i.e., that all elements and attributes and the type of data content adheres to a content model. So when should we use a Schema and when should we use a DTD?

The bad news is that XML schemas are not known for their brevity, so you have more to type in. However, they have many advantages over DTDs. We shall come across many of the advantages in later chapters, but here are a few:

- schemas are written in XML syntax whereas DTDs have a different syntax
- DTDs have only ten data types, but Schemas have over 40
- you can even create your own customised data types
- schemas have namespaces (see Chapter 20), DTDs do not

13: <u>XML Schemas</u>

For example, in an XML schema, you can specify that the content of an element or attribute must be ten digits (as in the case of an ISBN); that a number must be positive with two decimal places (as in the case of a purchase cost). This is not possible in a DTD, since it can only specify that a value content is a set of 'characters' but not what sort of characters. However, we shall look at all this and more as we progress. For the moment we shall concentrate on how to create a simple schema.

A First Example

There is no such thing as an internal schema unlike DTDs. Therefore, at least two files need to be created, the XML document and its accompanying schema.

In the example below, the standalone XML document provides a single book *root* element which can contain one child `authorname` and one child `title` element. Not much use as yet, but we shall soon expand upon it.

```
<?xml version="1.0" standalone="yes"?>
 <book>
  <authorname>Fred Jones</authorname>
  <title>My Day out in Bootle</title>
 </book>
            <!-- Ex13-1.xml -->
```

Here is a corresponding external DTD which can be used to validate an XML document:

```
<!ELEMENT book (authorname, title)>
<!ELEMENT authorname (#PCDATA)>
<!ELEMENT title (#PCDATA)>
            <!-- Ex13-1.dtd -->
```

In which case our XML document would need to include:

```
<?xml version="1.0" standalone="no"?>
<!DOCTYPE book SYSTEM "Ex13-1.dtd">
```

Here is an equivalent XML Schema version:

```
<?xml version="1.0"?>
<schema
targetNamespace="http://www.currency.org"
xmlns="http://www.w3.org/2001/XMLSchema"
xmlns:F="http://www.currency.org"
elementFormDefault="qualified">
<element name = "book">
 <complexType>
   <sequence>
    <element name = "authorname"
             type = "string"/>
    <element name = "title"
             type = "string"/>
   </sequence>
 </complexType>
</element>
</schema>   <!-- schema13-1.xds -->
```

The first thing we note is how lengthy it is. Secondly, we can see that it resembles an XML type document, which it is, and, therefore, is *well-formed*. That means that we no longer have to think in terms of a different syntax when writing schemas. *Do not forget that case is significant in an XML document and, therefore, in schemas.*

Let us now look at what is inside the above schema document. It was typed as it stands in Notepad (but you could use any editor or word processor) and saved as a text-only file with an *xsd* extension (.xsd). You can make up any extension for the schema file, but it is becoming conventional to use xsd.

The Schema
There is the standard declaration stating that this is an XML document. All XML schemas are, of course, XML documents. There is an optional encoding attribute:

13: XML Schemas

```
<?xml version="1.0" encoding = "UTF-8"?>
```

Next comes the root element - schema. All schema documents are enclosed in this root element. The opening schema element contains a lot of horrid looking things. They are horrid and we devote two chapters on namespaces in order to explain what they mean. For the moment try and forget them, unless you are trying out these examples and their corresponding XML documents in which case type them in as shown.

```
<schema
  targetNamespace="http://www.currency.org"
  xmlns="http://www.w3.org/2001/XMLSchema"
  xmlns:F="http://www.currency.org"
  elementFormDefault="qualified">

  .... the rest of the schema follows here ....

</schema>
```

The schema file must include at least two *namespaces* in the opening schema tag via two xmlns attributes, but for the moment we shall not discuss them. Just include them (or any variation) in your schema documents until we have had a chance to discuss their significance in Chapter 20.

Next comes:

```
<element name = "book">
```

The above sets the root element for the XML document. Since book will contain two child elements (authorname and title) and because only complexType[1] elements can have child elements, book has to be declared as a complexType element. Note the mandatory intercapping.

```
<element name = "book">
  <complexType>
```

---

[1] See Chapter 17.

The indentation is mine, although widely practised, to make it easier to read. Next comes:

```
<sequence>
 <element name="authorname" type="string"/>
 <element name="title"      type="string"/>
</sequence>
```

The `sequence` element (actually called a *compositor*) states that all the enclosed elements are child elements of the `book` element and must appear in the order given. In other words, `authorname` must come before the `title` element and, must appear in any XML document being validated against this schema. Because we have not said otherwise, the two elements can occur only once. (More of this later.)

A declared element must have a `name` attribute and a `type` attribute. We have chosen a `string` data type (equivalent to PCDATA in a DTD) for both child elements. The two elements cannot contain any child elements or attributes when used in the XML document. They can only contain text and are called *empty* elements. (Not to be confused with an empty element in a DTD.) That makes them `simpleTypes`.

In schemas, a simple type is said to be *empty* and this is denoted by the use of the closing forward slash. Any element which has child elements and/or attributes must be declared as *complexType*. (We have much to say about `simpleType` v. `complexType` in Chapter 17.)

```
<!-- in the schema -->
<element name="title"  type="string"/>
<!-- in the XML document -->
<title>Our day out in Bootle</title>
```

Finally, all the non-empty elements must be closed, as befits any well-formed XML document.

```
  </complexType>
 </element>
</schema>
```

Basically, that is how a simple schema is created. We need to discuss all the various types of data content that elements and attributes can contain. Learn how to create our own data types, how to link an XML document to a schema so that it can be validated, and find out about namespaces. Here is the final XML document.

```
<?xml version="1.0"?>
<!-- Schema-1.xml -->
 <book
xmlns="http://www.currency.org"
xmlns:xsi="http://www.w3.org/2001/XMLSchema-instance"
xsi:schemaLocation="http://www.currency.org
                 schema13-1.xsd">
  <authorname>Fred Jones</authorname>
  <title>My Day out in Bootle</title>
 </book>
                   <!-- Ex13-1.xml -->
```

Again there are several lines added to the root element book which needs to be discussed in Chapter 20.

A Second Example

Here is another XML document whose structure is based upon a schema. It simply provides information about a single book. Note the isbn attribute in the root element (book).

```
<?xml version="1.0" encoding="utf-8"?>
<book isbn="0836217462"
xmlns="http://www.currency.org"
```

```
xmlns:xsi="http://www.w3.org/2001/XMLSchema-instance"
xsi:schemaLocation="http://www.currency.org
                     schema13-2.xsd">
 <title>Our Day Out in Bootle</title>
  <authornames>
   <author> Fred Jones</author>
   <author> Mary Jones</author>
  </authornames>
 <details>
  <edition>2nd</edition>
  <pubDate>1950-10-04</pubDate>
  <cover>Hardback</cover>
 </details>
</book> <!-- Ex13-2.xml -->
```

Using an *internal* DTD the XML document would have looked like:

```
<?xml version="1.0" encoding="utf-8"
      standalone="yes"?>
<!DOCTYPE book [
<!ELEMENT book (title, authornames, details)>
<!ATTLIST book isbn CDATA #REQUIRED>
<!ELEMENT title    (#PCDATA)>
<!ELEMENT authornames (author+)>
<!ELEMENT author   (#PCDATA)>
<!ELEMENT details (edition, pubDate, cover)>
<!ELEMENT edition (#PCDATA)>
<!ELEMENT pubDate (#PCDATA)>
<!ELEMENT cover    (#PCDATA)>
]>
<book isbn="0836217462">
   <title>Our Day Out in Bootle</title>
   <authornames>
    <author> Fred Jones</author>
    <author> Mary Jones</author>
   </authornames>
   <details>
```

```
<edition>2nd</edition>
<pubDate>1950-10-04</pubDate>
<cover>Hardback</cover>
</details>
</book>
                <!-- bookDTD.xml -->
```

Any XML document can be opened in IE5 and it will show the parent-child relationship between the elements.

We can easily see that book has three child elements: title, authornames and details; authornames has one author child and details has three child elements, edition, pubDate and cover.

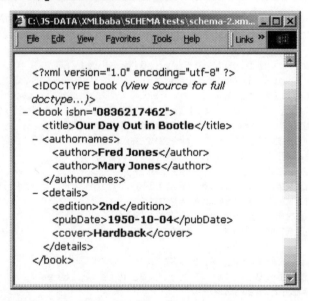

The XML schema is shown on the next page.

```
<?xml version="1.0" encoding="UTF-8"?>
<schema
targetNamespace="http://www.currency.org"
xmlns:F="http://www.currency.org"
xmlns="http://www.w3.org/2001/XMLSchema"
elementFormDefault="qualified">

<element name="book">
    <complexType>
      <sequence>
        <element name="title" type="string"/>
        <element name="authornames">
         <complexType>
           <sequence>
            <element name="author"
                       minOccurs="1"
                       maxOccurs="unbounded"/>
           </sequence>
          </complexType>
        </element> <!-- End of authornames -->
        <element name="details">
         <complexType>
           <sequence>
            <element name="edition"
                      type="string"/>
            <element name="pubDate"
                      type="date"/>
            <element name="cover"
                      type="string"/>
           </sequence>
          </complexType>
        </element>     <!-- End of details -->
      </sequence>
  <attribute name="isbn" type="string"/>
 </complexType>
 </element>              <!-- End of book -->
</schema>
          <!-- schema13-2.xds -->
```

13: XML Schemas

We can summarise the above in the following table, where the number shown is the order in which the elements (and the attribute) are declared in the schema.

Root Element	Contains	which contains
book [1]	title [2]	
	authornames [3]	authors [4] (one or more)
	details [5]	edition [6]
		pubDate [7]
		cover [8]
	an attribute isbn [9]	

There are three new features in this schema. First, we have specified the number of times that an author element can appear. In a DTD, this was done via the + occurrence symbol. But it can only mean at least once and possibly many. In a schema, we use the minOccurs and maxOccurs attributes. If they are left out, then they default to one occurrence. In our code, we have:

```
<element name="author"
        minOccurs="1" maxOccurs="unbounded"/>
```

This means that the author element must appear at least once because of the value of minOccurs and that any number of them may appear because of the unbounded value of maxOccurs.

But maxOccurs could also take a number. Thus:

```
<element name="author"
        minOccurs="1" maxOccurs="12"/>
```

Now, we could have any number of `author` elements in the range of 1-12. Because the default value of `minOccurs` is "1", we could have left it off. Here are a few more variations:

XML Schema	DTD equivalent
`minOccurs="0" maxOccurs="unbounded"`	*
`minOccurs="0" maxOccurs="1"`	?
`minOccurs="1" maxOccurs="unbounded"`	+
`minOccurs="1" maxOccurs="12"`	n/a

The second feature is that the `pubDate` element takes a `date` type.

```
<element name="pubDate" type="date"/>
```

Now, any XML document validated against this schema can enter only a date for the content of the `pubDate` element. In XML Schema a date is written in the following format: yyyy-mm-dd, but we shall see later that there are many other variations. It is not possible to restrict content to a date format using a DTD.

The third feature is the placement of the attribute declaration. Since all elements containing attributes must be a `complexType`, attributes must be placed after any child elements have been declared (if any) and before the closing `complexType` tag. *(There is apparently no logical reason for this, except that the* W3C *Working Group thought it was a more natural place to append attributes)*

```
    <attribute name="isbn" type="string"/>
  </complexType>
</element>   <!-- End of book -->
```

Notice, that unlike a DTD, no root element is specified in any formal way. The XML document author will have to type in the root element based on how the schema was written.

Note, too, that all attribute values are quoted, according to well-formed XML documents. The schema is, of course, an example of an XML document.

A Second way of writing XML schemas
Suppose we had a much more complex schema to create. Apart from ensuring that all the closing tags were present and correctly nested, indenting would become a nightmare. Fortunately, there is another way of writing schemas which allows us to keep all the simple elements in one part, all the attributes in another and all the complex type elements in yet another.

Instead of nesting elements from the top-down, sometimes called the *Russian doll design*, but officially known as *in-lining*, we can use a *flat catalogue design*. Here it is, first in a table format and then as a proper schema. It is a simple example but once we have looked at what is involved we will be able to re-write the earlier in-line example.

The XML document:

```
<?xml version="1.0"?>
<book
xmlns="http://www.currency.org"
xmlns:xsi="http://www.w3.org/2001/XMLSchema-instance"
xsi:schemaLocation="http://www.currency.org
                    schema13-3.xsd">
 <title>Our Day Out in Bootle</title>
 <author> Fred Jones</author>
</book>
            <!-- Ex13-3.xml -->
```

Complex elements	Simple elements
book (and root)	title
	author

The Schema:

```
<?xml version="1.0" encoding="UTF-8"?>
<schema
targetNamespace="http://www.currency.org"
xmlns:F="http://www.currency.org"
xmlns="http://www.w3.org/2001/XMLSchema"
elementFormDefault="qualified">

<!-- declarations of the simple type elements follow. -->
  <element name="title" type="string"/>
  <element name="author" type="string"/>

<!-- declaration of the root element. -->
  <element name="book">
    <complexType>
     <sequence>
      <element ref="F:title"/>
      <element ref="F:author"/>
     </sequence>
    </complexType>
  </element>       <!-- End of book -->
</schema>
            <!-- schema13-3.xsd -->
```

The main root element, book, takes children and, therefore, must be a complex type. It takes two child elements but this time it makes a reference to them via the ref attribute. This implies that they have been declared somewhere else. Like us, a parser will look through the schema looking for the declarations. The two elements have been declared at the start, both being of type string. In this way we can keep the simple types and the complex types in separate blocks of code.

13: XML Schemas

However, this approach, using the `ref` attribute requires that `title` and `author` be prefixed with `F`:

```
<element ref="F:title"/>
```

If you look in the opening `schema` element, you will see `xmlns:F`. It could have been any other letter or any valid XML name, I happened to choose F. The reason why the referenced elements in the `ref` attribute have to be prefixed is tied up with namespaces, a somewhat tricky topic better left to Chapter 20.

Applying the `ref` approach to `schema13-2.xsd`

We can apply the `ref` approach to an earlier example, `schema13-2.xsd`. In the following, all the simple elements come first, followed by any attribute definitions. Finally, we have the complex type elements. But we could type them in any order. The trick here is to marry up a `complexType` element with a simple type. This is achieved quite simply by using a *reference* (`ref` attribute).

```
<?xml version="1.0" encoding="UTF-8"?>
<schema
targetNamespace="http://www.currency.org"
xmlns:F="http://www.currency.org"
xmlns="http://www.w3.org/2001/XMLSchema"
elementFormDefault="qualified">

<!-- declarations for the simple type elements follow. -->
 <element name="edition" type="string"/>
 <element name="pubDate" type="date"/>
 <element name="cover"   type="string"/>
 <element name="title"   type="string"/>
 <element name="author"  type="string"/>

<!-- declarations for the complex type elements. -->
 <element name="authornames">
   <complexType>
   <sequence>
```

```
        <element ref="F:author" minOccurs="1"
                 maxOccurs="unbounded"/>
     </sequence>
    </complexType>
  </element> <!-- End of authornames -->

  <element name="details">
    <complexType>
      <sequence>
         <element ref="F:edition"/>
         <element ref="F:pubDate"/>
         <element ref="F:cover"/>
      </sequence>
     </complexType>
  </element>      <!-- End of details -->

  <element name="book">
    <complexType>
     <sequence>
      <element ref="F:title"/>
      <element ref="F:authornames"/>
      <element ref="F:details"/>
     </sequence>
      <attribute name="isbn" type="string"/>
    </complexType>
  </element> <!-- End of book -->
</schema>   <!-- schema13-2a.xsd -->
```

Notes:

1. It is now much easier to check for correct nesting.

2. Essentially, we are replacing the name attribute by the ref attribute. Notice how the ref attribute references one of the simple type element declarations.

3. The simple declarations do not (and must not) include anything apart from name and type attributes.

4. Be very, very careful about the use of the closing forward slashes for all the empty simple type elements.

5. The order in which the declarations are placed is arbitrary.

6. We had to add a prefix (F:) to those element names which are referenced via the ref attribute, (Chapter 20).

7. Finally, we have used another data type, namely date. This means that only a date in yyyy-mm-dd format will be valid as the content for element pubDate. There are 44 data types in XML Schema and are discussed in detail in Chapters 15 and 16.

Here is an XML document, Ex13-2a.xml, which has been validated against schema13-2a.xsd. Notice how the attribute isbn is included in the book element.

```
<?xml version="1.0"?>
<book isbn="1234567890"
xmlns="http://www.currency.org"
xmlns:xsi="http://www.w3.org/2001/XMLSchema-instance"
xsi:schemaLocation="http://www.currency.org
                    schema13-2a.xsd">
  <title>Our Day Out in Bootle</title>
  <authornames>
   <author> Fred Jones</author>
   <author> Mary Jones</author>
  </authornames>
  <details>
   <edition>2nd</edition>
   <pubDate>1950-10-04</pubDate>
   <cover>Hardback</cover>
  </details>
 </book>
            <!-- Ex13-2a.xml -->
```

It is difficult to validate XML documents against schemas until one has mastered namespaces and prefixes. These are discussed in detail in Chapters 20 and 21.

Compositors: `sequence`, `choice` & `all`

So far we have used only the `sequence` *compositor*, as it is officially called. But there are two more, *choice* and *all*. Remember that the `sequence` compositor dictates that the elements must occur in a particular order. The `choice` compositor provides a choice between several elements, but only one can be chosen. In the following, `authors` can take one or other of the elements `authorname` or `title`.

```
<?xml version="1.0" encoding = "UTF-8"?>
<schema ....... >
<element name = "authors">
 <complexType>
   <choice>
    <element name = "authorname"
             type = "string"/>
    <element name = "title" type = "string"/>
   </choice>
 </complexType>
</element>
</schema>
```

The above is similar to the following DTD:

```
<!ELEMENT authors (authorname | title)>
```

In the next example, we can begin to see just how powerful a combination of `choice` and `sequence` compositors can be. Here is the XML file with an internal DTD:

```
<?xml version="1.0" standalone="yes" ?>
<!DOCTYPE nameTypes
[
<!ELEMENT nameTypes (fullname | (firstname,
                    middlename*, lastname))>
<!ELEMENT fullname   (#PCDATA)>
```

```
<!ELEMENT firstname   (#PCDATA)>
<!ELEMENT middlename  (#PCDATA)>
<!ELEMENT lastname    (#PCDATA)>
]>
<nameTypes>
<!--fullname>John Smith</fullname-->
<firstname> John </firstname>
<!--middlename> Fred</middlename -->
<lastname> Smith</lastname>
</nameTypes>
               <!-- DTDchoice.xml -->
```

We can either have a `fullname`:

```
<nameTypes>
 <fullname>John Smith</fullname>
</nameTypes>
```

or: a `firstname`, an optional `middlename` followed by a `lastname`.

```
<nameTypes>
 <firstname> John </firstname>
 <middlename> Fred</middlename>
 <lastname> Smith</lastname>
</nameTypes>
```

The same can be achieved via an XML schema as follows:

```
<?xml version="1.0" encoding="UTF-8"?>
<schema
targetNamespace="http://www.currency.org"
xmlns:L="http://www.currency.org"
xmlns="http://www.w3.org/2001/XMLSchema"
elementFormDefault="qualified">
<element name = "nameTypes">
 <complexType>
   <choice>
    <element name = "fullname"
```

```
                type = "string"/>
    <sequence>
     <element name = "firstname"
                type = "string"/>
     <element name = "middlename"
                type = "string"
                minOccurs="0"/>
     <element name = "lastname"
                type = "string"/>
    </sequence>
   </choice>
 </complexType>
</element>
</schema> <!-- schema13-4.xsd -->
```

Because we have a `sequence` compositor within a `choice`, we can either have a `fullname` or a sequence of `firstname`, an optional `middlename` (because of `minOccurs="0"`) and a `lastname`.
Here is `Ex13-4.xml`:

```
<?xml version="1.0"?>
< nameTypes
xmlns="http://www.currency.org"
xmlns:xsi="http://www.w3.org/2001/XMLSchema-instance"
xsi:schemaLocation="http://www.currency.org
                    schema13-4.xsd">
<!--fullname>John Smith</fullname-->
<firstname> John </firstname>
<!--middlename> Fred</middlename -->
<lastname> Smith</lastname>
</nameTypes>
                <!-- Ex13-4.xml -->
```

The all Compositor
This is the same as the `sequence` compositor in that all elements must appear, but they are order independent.

```
<all>
    <element name = "firstname"
            type = "string"/>
    <element name = "middlename"
            type = "string"
            minOccurs="0"/>
    <element name = "lastname"
            type = "string"/>
</all>
```

Usually, it is better to avoid using this one since an XML author could choose any order for the elements, such as first-last-middle or middle-last-first, etc.

Summary

We have introduced XML schemas and seen how to create in-line schemas and flat catalogue schemas.

We have seen that elements which contain child elements and/or attributes must be complex types. Those with neither child elements nor attributes (*empty* in XML Schema terminology) are simple types.

The actual number of occurrences of an element can be stated with the `minOccurs` and `maxOccurs` attributes. if they are omitted, they both have a default value of 1.

Finally we looked at the three various types of compositors, `all`, `choice` and `sequence`.

Caution: Perhaps you already have a product like XML Spy which automatically validates XML documents against DTDs and schemas. It will also validate a DTD and/or schema without needing to reference an XML document.

If you are trying to validate your XML documents against a schema, as opposed to a DTD, you may well run into problems (as I did, frequently) until you have mastered namespaces and prefixes. It is quite a complex affair which I have left until Chapters 20 onwards. To fully understand the namespace problem, you also need to know a fair amount about schemas. So the approach adopted here is to cover schemas as far as possible, and then delve into namespaces. If you are trying out my examples, just be careful to use the prefixes where they are shown.

simpleType	no child elements, no attributes
complexType	used with child elements and/or attributes
sequence	all must appear in order given
all	all must appear but in any order
choice	restricts the choice to one of two or more elements, rather like the enumeration feature for DTDs
minOccurs	minimum number of times an element can appear
maxOccurs	maximum number of times an element can appear
name	name of element
type	type of data an element can contain
string	any sequence of characters may be used for this data type
date	a date in strict yyy-mm-dd format

Test 13:

1. How could you say that an element can occur exactly 3 times?

2. What is the root element for an XML Schema?

3. How is a simple type recognised by a parser?

4. What is the equivalent of #PCDATA in an XML Schema?

13: <u>XML Schemas</u>

5. What is the formal jargon term for `sequence`, `all` and `choice`?

6. What is the difference between `sequence` and `all`?

7. Can an empty simple type element contain any content?

8. What is the difference between a simple type element and a complex type element?

9. Where is an attribute declared in an XML Schema?

10. How would you offer an XML author the choice between entering either a `telephone` or `email` contact?

FOURTEEN

Creating Your Own Data Types

One of the advantages of XML schemas is that it allows us to create our own data types. Here is one of our earlier examples. The root element `booklist` can take one or many `book` elements, we just show one in the following XML instance document:

```
<?xml version="1.0" encoding="utf-8"?>
<L:booklist
xmlns:L="http://www.currency.org"
xmlns:xsi="http://www.w3.org/2001/XMLSchema-instance"
xsi:schemaLocation="http://www.currency.org
                    schema14-1.xsd">

<book>
  <title>Our Day Out in Bootle</title>
  <author> Fred and Mary Jones</author>
  <edition>2nd</edition>
  <pubDate>2002-10-19</pubDate>
  <cover>Hardback</cover>
 </book>
</L:booklist>
              <!-- Ex14-1.xml -->
```

14: Creating Your Own Data Types

Here is an in-line schema which could be used for the XML document `Ex14-1.xml`:

```
<?xml version="1.0" encoding="UTF-8"?>
<schema
targetNamespace="http://www.currency.org"
xmlns="http://www.currency.org"
xmlns="http://www.w3.org/2001/XMLSchema"
elementFormDefault="unqualified">

<element name="booklist">
 <complexType>      <!-- anonymous -->
  <sequence>
   <element name="book"
             maxOccurs="unbounded">
    <complexType> <!-- anonymous -->
     <sequence>
      <element name="title" type="string"/>
      <element name="author"
                type="string"/>
      <element name="edition"
                type="string"/>
      <element name="pubDate" type="date"/>
      <element name="cover" type="string"/>
     </sequence>
    </complexType>
   </element>  <!-- End of book -->
  </sequence>
 </complexType>
</element>       <!-- End of booklist -->
</schema>
             <!-- schema14-1.xsd -->
```

Notice that the `complexTypes` are *anonymous*, they have no names. But, it is possible to give *names* to complex types and refer to those names as a *data type definition* in an element declaration. It is yet a third way of creating schemas (and the last!). Here is an equivalent version of the in-line schema (schema14-1.xsd) but with a *named* complex type. I can refer to this type within an element declaration. The following schema14-2.xsd can be used with the XML document Ex14-1.xml:

```
<?xml version="1.0" encoding="UTF-8"?>
<schema
targetNamespace="http://www.currency.org"
xmlns:X="http://www.currency.org"
xmlns="http://www.w3.org/2001/XMLSchema"
elementFormDefault="unqualified">

<element name="booklist">
 <complexType>
   <sequence>
    <element name="book"
              type="X:bookDefinition"
              maxOccurs="unbounded"/>
   </sequence>
 </complexType>
</element> <!-- Eof booklist -->
<!-- Here is my own data type definition
              for bookDefinition -->
<complexType name="bookDefinition">
      <sequence>
        <element name="title" type="string"/>
        <element name="author"/>
        <element name="edition"
                 type="string"/>
        <element name="pubDate" type="date"/>
        <element name="cover" type="string"/>
      </sequence>
      </complexType>
</schema>
            <!-- schema14-2.xsd -->
```

What we have done here is to create a data type named bookDefinition. In practice, it is identical to the anonymous `complexType` except that it has been given a name:

```
<complexType name="bookDefinition">
... etc ...
</complexType>
```

It has been placed on its own. The complex type element `booklist` can now refer to this new type via the *type* attribute to see what content model it contains.

```
<element name="booklist">
 <complexType>
   <sequence>
    <element name="book"
             type="bookDefinition"
             maxOccurs="unbounded"/>
   </sequence>
 </complexType>
</element>
```

This, therefore, is yet a third way of writing schemas. Each of the three methods have their pros and cons. But we cannot discuss them until we see how each impacts on namespaces and that is left until Chapter 20.

Another Example

Here is an in-line schema example from Chapter 13, but extended to allow for any number of books in a book list and an `isbn` attribute. It also has `xs:` prefixed to many of the elements. This is a common approach to do with namespaces and we shall why later in Chapter 20.

```
<?xml version="1.0" encoding="UTF-8"?>
<xs:schema
targetNamespace="http://www.currency.org"
xmlns="http://www.currency.org"
xmlns:xs="http://www.w3.org/2001/XMLSchema"
```

```
elementFormDefault="unqualified">
<xs:element name="bookList">
 <xs:complexType>
  <xs:sequence>
   <xs:element name="book">
    <xs:complexType>
     <xs:sequence>
      <xs:element name="title"
                  type="xs:string"/>
      <xs:element name="authornames">
       <xs:complexType>
        <xs:sequence>
         <xs:element name="author"
                     minOccurs="1"
                     maxOccurs="unbounded"/>
        </xs:sequence>
       </xs:complexType>
      </xs:element> <!-- End of authornames -->
      <xs:element name="details">
       <xs:complexType>
        <xs:sequence>
         <xs:element name="edition"
                     type="xs:string"/>
         <xs:element name="pubDate"
                     type="xs:date"/>
         <xs:element name="cover"
                     type="xs:string"/>
        </xs:sequence>
       </xs:complexType>
      </xs:element> <!-- End of details -->
     </xs:sequence>
     <xs:attribute name="isbn"
                   type="xs:string"/>
    </xs:complexType>
   </xs:element>    <!-- End of book -->
  </xs:sequence>
 </xs:complexType>
```

14: Creating Your Own Data Types

```
</xs:element>   <!-- End of booklist -->
</xs:schema>    <!-- schema14-3.xds -->
```

The above is the in-line approach. We shall re-write it as
`schema14-4.xsd` using data type definitions. First, we
have to identify what our data types will be. We shall have
three, `book`, `authornames` and `details`. I shall append
'Type' to these three to indicate that they are my own data
types.

- bookType
- authornamesType
- detailsType

Here is an XML document instance (`Ex14-4.xml`) which
will work with `schema14-3.xsd` and `schema14-4.xsd`:

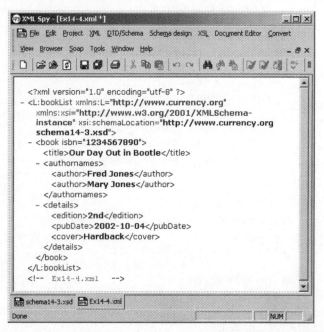

The main (root) element, `bookList` will take `bookType` as its child. This child will take both `authornamesType` and `detailsType` as its children. Study the following:

```xml
<?xml version="1.0" encoding="UTF-8"?>
<xs:schema
targetNamespace="http://www.currency.org"
xmlns="http://www.currency.org"
xmlns:xs="http://www.w3.org/2001/XMLSchema"
elementFormDefault="unqualified">
<xs:element name = "bookList">
 <xs:complexType>
   <xs:sequence>
    <xs:element name = "book"
                type="bookType"
                maxOccurs="unbounded"/>
    </xs:sequence>
   </xs:complexType>
</xs:element>
<!-- Here follows our data Types -->
            <!-- bookType -->
<xs:complexType name="bookType">
 <xs:sequence>
   <xs:element name="title"
               type="xs:string"/>
   <xs:element name="authornames"
               type="authornamesType"/>
   <xs:element name="details"
               type="detailsType"/>
</xs:sequence>
<xs:attribute name="isbn" type="xs:string"
              use="optional"/>
</xs:complexType>
            <!-- End of bookType -->

            <!-- authornamesType -->
<xs:complexType name="authornamesType">
```

```
<xs:sequence>
  <xs:element name="author" type="xs:string"
              maxOccurs="unbounded"/>
 </xs:sequence>
</xs:complexType>
        <!-- End of authornamesType -->
            <!-- detailsType -->
<xs:complexType name ="detailsType">
 <xs:sequence>
  <xs:element name="edition"
              type="xs:string"/>
  <xs:element name="pubDate" type="xs:date"/>
  <xs:element name="cover" type="xs:string"/>
 </xs:sequence>
</xs:complexType>
        <!-- End of detailsType -->
</xs:schema>
            <!-- schema14-4.xsd -->
```

In the table below, we can see that bookList takes one child element of type bookType. In turn, this has three children, a simple title element and two data types, authornamesType and detailsType. Both of these have simple elements as their children.

Element	Children
bookList (*root*)	bookType
bookType	title authornamesType detailsType *attribute* isbn
authornamesType	author +
detailsType	edition pubdate cover

Table 14.1

Is it worth going to the trouble of writing schemas using this third approach? We shall give some reasons in later Chapters. Again, it is a question of namespaces.

A Third Example
Let us suppose that we have to maintain a list of resources for a particular subject, such as, tennis, wild flowers, environmental issues, arthritis, or whatever. The resources could come from any of the following: books, journals, magazines, conference papers, newspapers, web sites, etc.

We would like to identify which source it belongs to - book, journal, etc. So, we introduce an element called medium. Finally, only a book can have an ISBN attribute, so we shall have to take that into account.

resourcesList becomes the root element and it takes one or many source elements. It also takes an attribute named topic.

source takes a sourceType data type and an isbn attribute which is optional so that it will only be entered when the medium is a book

sourceType takes a details element
in turn, the details element takes the following child elements: title, author (maximum ten), medium, edition, pubDate, publisher, description

The XML document as viewed in IE6 can be seen on page 180.

```
<?xml version="1.0" encoding="UTF-8"?>
<xs:schema
targetNamespace="http://www.currency.org"
xmlns="http://www.currency.org"
xmlns:xs="http://www.w3.org/2001/XMLSchema"
elementFormDefault="unqualified">
```

14: <u>Creating Your Own Data Types</u>

```
<xs:element name="resourcesList">
 <xs:complexType>
  <xs:sequence>
   <xs:element name="source"
               type="sourceType"
               maxOccurs="unbounded"/>
  </xs:sequence>
  <xs:attribute name="topic"
                type="xs:string"/>
 </xs:complexType>
</xs:element>
     <!-- Here follows our sourceType -->
<xs:complexType name="sourceType">
 <xs:sequence>
  <xs:element name="details">
   <xs:complexType>
    <xs:sequence>
  <xs:element name="title" type="xs:string"/>
  <xs:element name="author"
               type="xs:string"
               maxOccurs="10"/>
  <xs:element name="medium"
                type="xs:string"/>
  <xs:element name="edition"
               type="xs:string"
               minOccurs="0"/>
  <xs:element name="pubDate"
             type="xs:date"/>
  <xs:element name="publisher"
              type="xs:string"/>
  <xs:element name="description"
             type="xs:string"/>
    </xs:sequence>
   </xs:complexType>
  </xs:element>
 </xs:sequence>
```

```
<xs:attribute name="isbn" type="xs:int"
              use="optional"/>
</xs:complexType>
</xs:schema>
            <!-- schema14-5.xsd -->
```

Notes:

1. `resourcesList` takes 1 or any number (unbounded) of `source` elements together with one attribute, `topic`. Remember that `minOccurs` has a default value of 1 if it is omitted. Note where the attribute `topic` has been declared.

2. The `source` element is of type `sourceType`.

3. `sourceType` takes a `details` child element

4. `details` takes seven simple type elements:

Element	Occurrences	Type
title	one	string
author(s)	1 to maximum 10	string
medium	one	string
edition	none or one	string
pubDate	one	date
publisher	one	string
description	one	string

5. Note how the placement of the attributes means that only the `resourcesList` and `source` elements can take attributes.

The use attribute in attribute declarations

XML schemas allow the author to define how an attribute is to be used. The `optional` value of the `use` attribute is equivalent to the #IMPLIED DTD keyword. It means that you are not forcing the XML author to use the attribute and, if it is not used, there is no default value.

14: Creating Your Own Data Types

```
C:\JS-DATA\XMLbaba\SCHEMAtests\xml-14-5.xml - Microsoft Internet Explorer provi...
File  Edit  View  Favorites  Tools  Help                              Links »

<?xml version="1.0" encoding="utf-8" ?>
- <L:resourcesList topic="XHTML" xmlns:L="http://www.currency.org"
    xmlns:xsi="http://www.w3.org/2001/XMLSchema-instance"
    xsi:schemaLocation="http://www.currency.org schema-14-5.xsd">
    <!--  xml-14-5.xml  -->
- <source isbn="1234567890">
    <!-- cover="softback" -->
  - <details>
      <title>XHTML & CSS explained</title>
      <author>John Shelley</author>
      <medium>book</medium>
      <edition>2nd</edition>
      <pubDate>2002-05-23</pubDate>
      <publisher>Babani Books</publisher>
      <description>An excellent treatment by ...</description>
    </details>
  </source>
- <source>
  - <details>
      <title>XHTML 1.0</title>
      <author>W3C</author>
      <medium>web</medium>
      <pubDate>1996-01-20</pubDate>
      <publisher>W3 Org</publisher>
      <description>recommendation ...</description>
    </details>
  </source>
- <source>
  - <details>
      <title>XHTML v. HTML</title>
      <author>Fred Doe</author>
      <author>Sally Hardcastle</author>
      <medium>newspaper</medium>
      <pubDate>2001-11-02</pubDate>
      <publisher>Computer Quarterly</publisher>
      <description>Fred has a succinct style ...</description>
    </details>
  </source>
</L:resourcesList>
<!--  basic XML14-5  -->
```

The string type is equivalent to CDATA.

```
<attribute name="ISBN" type="string"
           use="optional"/>
```

The corresponding DTD version would be:

```
<!ATTLIST source ISBN CDATA #IMPLIED>
```

The `use` attribute can take three values:

Values for use	Explanation	Equivalent DTD
optional	attribute is not required	#IMPLIED
required	attribute is required	#REQUIRED
prohibited	attribute cannot be used	not available

default & fixed values

In the following, the attribute `version` has a default value and is `optional`:

```
<attribute name="version" type="string"
           default="2.3"  use="optional"/>
```

Without the use attribute, the default value would be supplied by the parser if the attribute was not present in the XML document.

The next example shows a fixed value that *must* be used:

```
<attribute name="version" type="string"
           fixed="2.3"    use="required"/>
```

Conditions for Attribute Declarations

According to the W3C Recommendation[1], an attribute with a default value can take only the `optional use` value or be omitted.

> "Note that default values for attributes only make sense if the attributes themselves are optional, and so it is an error to specify both a default value and anything other than a value of `optional` for use."

If an attribute has a default value, the schema processor will supply that value only if the attribute is missing in the XML document. If the attribute is present and the XML

---

[1] XML Schema Part 0: Primer, 2.2.1 Occurrence Constraints.

author provides some value other than the default, that other value is the one which will apply. In other words, it will not be replaced with the default value.

Conditions for element declarations

1. In an element declaration, *"one of* ref *or* name *must be present, but not both".*

2. If ref is present, only minOccurs, maxOccurs and id (yet to be discussed) are allowed.

3. An element declaration can have either a type attribute, (to refer to a data type content model), or a complexType child element, but not both. Consequently:

```
<element name="abc"
         type="xyz"/>
```

and:

```
<element name="abc">
 <complexType>
  ... content model ... etc ...
 </complexType>
```

are both valid, but the following is ***incorrect***:

```
<element name="abc" type="defg">
 <complexType>
  ... etc ...
 </complexType>
```

Summary

We have seen a third way to create schemas by defining our own data types and giving the complexType a name. The reference to the data type is made via the type attribute in the element declaration.

Three ways to create schemas

The same XML document can be validated against any one of the following three schemas. I have deliberately minimised the use of prefixes in the following schemas. A complete discussion about prefixes and why we must use them is given in Chapters 20 and 21. L: is my chosen prefix, but it could have been any other letter or, indeed, any valid XML name.

```
<?xml version="1.0"?>
<abc
xmlns="http://www.books.org"
xmlns:xsi="http://www.w3.org/2001/XMLSchema-instance"
xsi:schemaLocation="http://www.books.org
                         schema14-6a.xsd">

  <bbb>BBB</bbb>
  <ccc>2003-05-21</ccc>
</abc>
```

Schema 1: The *in-line* approach does not require a prefix in the XML document, but does in the schema:

```
<?xml version="1.0"?>
                 <!-- IN-LINING -->
<schema
targetNamespace="http://www.books.org"
xmlns="http://www.w3.org/2001/XMLSchema"
xmlns:L="http://www.books.org"
elementFormDefault="qualified">
<element name="abc">
 <complexType>
  <sequence>
   <element name="bbb" type="string"/>
   <element name="ccc" type="date"/>
  </sequence>
 </complexType>
</element>
</schema> <!-- schema14.6a.xsd -->
```

Schema 2: By a `ref` attribute which does requires a prefix:

14: <u>Creating Your Own Data Types</u>

```
<?xml version="1.0"?>
                <!-- by REF -->
<schema
targetNamespace="http://www.books.org"
xmlns="http://www.w3.org/2001/XMLSchema"
xmlns:L="http://www.books.org"
elementFormDefault="qualified">
<element name="bbb" type="string"/>
<element name="ccc" type="date"/>

<element name="abc">
 <complexType >
  <sequence>
  <element ref="L:bbb"/>
  <element ref="L:ccc"/>
 </sequence>
</complexType>
</element>
</schema>         <!-- schema14-6b.xsd -->
```

Schema 3: Using `type` which also requires a prefix:

```
<?xml version="1.0"?>
         <!-- define a data type -->
<schema
targetNamespace="http://www.books.org"
xmlns="http://www.w3.org/2001/XMLSchema"
xmlns:L="http://www.books.org"
elementFormDefault="qualified">

<element name="abc" type="L:abcType"/>

<complexType name="abcType">
  <sequence>
  <element name="bbb" type="string"/>
  <element name="ccc" type="date"/>
 </sequence>
</complexType>
</schema>    <!-- schema14-6c.xsd -->
```

FIFTEEN

Further Use of Data Types

We have seen how we can define our own types to create complete schemas. In this section, we shall look at how we can create our own data types to ensure that XML document authors enter only valid data. For example, a telephone number consists of numbers and must not include letters or any other characters apart from hyphens. In a DTD, it would not be possible to restrict a telephone number to just numbers since DTDs mainly use just one data type, namely text-strings, which can include any character: digits, letters, punctuation symbols, etc.

XML schemas, on the other hand, have 44 different data types, see the next Chapter. This means that XML authors can be forced to enter data in a very strict format, otherwise their documents will not be valid. However, in addition to the 44 XML Schema data types, we can create our own, usually based on one of the 44. This is what we examine in this chapter and hope to illustrate one of the main advantages of schemas over DTDs.

Previously, we made an ISBN of type `string`:

```
<attribute name="isbn" type="string"/>
```

15: Further use of Data Types

This `string` type means that almost any character could be entered. In a DTD, the CDATA data type is all we have access to. So, as it stands, there is no difference between the string `type` and the following DTD equivalent:

`<!ATTLIST book isbn CDATA>`

An ISBN consists mainly of a ten-digit number. Suppose we wanted to constrain an XML author to enter just digits and, furthermore, that *ten* digits are required. We shall forget the hyphens for the time being, we simply want the ten digits.

We begin by defining our ISBN attribute (alternatively it could have been an element). I chose to call its *type* isbnType:

```
<attribute name="ISBN" type="isbnType"
           use="required"/>
```

Somewhere, we have to define the `isbnType` data type, and enclose it within a `simpleType` element as follows:

```
<simpleType name="isbnType">
  <restriction base="string">
    <pattern value="[0-9]{10}"/>
 </restriction>
</simpleType>
```

The first thing to mention is that attributes are always defined as *simple types* because they do not contain child elements. Elements which contain only text are also simple types but they do not need to be nested within the `simpleType` element, thus, in the following `authors` is by default a simple type:

```
<element name="authors" type="string"/>
```

We shall discuss `simpleType` versus `complexType` in detail in the next Chapter.

The next thing to appreciate is that when creating our new data type, the new type must be based on *an existing data type* known to the schema processor. In our case this is the *string* type. We shall derive a new type based on this string type by *restricting* what it can consist of. By default, the `string` data type can take any kind of character, letters, numbers, etc., but we want to tell the processor that to *restrict* this base `string` type:

```
<restriction base="string">
 ... etc ...
</restriction>
```

But what restrictions shall we impose? Well, that is done via a `pattern`:

```
<pattern value="[0-9]{10}/>
```

where the content of value spells out our restriction, namely any digits between 0-9, enclosed in square brackets and, in curly brackets, the required number, 10. There must be no space between the closing square bracket and the opening curly bracket.

Now suppose we wanted to force people to input an ISBN number with hyphens. Here are some of the valid formats used by publishers, where 'd' stands for a decimal digit:

d-dddd-dddd-d, or, d-ddddd-ddd-d, or, d-dd-dddddd-d

```
<simpleType name="isbnType">
  <restriction base="string">
  <pattern value="\d{1}-\d{4}-\d{4}-\d{1}"/>
  <pattern value="\d{1}-\d{5}-\d{3}-\d{1}"/>
  <pattern value="\d{1}-\d{2}-\d{6}-\d{1}"/>
  </restriction>
</simpleType>
```

An alternative method for specifying a digit is to use the '\d{5}' format instead of '[0-9]{5}'. The first pattern specifies a single digit followed by a hyphen (or dash), followed by 4 digits followed by a dash, followed by another set of four digits and a dash, followed by a single digit. No spaces have been allowed.

The second pattern specifies one digit, followed by a hyphen, followed by five digits, followed by a hyphen, followed by 3 digits, followed by a hyphen and one digit; and so on. We have used three patterns but only one can be chosen by an XML author and used in a given instance.

There is an alternative way of writing the above, using just one pattern value but separating each pattern by the *or* symbol (| - a vertical bar).

```
<pattern value="\d{1}-\d{4}-\d{4}-\d{1}|
\d{1}-\d{5}-\d{3}-\d{1}|\d{1}-\d{2}-\d{6}-
\d{1}"/>
```

It can be more difficult to read. When more than one pattern is used, the implication is that one and only one can be used at any one time. It is also important not to press the Enter Key anywhere between the double quotes of the pattern's value.

There must not be any spaces before or after the bar symbol. If you do, then a space must appear in the XML instance document. thus:

```
<pattern value="\d{3} | \d{3}"/>
```

would require: 123^ or ^123 where a space is shown by the ^ symbol in this text. So take great care about spaces.

Date type
Like the string type, the date type is another example of a built-in data type which schema validators can recognise. However, it has a strict format. The date type is used to represent a specific date in year-month-day

format and must be typed as CCYY-MM-DD (e.g.: 2003-11-28) where:

Symbol	meaning	range
CC	century	00-99
YY	year	00-99
MM	month	01-12
DD	day - if month 2	0-28
	if leap year month 2	0-29
	if month 4,6,9,11	0-30
	if month 1,3,5,7,8,10 or 12	0-31

(XML Spy allows the CC to be omitted when validating a date type. But this is contrary to the W3C Recommendation.)

gYear (the Gregorian calendar year) is yet another built-in data type. Elements declared to be of type gYear must follow the form CCYY, for example, 1999 or 2003. If we wanted our date to be of type gYear, as for a typical copyright: 2003 ©, we would simply use the following:

```
<element name="copyright" type="gYear"/>
```

There are many more variations of a date type and these are examined in the next Chapter.

complexType v. simpleType
Just to summarise:

a complexType is used when an element has child elements and/or attributes.

a simpleType is used when we need to derive a new data type of our own which is based upon one of the built-in type, such as date, gYear or string.

A Telephone data type
We shall do one more example and then introduce some jargon terms which you need to know about. Then we can

15: <u>Further use of Data Types</u>

begin to discuss some of the many other built-in data types and see what we can do with them. Here is an example of a telephone data type which I have chosen to call `TelephoneNumber`. It is a standard type of 3-4-4 pattern for London and outer London telephone numbers. (The numbers are meant to be fictitious!) Note how the pattern includes hyphens.

020-7569-4321   020-8123-4567

```
<simpleType name="TelephoneNumber">
 <restriction base="string">
   <length value="13"/>
   <pattern value="\d{3}-\d{4}-\d{4}"/>
 </restriction>
</simpleType>
```

`length` states that the base `string` must be exactly 13 characters. In fact, it is made redundant because the `pattern` fixes the number of characters as well. However, it has introduced the length *facet*. Yes, that is what it is called, not an element. The `pattern` is also called a facet. The `string` and `date` data types are formally known as a *primitive data types*. So we now have these two jargon terms, *primitive data types* and *facets*. There are 19 primitive data types and they form the basis (the base) for the other 25 XML Schema data types, as we shall see later in the next Chapter.

The *string* data type & its facets
The `string` data type represents a finite length sequence of characters. It can take the following facets:

length	enumeration
minLength	maxLength
pattern	whiteSpace

There are twelve facets in XML Schema, of which only six apply to the `string` data type.

Primitive data types

There are 19. Those marked with an asterisk are used for specific applications and are not covered in this text, but for details, see the W3C reference given in Appendix A.

Primitive Data Type	Example/Format
string	Babani Books
boolean	true, false, 1, 0
decimal	23.45
float	13.56E12, 12.34, -12, 13.56e15
*double	a 64-bit double precision IEEE floating point number e.g. 133.456e12
duration	represents a duration in this order: year, month, day, hour, minute and second P10D2H30M45S
dateTime	CCYY-MM-DDThh:mm:ss 2003-12-25T12:30:45
time	hh:mm:ss 12:30:45
date	CCYY-MM-DD 2003-12-25
gYearMonth	CCYY-MM 2003-12
gYear	CCYY 2003
gMonthDay	--MM-DD --12-25
gDay	---DD ---25
gMonth	--MM-- --02--
*hexBinary	FFCC69
*base64Binary	AC2xaQ
anyURI	http://www.w3.org/TR/xmlschema-2
*QName	a namespace qualified name
*NOTATION	a NOTATION from the XML spec

As you can see, some of them look terrifying and are used in special circumstances, beyond the scope of this text.

15: <u>Further use of Data Types</u>

Facets

We shall now look at the twelve facets. In the next Chapter, we specify which facets apply to which data type.

length	enumeration
minLength	maxLength
pattern	whiteSpace
maxInclusive	minInclusive
maxExclusive	minExclusive
totalDigits	fractionDigits

length: specifies the *exact* number of characters allowed and must be a non-negative integer (whole) number. In other words, the value must be equal to or greater than zero. If length is specified for a data type, neither minLength nor maxLength can be used for that data type.

Example: I have an element called password based on the string data type. However, it needs to be restricted to exactly 8 characters. The length facet is ideal:

```
<element name="password">
 <simpleType>
  <restriction base="string">
    <length value="8"/>
  </restriction>
 </simpleType>
</element>
<!-- in an XML instance -->
<password>1234abcd</password>
```

maxLength & minLength: specifies the maximum/minimum number of characters allowed. It must be equal to or greater than zero. These cannot be used if the length facet is used.

Example: a password must be between 6 and 10 characters
inclusive

```
<element name="password">
 <simpleType>
  <restriction base="string">
    <minLength value="6"/>
    <maxLength value="10"/>
  </restriction>
 </simpleType>
</element>
<!-- in an XML instance -->
<password>12abcd</password>
```

pattern: restricts via a regular expression the possible
content of a data type. If multiple patterns are present,
only one of the patterns may be used in the XML
document. Multiple patterns act as an 'or'.

Example 1: a gender element can contain either *male* or
female. The bar symbol denotes 'or'. Be careful not to put
spaces before or after the bar, otherwise they become part of
the pattern

```
<element name="gender">
 <simpleType>
  <restriction base="string">
    <pattern value="male|female"/>
  </restriction>
 </simpleType>
</element>
<!-- in an XML instance -->
<gender>female</gender>
```

Example 2: a password must contain exactly 8 characters
and the characters must be lowercase a-z, or uppercase A-Z
or a number from 0-9, in any order and mixture.

15: Further use of Data Types

```
<element name="password">
 <simpleType>
  <restriction base="string">
    <pattern value="[a-zA-Z0-9]{8}"/>
  </restriction>
 </simpleType>
</element>
<!-- in an XML instance any of the following would be valid
-->
<password>11111111</password>
<password>aaaaaaaa</password>
<password>1123aBC7</password>
```

There are many variations possible using regular expressions with the pattern facet. Allowable characters are placed within square brackets. The number of times they can recur is placed within curly brackets.

enumeration: specifies an acceptable set of valid values for the XML document instance. Like the pattern facet, only one may be used.

Example: a *car* element in an XML document, may contain any one of the enumerated values

```
<element name="car">
<simpleType>
  <restriction base="string">
    <enumeration value="Jeep"/>
    <enumeration value="Toyota"/>
    <enumeration value="Hyundai"/>
  </restriction>
</simpleType>
</element>
<!-- in an XML instance -->
<car>Toyota</car>
```

whiteSpace: this facet specifies how the processor is to treat whitespace - tabs, line feeds, carriage returns and multiple consecutive spaces. One of three values may be applied:

> **preserve:** no modification takes place by the processor, so that all whitespace is preserved.
>
> **replace:** replace tabs, line feeds and carriage returns with single spaces.
>
> **collapse**: after tabs, line feeds and carriage returns are replaced with single spaces, sequences of spaces are collapsed into a single space. Furthermore, leading and trailing spaces are removed.

Example 1: The following `name` element will have all forms of white space preserved.

```
<element name="name">
<simpleType>
  <restriction base="string">
    <whiteSpace value="preserve"/>
  </restriction>
</simpleType>
</element>
<!-- in an XML instance -->
<name>  John
        Smith   </name>
```

It would probably be better to use a `collapse` value, especially if the data is destined for a database:

Example 2:

```
<simpleType>
  <restriction base="string">
    <whiteSpace value="collapse"/>
  </restriction>
</simpleType>
```

15: Further use of Data Types

maxInclusive & minInclusive: sets the upper/lower, respectively, bounds for the range of values. The values are *included* in the range.

Example: An age element is restricted to integer values in the range 0-100. (*integer* is a data type derived from the primitive decimal data type, see the next Chapter.)

```
<element name="age">
<simpleType>
  <restriction base="integer">
    <minInclusive value="0"/>
    <maxInclusive value="100"/>
  </restriction>
</simpleType>
</element>
<!-- in an XML instance -->
<age>100</age>
```

maxExclusive & minExclusive: as above, but the values are not included in the range.

Example: zero and 100 are excluded.

```
<element name="age">
<simpleType>
  <restriction base="integer">
    <minExclusive value="0"/>
    <maxExclusive value="100"/>
  </restriction>
</simpleType>
</element>
<!-- in an XML instance -->
<age>99</age>
```

totalDigits: this facet is used for data types derived from the decimal data type. It sets the *maximum* total number of digits in the entire number and must be a positive integer. See example below.

fractionDigits: this facet is used for data types derived from the `decimal` data type, but sets the *maximum* total number of digits in the fractional part of the number. Its value must be a non-negative number (i.e. it can be zero). If it is set to zero, then the number cannot contain a decimal point or any fraction digit.

Example: using the above two facets we can restrict a `purchase` element to a value between 0.00 and 999.99:

```
<element name="purchase">
 <simpleType>
   <restriction base="decimal">
    <totalDigits value="5"/>
    <fractionDigits value="2"/>
   </restriction>
 </simpleType>
</element>
<!-- in an XML instance any of the following is valid-->
<purchase>155.99</purchase>
<purchase>15.9</purchase>
<purchase>5.99</purchase>
<purchase>.99</purchase>
<!-- in an XML instance the following are invalid-->
<purchase>1234.99</purchase>
<purchase>2.919</purchase>
```

Derived data types

We have seen that there are 19 primitive data types and mentioned that XML Schema allows for 44 built-in data types. So what and where are the other 25? Twelve of them derive from the *primitive* `string` data type and the other 13 from the `decimal` data type. The correct terminology is to say that they are *derived* from these two.

15: <u>Further use of Data Types</u>

`string` **derived data types**

normalizedString	token
language	*NMTOKEN
*NMTOKENS	Name
*NCName	ID
IDREF	IDREFS
ENTITY	ENTITIES

`decimal` **Derived data types**

integer	
positiveInteger	nonPositiveInteger
negativeInteger	nonNegativeInteger
int	unsignedInt
byte	unsignedByte
short	unsignedShort
long	unsignedLong

In the next Chapter we examine the various primitive and derived data types.

Examples

Here are two examples of user defined data types derived from the `string` primitive data type. The first is applied to an attribute.

In an XML document, the author *must* choose one of the three patterns based on the following schema, otherwise the document will not be valid.

```
<?xml version="1.0" encoding="UTF-8"?>
<xsd:schema
targetNamespace="http://www.currency.org"
xmlns:xsd="http://www.w3.org/2001/XMLSchema"
xmlns="http://www.currency.org"
elementFormDefault="qualified">
<xsd:element name="xcost">
   <xsd:complexType>
     <xsd:sequence>
```

```
      <xsd:element name="cost"
                    type="xsd:string"/>
    </xsd:sequence>
      <xsd:attribute name="isbn"
           type="isbnType" use="optional"/>
  </xsd:complexType>
 </xsd:element>
 <xsd:simpleType name="isbnType">
 <xsd:restriction base="xsd:string">
 <xsd:pattern
           value="\d{1}-\d{4}-\d{4}-\d{1}"/>
  <xsd:pattern
           value="\d{1}-\d{5}-\d{3}-\d{1}"/>
  <xsd:pattern
           value="\d{1}-\d{2}-\d{6}-\d{1}"/>
 </xsd:restriction>
</xsd:simpleType>
</xsd:schema> <!-- schemaEx15-1.xsd -->
```

```
          <!-- in the XML instance -->
<xcost isbn="1-2345-6789-0"> or
<xcost isbn="1-23456-789-0"> or
<xcost isbn="1-23-456789-0">
```

Based on the following schema, an XML document author must choose just one of the enumerations otherwise the document will not be valid.

```
<xs:element name="details">
 <xs:complexType>
  <xs:sequence>
   <xs:element name="title"
               type="xs:string"/>
   <xs:element name="author"
               type="xs:string"
               maxOccurs="10"/>
   <xs:element name="medium"
               type="mediumType"/>
```

```
    <xs:element name="edition"
                type="xs:string"
                minOccurs="0"/>
    <xs:element name="pubDate"
                type="xs:date"/>
    <xs:element name="publisher"
                type="xs:string"/>
    <xs:element name="description"
                type="xs:string"/>
  </xs:sequence>
 </xs:complexType>
</xs:element>
            <!-- mediumType definition -->
<xs:simpleType name="mediumType">
  <xs:restriction base="xs:string">
    <xs:enumeration value="book"/>
    <xs:enumeration value="web"/>
    <xs:enumeration value="newspaper"/>
  </xs:restriction>
</xs:simpleType>

            <!-- in the XML instance -->
<medium>newspaper</medium> or
<medium>web</medium>    or
<medium>book</medium>
```

Perhaps we can now begin to appreciate just why XML
Schemas are becoming so popular, despite their
verbosity.

SIXTEEN

Primitive and Derived Data Types

The Primitive data types

Within an element or an attribute, the primitive data types are used as a *value* of the `type` attribute. They express how data can appear in an XML instance document and how they can be constrained by the use of facets. We have seen some in the previous chapter, `pattern`, `enumeration`, `length`, but now we shall look at the data types in detail.

Each of the following has its own permissible set of facets. In the following, for example, `string` has six out of the possible twelve.

string: represents a finite-length sequence of characters.

constraining facets:

length	enumeration
minLength	maxLength
pattern	whiteSpace

```
<element name="codenumber">
 <simpleType>
   <restriction base="string">
    <length value="5"/>
   </restriction>
```

```
  </simpleType>
</element>

            <!-- in an XML instance -->
<codenumber>AB123</codenumber>
```

boolean: used for binary logic (true or false | 1 or 0)

constraining facets:

pattern	whiteSpace

```
<element name="valid" default="true"
        type="boolean"/>
or
<element name="valid" default="1"
        type="boolean"/>

  <!-- in an XML instance but not using the default -->
<valid>false</valid> or <valid>0</valid>
      <!-- in an XML instance using the default -->
<valid/>
```

decimal: a finite sequence of digits separated by a period. Leading and trailing zeroes are optional. An optional leading + or - is also allowed. If no leading sign is used, it is assumed to be +. The *maximum* number of digits is usually set at 18, but it can vary depending on the operating system.

constraining facets:

pattern	whiteSpace
maxInclusive	minInclusive
maxExclusive	minExclusive
totalDigits	fractionDigits
enumeration	

```
<element name="myNumber" default="999"
        type="decimal"/>
```

```
<!-- in an XML instance any of the following are valid  -->
<myNumber>999.50</myNumber>
<myNumber>+999.50</myNumber>
<myNumber>-999.5009</myNumber>
<myNumber>999</myNumber>
<myNumber>0</myNumber>
      <!-- in an XML instance using the default  -->
<myNumber/>
```

`float:` represents a 32-bit, single-precision IEEE floating point number. Its value is in the range: $m \times 2^e$ where m is an integer whose absolute value is less than 2^{24} and e is an integer between -149 and 104 inclusive.

`double:` represents a 64-bit, double-precision IEEE floating point number. Its value is in the range: $m \times 2^e$ where m is an integer whose absolute value is less than 2^{53} and e is an integer between -1075 and 970 inclusive

constraining facets for float & double:

pattern	whiteSpace
maxInclusive	minInclusive
maxExclusive	minExclusive
enumeration	

If you need numbers which look like 3.97E25, see the finer details in the XML Schema Part 2: Data types (see Appendix A).

`duration:` is used to specify a time interval. It must be specified in the following form:

`PnYnMnDTnHnMnS` where:

P	indicates the period (required)
nY	indicates the number of years
nM	indicates the number of months

16: <u>Primitive and Derived Data Types</u>

nD   indicates the number of days
T   indicates the start of the time section (required
       when a time is specified)
nH   indicates the number of hours
nM   indicates the number of minutes
nS   indicates the number of seconds

constraining facets:

pattern	whiteSpace
maxInclusive	minInclusive
maxExclusive	minExclusive
enumeration	

```
<element name="period" type="duration"/>
<!-- in an XML instance any of the following are valid -->
<period>P5Y</period>
     <!-- 5 years -->
<period>P5Y3M12D</period>
     <!-- 5 years, 3 months and 12 days -->
<period>P5M10DT2H30M</period>
     <!-- 5 months, ten days, 2 hours and 30 minutes
          and note the use of the T separator -->
<period>PT2H</period>
     <!-- 2 hours -->
<period>-P10D</period>
     <!-- minus ten days -->
```

Here is an example where a duration data type is restricted by a pattern. In a regular expression \d specifies one or more digits, the + specifies the content to follow. Thus \d+M means one or more digits followed by M. Appendix C discusses regular expressions in some detail.

```
<element name="sabbatical">
 <simpleType>
   <restriction base="duration">
```

```
    <pattern value="P\d+M\d+D"/>
   </restriction>
 </simpleType>
</element>
<!-- in an XML instance 12 months, 5 days-->
<sabbatical>P12M5D</sabbatical>
```

\D means any non-digit character including blank.

Here is a delivery date pattern:

```
<element name="deliverTime">
 <simpleType>
   <restriction base="duration">
    <pattern value="P\d+D"/>
   </restriction>
 </simpleType>
</element>
<!-- in an XML instance  25 days -->
<deliverTime>P25D</deliverTime>
```

dateTime: represents a specific date and time in the following form:

CCYY-MM-DDThh:mm:ss where:

CC indicates the century
YY indicates the year
MM indicates the month
DD indicates the day
T indicates the start of the *required* time section
hh indicates the hours
mm indicates the minutes
ss indicates the seconds

Note: all components are required.

constraining facets:

pattern	whiteSpace
maxInclusive	minInclusive

maxExclusive	minExclusive
enumeration	

```
<element name="startDate" type="dateTime"/>
        <!-- in an XML instance -->
<startDate>2003-05-16T09:30:00</startDate>
```

time: represents a specific time in the following form:

hh:mm:ss where:

hh indicates the hours
mm indicates the minutes
ss indicates the seconds

Note: all components are required, and leading zeroes.

constraining facets:

pattern	whiteSpace
maxInclusive	minInclusive
maxExclusive	minExclusive
enumeration	

```
<element name="startTime" type="time"/>
        <!-- in an XML instance -->
<startTime>09:30:00</startTime>
```

date: represents a specific date in the following form:

CCYY-MM-DD where:

CC indicates the century
YY indicates the year
MM indicates the month
DD indicates the day

Note: all components are required.

constraining facets:

pattern	whiteSpace
maxInclusive	minInclusive

maxExclusive	minExclusive
enumeration	

```
<element name="anniversary" type="date"/>
```
            <!-- in an XML instance -->
```
<anniversary>2003-05-16</anniversary>
```

Time Zones
The `datetime`, `date` and `time` data types may take an optional time zone to indicate a value in UTC (Coordinated Universal Time) time. You can either add a Z after the value:

```
<element name="anniversary" type="date"/>
```
            <!-- in an XML instance -->
```
<anniversary>2003-05-16Z</anniversary>
```

or, follow the format with a minus or plus sign to indicate a UTC time offset represented as hh:mm:

```
<element name="startDate" type="dateTime"/>
```
            <!-- in an XML instance -->
```
<startDate>2003-05-16T09:30:00+06:00
</startDate>
<startDate>2003-05-16T09:30:00-06:00
</startDate>
```

Gregorian dates
All the Gregorian data types may also take an optional time zone as discussed above.
They are all based on the Gregorian Calendar.
They all have the same constraining facets.

constraining facets:

pattern	whiteSpace
maxInclusive	minInclusive
maxExclusive	minExclusive
enumeration	

16: Primitive and Derived Data Types

gYearMonth: represents a specific year and month in the Gregorian Calendar, in the following form:

CCYY-MM where:

CC indicates the century
YY indicates the year
MM indicates the month

To specify May, 2003 one would type: 2003-05

Note: all components are required. A preceding minus sign is allowed.

```
<element name="grandOpening"
        type="gYearMonth"/>

        <!-- in an XML instance -->
<grandOpening>2003-05Z</grandOpening>
```

gYear: represents a specific *year* in the following form:

CCYY where:

CC indicates the century
YY indicates the year

```
<element name="anniversary" type="gYear"/>

        <!-- in an XML instance -->
<anniversary>2003</anniversary>
```

gMonthDay: this data type can be used to represent a specific day in a month, for example, an anniversary date which occurs every 14th February. It takes the following form:

--MM-DD where:

MM indicates the month
DD indicates the day

No preceding sign (i.e. a plus or minus) is allowed but it requires the two preceding hyphens.

```
<element name="anniversary"
         type="gMonthDay"/>
            <!-- in an XML instance -->
<anniversary>--05-16</anniversary>
```

gDay: represents a specific day of the month, For example, I get paid on 24th of each month. It takes the following form:

`---DD` where:

DD indicates the day. No preceding sign is allowed but it requires the three preceding hyphens.

```
<element name="payday"
         type="gDay"/>
            <!-- in an XML instance -->
<payday>---24</payday>
```

gMonth: represents a specific month. For example, I may always take my holidays during the month of August. It takes the following form:

`--MM--` where:

MM indicates the month

No preceding sign is allowed but it requires the two preceding and trailing hyphens.

```
<element name="holiday"
         type="gMonth"/>
            <!-- in an XML instance -->
<holiday>--08--</holiday>
```

anyURI: used to represent a URI (Uniform Resource Identifier). (See XML Schema Part 2: Data types for details.) This is a useful data type should you need to refer to a web site. A parser makes certain that the content looks like a valid URI.

constraining facets:

pattern	whiteSpace
enumeration	length
minLength	maxLength

```
<element name="webSite" type="anyURI"/>
        <!-- in an XML instance -->
<webSite>http://www.w3.org/TR/xmlschema-2/
</webSite>
```

For details of how and when to use the following data types, see Part 2 of the XML Schema: `QName`, `NOTATION`, `hexBinary` and `base64Binary`. They are used for more specialised areas which are beyond the scope of this text.

The 25 Derived Built-in Data Types
It is convenient to gather twelve of the data types under the umbrella of the `string` data type. However, it is not strictly accurate. For example, `normalizedString` is derived from the `string` type, but `token` is actually derived from the `normalizedString` which is derived from `string`. The Chart on page 223 shows the precise derivations.

The string derived data types

normalizedString	token
language	*NMTOKEN
*NMTOKENS	Name
*NCName	ID
IDREF	IDREFS
ENTITY	ENTITIES

normalizedString: The base type for this is `string`. The value is a set of strings which do not contain carriage returns, line feeds or tabs. It is equivalent to the use of `string` with a `whiteSpace` facet set to the `replace` value. Its derived data type is `token`.

constraining facets:

pattern	length
maxLength	minLength
enumeration	whiteSpace

```
<element name="myString">
 <simpleType>
  <restriction base="normalizedString">
    <maxLength value="25"/>
   </restriction>
  </simpleType>
</element>
    <!-- in an XML instance mystring cannot exceed 25
                    characters-->
<myString>Here is an example.</myString>
```

token: derived from `normalizedString`. It represents strings which do not contain carriage returns, line feeds, tabs or internal sequences of two or more spaces. Equivalent to `string` with a `whiteSpace` facet set to a value of `collapse`. The derived data types from the token type are `language`, `NMTOKEN` and `Name`.

constraining facets:

pattern	length
maxLength	minLength
enumeration	whiteSpace

```
<element name="myToken" base="token"/>
```

16: Primitive and Derived Data Types

```
              <!-- in an XML instance -->
<myToken>Rather like normalizedString.
</myToken>
```

language: derived from token. It represents language identifiers from the set of valid language identifiers. It has no derived data types.

constraining facets:

pattern	length
maxLength	minLength
enumeration	whiteSpace

```
<element name="nativeLang">
 <simpleType>
  <restriction base="language">
   <enumeration value="de"/>
   <enumeration value="fr"/>
   <enumeration value="en-GB"/>
   <enumeration value="en-US"/>
  </restriction>
 </simpleType>
</element>
              <!-- in an XML instance -->
<nativeLang>fr</nativeLang>
```

In the above, our schema is restricting the allowed languages to one of the following fr (French), de (German), en-GB (English - UK) or en-US (American English.

In the following, we refer to the base type token and, via a pattern, restrict the choice to any two-letter language identifier.

```
<element name="nativeLang">
 <simpleType>
  <restriction base="token">
```

```
   <pattern value="[a-zA-Z]{2}"/>
  </restriction>
 </simpleType>
</element>
          <!-- in an XML instance -->
<nativeLang>en</nativeLang>
```

NMTOKEN: derived from token. It represents the XML NMTOKEN, i.e. any valid characters from the following: Unicode letters, digits and any of the four punctuation characters: underscore (_), colon (:), hyphen (-) and period (.). Any of these characters may appear as the first character. NMTOKEN values must not include any white space. It has a derived data type NMTOKENS.

Note: The W3C advises that NMTOKEN should be used only with attributes.

constraining facets:

pattern	length
maxLength	minLength
enumeration	whiteSpace

```
<element name="title">
 <complexType>
  <simpleContent>
   <extension base="string">
    <attribute name="degree" type="NMTOKEN"/>
   </extension>
  </simpleContent>
 </complexType>
</element>
          <!-- in an XML instance -->
<title degree="MSc">Master of Science</title>
```

NMTOKENS: derived from NMTOKEN. It is identical to NMTOKEN except that more than one NMTOKEN value can be included, each separated by white space.

16: <u>Primitive and Derived Data Types</u>

```
. . . . . . .
<attribute name="degree" type="NMTOKENS"/>
. . . . . .
            <!-- in an XML instance -->
<title degree="MSc BA BSc MPhil">
Master of Philosophy</title>
```

By using the NMTOKEN and NMTOKENS types we can ensure that only valid XML name characters can appear. Therefore, any program using the content will know that it consists of characters from a given set.

`ID:` derived from NCName. `ID` is a unique identifier. Its content may be used only once in an instance document.

Note: The W3C advises that `ID` should be used only with attributes. It must be a valid XML name, not just a valid XML name character, i.e. it must begin with a letter.

constraining facets:

pattern	length
maxLength	minLength
enumeration	whiteSpace

```
<attribute name="staffid" type="ID"
           use="required"/>
            <!-- in an XML instance -->
<staffMember staffid="A1234">K. Jones
</staffMember>
```

Name, NCName, ENTITY, ENTITIES, IDREFS are not discussed in this text. They have more advanced uses and you are better advised to defer their purpose until you have become familiar with the basics of schemas and are ready to move on. ID is shown in an example on page 255.

`decimal` derived data types

integer	
positiveInteger	nonPositiveInteger
negativeInteger	nonNegativeInteger
int	unsignedInt
byte	unsignedByte
short	unsignedShort
long	unsignedLong

It is convenient to gather the above thirteen data types under the umbrella of the `decimal` data type. But, again, that is not strictly accurate. For example, `integer` is derived from the `decimal` type, but `long` is derived from the `integer` type. The Chart on page 224 shows the precise derivations. *They all have the same constraining facets as the integer type below.*

`integer`: derived from the `decimal` primitive data type by setting the `fractionDigits` to be zero. It is used to represent the mathematical concept of an integer, i.e. a whole number, positive or negative with no fractional part, e.g.: -999, 0, +123 or 123. If the value has no preceding sign, it is assumed to be positive. The base type of `integer` is `decimal`.

constraining facets:

length	enumeration
minLength	maxLength
pattern	whiteSpace
maxInclusive	minInclusive
maxExclusive	minExclusive
totalDigits	fractionDigits

```
<element name="age">
 <simpleType>
  <restriction base="integer">
```

```
    <minInclusive value="0"/>
    <maxInclusive value="110"/>
   </restriction>
 </simpleType>
</element>
                <!-- in an XML instance -->
<age>65</age>
```

nonPositiveInteger

Derived from the `integer` type by setting the value of `maxInclusive` to be zero. A set of integers less than and including zero. The following will allow any negative integer from -2110. Therefore, -2109 and -3111 would be illegal. The base type is `integer`.

```
<element name="BC">
 <simpleType>
  <restriction base="nonPositiveInteger">
   <minInclusive value="-3110"/>
   <maxInclusive value="-2110"/>
  </restriction>
 </simpleType>
</element>
                <!-- in an XML instance -->
<BC>-2232</BC>
```

negativeInteger

Derived from the `nonPositiveInteger` type by setting the value of `maxInclusive` to be -1. A set of integers less than or equal to -1. The following will allow any negative two-digit value and must be preceded by a minus sign. No types are derived from `negativeInteger`. Leading zeroes are prohibited.

```
<element name="negNum">
 <simpleType>
  <restriction base="negativeInteger">
```

```
   <pattern value="-\d{2}"/>
   </restriction>
 </simpleType>
</element>
                <!-- in an XML instance -->
<negNum>-15</negNum>
```

long

Derived from the `integer` type. A set of integers from
-9223372036854775808 to 9223372036854775807
by setting the `minInclusive` and `maxInclusive`,
respectively, to the above values. The base type of `long`
is `integer`.

int

Derived from the `long` type. A set of integers from
-2147483648 to 2147483647
by setting the `minInclusive` and `maxInclusive`,
respectively, to the above values. The base type of `long`
is `integer`. In the following, a maximum of a five-digit
code number is expected.

```
<element name="code5">
 <simpleType>
   <restriction base="int">
     <totalDigits value="5"/>
   </restriction>
 </simpleType>
</element>
                <!-- in an XML instance -->
<code5>55565</code5>
```

short

Derived from the `int` type. A set of integers from
-32768 to 32767
by setting the `minInclusive` and `maxInclusive`,
respectively, to the above values. The base type of `short`

is `int`. In the following, a maximum of a five-digit code number is expected in the range of `short`.

```
<element name="code5">
 <simpleType>
  <restriction base="short">
    <totalDigits value="5"/>
  </restriction>
 </simpleType>
</element>
            <!-- in an XML instance -->
<code5>12565</code5>
```

byte

Derived from the `long` type. A set of integers from
-128 to 127
by setting the `minInclusive` and `maxInclusive`, respectively, to the above values. The base type of `byte` is `short`.

nonNegativeInteger

Derived from the `integer` type. A set of integers greater than or equal to zero, by setting the `minInclusive` to zero. The base type of `nonNegativeInteger` is `integer`. In the following we want orders to be positive, at least 1 and less than 99 per household.

```
<element name="order">
<simpleType>
  <restriction base="nonNegativeInteger">
    <totalDigits value="2"/>
    <minInclusive value="1"/>
  </restriction>
 </simpleType>
</element>
            <!-- in an XML instance -->
<order>55</order>
```

unsignedLong

Derived from the `integer` type. A set of integers greater than or equal to zero, or less than or equal to:
18446744073709551615
by setting the `maxInclusive` to the above. The base type of `unsignedLong` is `nonNegativeInteger`. Leading zeroes are prohibited.

unsignedInt

Derived from the `unsignedLong` type. A set of integers greater than or equal to zero, or less than or equal to:
4294967295
by setting the `maxInclusive` to the above. The base type of `unsignedInt` is `unsignedLong`. Leading zeroes are prohibited.

unsignedShort

Derived from the `unsignedInt` type. A set of integers greater than or equal to zero, or less than or equal to:
65535 (i.e.: 32767*2 +1)
by setting the `maxInclusive` to the above. The base type of `unsignedShort` is `unsignedInt`. Leading zeroes are prohibited.

```
<element name="order"
         type=" unsignedShort "/>
           <!-- in an XML instance -->
<order>55565</order>
```

unsignedByte

Derived from the `unsignedShort` type. A set of integers greater than or equal to zero, and less than or equal to:
255, (i.e.: 127*2 + 1)
by setting the `maxInclusive` to the above. The base type of `unsignedByte` is `unsignedShort`. Leading zeroes are prohibited.

```
<element name="order"
          type="unsignedByte"/>
  </restriction>
 </simpleType>
</element>
            <!-- in an XML instance -->
<order>255</order>
```

positiveInteger
Derived from the nonNegativeInteger type. A set of
integers greater than or equal to 1.
It is derived by setting the minInclusive to 1. The base
type of positiveInteger is nonNegativeInteger.

Test 16:
1. Using XML Schema, how could you make certain that in a
London telephone number, only 7 or 8 could appear after
020- in a valid XML document?

2. If this was in a pattern: \d {3} rather than \d{3} what
difference would it make?

3. How would you force a code number to have two leading
uppercase characters in the range A-D followed by a three
digit number?

4. How would you force a code number to have two leading
uppercase characters in the range A-D followed by a space
and then by a three digit number?

5. How would force a date to be in the range 1960 – 2006?

6. What is the difference between these three patterns:?
```
<pattern value="ab{3}"/>
<pattern value="(ab){3}"/>
<pattern value="[a|b]{3}"/>
```

SEVENTEEN

Simple and Complex Content

Until now, we have been using a default abbreviation for creating schemas via data types. What we shall now do is to look at what has really been going on behind the scene. Bear in mind that any element in an XML document has some form of content, unless we choose to use an empty element (no content). The content of the element is based on some form of content model as defined by a schema. The content model can be one of the 44 XML Schema data types or a user defined data type which either restricts or extends some base type.

Hierarchy of all types

Behind W3C schemas is the type hierarchy. The syntax for expressing types in schemas follows from this type hierarchy. For a full-page diagrammatic representation, see:

```
http://www.w3.org/TR/xmlschema-2/#built-in-
data types
```

From the Table 17.1, on the next page, we can see that there is a root data type called anyType.

17: Simple and Complex Content

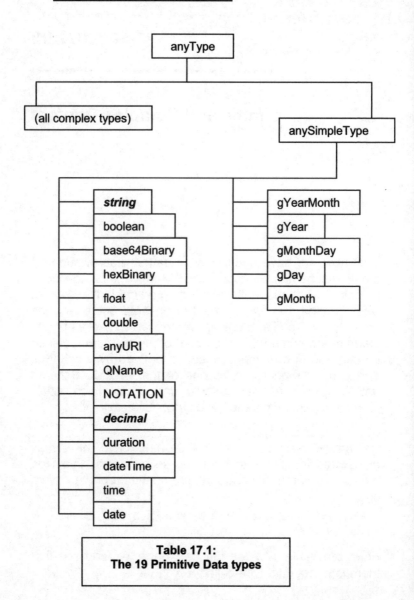

Table 17.1:
The 19 Primitive Data types

All types are derived directly or indirectly from this root type. Indeed, we can actually make use of `anyType`, as shown on the previous page. From the root, there are two branches, `anySimpleType` and 'all complex types'. All of the 19 primitive data types are derived from `anyType`.

To derive a type means to take an existing type, called the *base*, and to modify it in some way. There are four kinds of derivation: `restriction`, `extension`, `list` and `union`. We have already seen how to use restriction and extension, we shall look at `list` and `union` later.

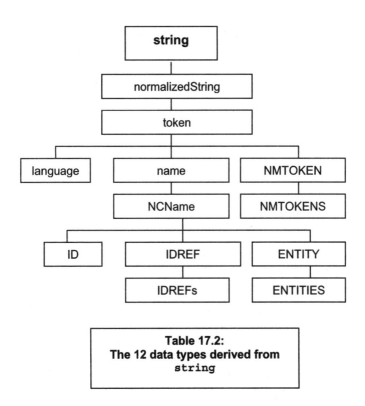

Table 17.2:
The 12 data types derived from
`string`

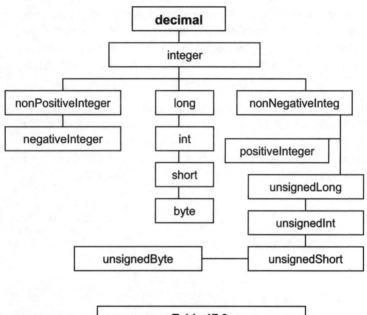

**Table 17.3:
The 13 data types derived from
decimal**

Derivation by restriction implies taking an existing type as the base and creating a new type by limiting (restricting) its content to a subset of whatever the base type permits.

Derivation by extension implies taking an existing type as its base and creating a new type by adding to (extending) whatever that base type allows.

Simple Type v. Complex Type
Simple types can have neither child elements nor attributes. Complex types may have child elements and/or attributes. Tracing the hierarchy down, we can see that the 44 built-in data types are all simple types, each of which is derived from anySimpleType. To derive a new

type from any of the 44 simple types, it must be done by *restriction*. Let us take this example. I need to create a new simple type for the name of an employee. If I simply type:

```
<element name="employee" type="string"/>
```

the employee's name could take any mixture of characters, including digits and punctuation characters. But I employ just two people, so I would like to create a new type based on string but restricting the names to the two people. enumeration will be the facet required, thus:

```
<simpleType name="EmployeeType">
  <restriction base="string">
    <enumeration value="John Doe" />
    <enumeration value="Susan Smith" />
  </restriction>
</simpleType>
```

The above is the definition for EmployeeType. What we now need is to associate a declared element with this definition, thus:

```
<element name="employee"
         type="EmployeeType"/>
```

In an XML document instance, I can now use:

```
<employee>Susan Smith</employee>
```

Because employee has neither child elements nor attributes and because we need to restrict the base type string via an enumeration facet, we must use a simple type definition.

Definition v. Declaration

Any element or attribute used in an XML document has to be *declared* in a corresponding XML schema. Thus, because I am using <employee> in my XML document, it must be declared in the schema. All the declared elements and attributes in a schema form the *vocabulary* which an XML document author uses.

```
<schema ......>
      <!-- definition of EmployeeType -->
<simpleType name="EmployeeType">
  <restriction base="string">
    <enumeration value="John Doe" />
    <enumeration value="Susan Smith" />
  </restriction>
</simpleType>
      <!-- declaration for employee -->
<element name="employee"
        type="EmployeeType"/>
</schema>
```

A component which is used within a schema document but which does *not appear* in an XML document instance is a *definition*. Thus, the simple type EmployeeType is used in the schema as a definition for use in the declared employee element, but it will not appear in an XML document.

Two forms of the Complex Type
Complex types are divided into two groups, those with *simple content* and those with *complex content*. Both forms of the complex type allow for attributes, but only complex content can take child elements. Simple content allows only character content. In other words, only complex content of the complex type can take child elements.

Let us add a *position* attribute to the employee element.

```
<employee position="finance">
        Susan Smith</employee>
```

What will now be our definition? Because we add an
attribute, we can no longer use the simpleType, so, our
definition must move into the complexType. Once we
move into the complex type branch, we now have to
choose whether to use simple content or complex content.
It is simply a matter of deciding whether this new type will
contain child elements or not. I do not want child
elements, just an attribute. So, I choose a complexType
with simple content, thus:

```
<schema ......>
     <!-- definition of EmployeeType -->
<simpleType name="EmployeeType">    ◄─────────┐
  <restriction base="string">
    <enumeration value="John Doe" />
    <enumeration value="Susan Smith" />
  </restriction>
</simpleType>
     <!-- definition of newEmployeeType --▶
<complexType name="newEmployeeType">   ◄───┐  │
  <simpleContent>                            │  │
    <extension base="EmployeeType"> ─────────┘  │
      <attribute name="position"                │
                 type="string" />               │
    </extension>                                │
  </simpleContent>                              │
</complexType>                                  │
     <!-- declaration for employee -->          │
<element name="employee"                        │
        type="newEmployeeType"/>  ──────────────┘
</schema>
```

```
     <!-- in an XML document instance -->
<employee position="finance">Susan
Smith</employee>
```

17: Simple and Complex Content

We have extended the base, the simple type `employeeType`, by adding an attribute to it via the `<extension>` element. It has no child elements, just an attribute, so we make use of the simple content form of the complex type.

Finally, let us modify our employee element so that it *does* have child elements:

```
<employee position="finance">
<name>Susan Smith</name>
<location>Watford, UK</location>
</employee>
```

What do we do now? Clearly, it still has to be a complex type, but it must take *complex content*.

```
<?xml version="1.0" encoding = "UTF-8"?>
<!-- Schema-x.xsd -->
<schema ......>
        <!-- definition of EmployeeType -->
<simpleType name="EmployeeType">
  <restriction base="string">
    <enumeration value="John Doe" />
    <enumeration value="Susan Smith" />
  </restriction>
</simpleType>

      <!-- definition of newEmployeeType -->
<complexType name="newEmployeeType">
  <complexContent>
    <extension base="EmployeeType">
      <sequence>
      <element name="name" type="string" />
    <element name="location" type="string" />
   </sequence>
    <attribute name="position"
                type="string" />
  </extension>
```

```
  </complexContent>
</complexType>

          <!-- declaration for employee -->
<element name="employee"
          type="newEmployeeType"/>
</schema>
```

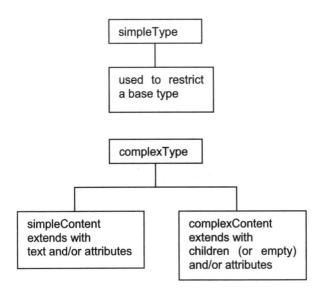

Using anyType

In a large organisation, employees come and go and there will be many names. Let us suppose that we simply want to use string without any restrictions. In case you are trying out the examples, here is a valid schema. Note that there is an L: and a :L. Their purpose is the subject of Chapters 20 and 21.

```
<?xml version="1.0" encoding="UTF-8"?>
<schema
```

17: Simple and Complex Content

```
targetNamespace="http://www.currency.org"
xmlns:L="http://www.currency.org"
xmlns="http://www.w3.org/2001/XMLSchema"
elementFormDefault="unqualified">
        <!-- definition for EmployeesType -->
<element name="employeeList">
<complexType>
<sequence>
<element name="employee"
        type="L:EmployeesType"
        maxOccurs="unbounded"/>
        </sequence>
</complexType>
</element>
<complexType name="EmployeesType">
  <complexContent>
    <restriction base="anyType">
    <sequence>
    <element name="name" type="string" />
    <element name="location" type="string" />
    </sequence>
     <attribute name="position"
                type="string" />
  </restriction>
 </complexContent>
</complexType>
        <!-- declaration for employee -->
</schema>
        <!-- schema17-1.xsd -->
```

We need to create an employee definition. It will contain an attribute, so we must have a *complex type*. It will have two child elements, namely, name and location, therefore we need to have complex content. So far so good. However, what base type are we going to use? We have no existing type to use as a base.

Previously, we based the `employee` element on a `newEmployeeType` which extended an `EmployeeType` by adding two child elements and an attribute. In turn, this `EmployeeType` restricted the type `string` via an `enumeration`. But now, what base type do we use for the `EmployeesType`? This is where the `anyType` can be useful.

```
<complexType name="EmployeesType">
  <complexContent>
   <restriction base="anyType">
```

However, it needs to be restricted rather than extended. `anyType` is the grand-daddy of all types and, therefore, cannot be extended, only restricted. We limit `anyType` to two child elements and one attribute. So, our declared element, `employee`, can now take an element called `name`, followed by an element called `location`. In addition, it takes an attribute called `position`.

Here is the relevant XML instance validated against the schema: `schema17-1.xsd`

```
<?xml version="1.0" encoding="utf-8"?>
<L:employeeList
xmlns:L="http://www.currency.org"
xmlns:xsi="http://www.w3.org/2001/XMLSchema-instance"
xsi:schemaLocation="http://www.currency.org
                    schema17-1.xsd">
<employee position="training">
 <name>Any Name</name>
 <location>Any Place</location>
</employee>
<employee position="finance">
 <name>Susan Phillpotts</name>
 <location>Herts.UK</location>
</employee>
```

```
<!-- etcetera -->
</L:employeeList>
<!-- Ex17.1.xml -->
```

Wait a moment. Perhaps you are remembering the format shown in previous chapters, where we were able to express the above more concisely, thus:

```
<complexType name="EmployeesType">
     <sequence>
   <element name="name" type="string" />
   <element name="location" type="string" />
   </sequence>
    <attribute name="position"
                type="string" />
  </complexType>
```

The above is equivalent to the longer method below:

```
<complexType name="EmployeesType">
  <complexContent>
   <restriction base="anyType">
   <sequence>
   <element name="name" type="string" />
   <element name="location" type="string" />
   </sequence>
    <attribute name="position"
                type="string" />
  </restriction>
 </complexContent>
</complexType>
```

Up until now, we have been using the abbreviated version. We simply left out the following:

```
<complexContent>
```
`<restriction base="anyType">` elements.

The abbreviated format has a default syntax for complex types whereby it is complex content which restricts `anyType`.

We could have used a `string` data type instead of `anyType`, in which case we would have used `extension` rather than `restriction`.

Empty Elements
One final point. Empty elements are ones which have no data content and no child elements, although they may contain attributes. Suppose we want an empty element which does not have even an attribute. (It does very little in the XML document, but may be a program which is reading such an XML document will pick it up as a marker or flag and react in some way.)

Here is an empty element in an XML document:

```
<emptyElement/>
```

How is this going to be defined in an XML schema? Perhaps as a simple type? No. Because simple types contain data content and we need to say that this element *cannot* contain data. So, it must be a complex type. We now ask whether this element will be allowed to contain child elements. The answer, of course, is no. Do we, therefore, use a complex type with simple content? Again, no! Complex types with simple content can also contain data. so the only thing left is a complex type with complex content. "But,", you cry, "complex types with complex content can have child elements and we need to define the complex content as having no data, no attributes and no child elements." The point is, that complex types with complex content are *not required* to have any data content, child elements or attributes. So that is what we have to specify, as follows:

17: Simple and Complex Content

```
<complexType name="programFlag">
  <complexContent>
    <restriction base="anyType">
    </restriction>
  </complexContent>
</complexType>
<element name="aTriggerToApp"
        type="programFlag" />
<!-- in an XML instance this may trigger some
     action by the reading program -->
<aTriggerToApp/>
```

In the above, we have simply left out any content whatsoever. It has to be empty and cannot contain any data content.

Here is the equivalent abbreviated version, which without knowing what lies behind it, could look very peculiar:

```
<complexType name="programHook">
  </complexType>
```

Here is an example of an empty element with an attribute:

```
<xsd:element name="gallery">
 <xsd:complexType>
  <xsd:sequence>
   <xsd:element name="image"
                maxOccurs="unbounded">
    <xsd:complexType>
     <xsd:attribute name="href"
          type="xsd:anyURI" use="required"/>
    </xsd:complexType>
   </xsd:element>
  </xsd:sequence>
 </xsd:complexType>
</xsd:element>
```

Prohibiting derivations

Sometimes we may create a type and wish to prohibit any form of derivations. This can be done by using a `final` attribute. Suppose I have a complex type and make it publicly available. I may want to prohibit anyone from extending it or restricting it. For example, it may contain some copyright information.

We can specify three values for the `final` attribute:

```
final="#all"        - to prohibit any extension or restriction
final="restriction" - to prohibit any restriction
final="extension"   - to prohibit any extension
```

In the following, we prevent any restriction to the `address` type. We may intend to use this as a base type for an address and wish only to allow people to extend it by adding in a country element, an e-mail address, etc.

```
<complexType name="address"
             final="restriction">
<sequence>
 <element name="address1" type="string"/>
 <element name="address2" type="string"/>
 <element name="town"     type="string"/>
 </sequence>
</complexType>
```

Summary

We looked at the hierarchy of data types so that we could see which types have to be derived by a `simpleType`. Simple types can only be restricted; complex types can be extended with child elements or attributes. But we can extend a `simpleType` by making it the base and adding extensions via a new complexType with either simple content or complex content as the case may be.

17: Simple and Complex Content

We discussed the real meaning of declarations and definitions.

Complex types can take either simple content or complex content, depending on whether the content includes child elements. Both are allowed attributes.

`anyType` can prove useful in certain circumstances.

Finally we saw how to create elements which have no content.

Extension means to extend a parent with more elements.

Restriction means create a type which is a subset of the base type

Test 17:

1. When is a `simpleType` used?

2. When is a `complexType` used?

3. When is `ref` used?

4. When is `type` used?

5. When is `simpleContent` used?

6. When is `complexContent` used?

7. Given this:

`<enumeration value="Susan Smith" />`

if I type:

`<employee> Susan Smith </employee>`

into an XML instance, will it be valid?

EIGHTEEN

Element Substitution

In daily conversation there are sometimes several ways of expressing the same thing. For example, Londoners might talk about the London Underground, others may refer to the London Underground as a metro or subway. XML Schema allows a similar type of substitution. We shall take a simple example to see how the process works and then look at a more practical example.

Let us suppose that we have an element called LU standing for the London Underground and which can contain the name for any specific line on the underground, such as the Central or Circle Line.

Here is our LU element declaration:

```
<element name="LU" type="string"/>
```

Here is its use in an XML instance:

```
<LU>Circle Line</LU>
```

18: Element Substitution

We would like to make it possible to substitute either `metro` or `subway` for `LU`, thus:

```
<metro>Circle Line</metro>
<subway>Circle Line</subway>
```

We can do so by the following. The `LU` element is known as the *head*, and can be *substituted* by other named elements via a `substitutionGroup` attribute. Nothing special is done to the head element, it is the others which need special treatment:

```
<element name="LU" type="string"/>
<element name="metro" substitutionGroup="LU"
         type="string"/>
<element name="subway" substitutionGroup="LU"
         type="string"/>
```

Now anywhere that the head element `LU` can be used, either `metro` or `subway` can substituted.

In the following, a `transport` element has been declared with a child element `LU`:

```
<element name="LU" type="string"/>
<element name="metro" substitutionGroup="LU"
         type="string"/>
<element name="subway" substitutionGroup="LU"
         type="string"/>
<element name="transport">
 <complexType>
  <sequence>
   <element ref="LU"/>
  </sequence>
 </element>
</complexType>
```

In an XML document instance, any of the following could be used:

```
<transport>
  <LU>City Line</LU>
</transport>

or <transport>
     <subway>Central Line</subway>
   </transport>

or <transport>
     <metro>City Line</metro>
   </transport>
```

Here is an example whereby we could allow international clients to customise their XML documents, for example, a Spanish client may prefer to use `transporte` instead of `transport`

Note that two sets of `substitutionGroup` are being used:

```
<element name="LU" type="string"/>
<element name="metro" substitutionGroup="LU"
         type="string"/>
<element name="subway" substitutionGroup="LU"
         type="string"/>
<complexType name="transport">
 <sequence>
  <element ref="LU"/>
  </sequence>
</complexType>
<element name="transportation"
         type="transport"/>
<element name="transporte"
         substitutionGroup="transportation"/>
```

When a validator meets an element `transportation` in an XML document, it finds the schema stating that it is a `transport` type. The `transport` type definition states that it must consist of a single `LU` element via the `ref` attribute. The actual declaration for `LU` states that it must contain `string` type content. If it meets `subway` or `metro` rather than `LU`, the validator is told that either can be substituted for `LU`. So the XML document is valid.

```
<transportation>
  <subway>Red Line</subway>
</transportation>
```

Suppose the validator meets a `transporte` element, it checks the schema and discovers that `transporte` can be substituted for `transportation` which is of type `transport` which takes an `LU` element. However, instead of `LU` it finds a `metro` element. It looks for a `metro` element and finds that it can be substituted for an LU element. Again, the XML document is valid.

```
<transporte>
  <metro>Linea Roja</metro>
</transporte>
```

Notes on using `substitutionGroup`

1. The *head* element must be declared as a *global* element, see global versus local later in this Chapter. The elements which are in the `substitutionGroup` must also be declared as global elements.

2. If the type of the substitutable element is the same as the type of the *head* element, it can be omitted. Thus:

```
<element name="LU" type="string"/>
<element name="metro" substitutionGroup="LU"
         type="string"/>
<element name="subway" substitutionGroup="LU"
         type="string"/>
```

could be written as:

```
<element name="LU" type="string"/>
<element name="metro"
         substitutionGroup="LU"/>
<element name="subway"
         substitutionGroup="LU"/>
```

3. Finally, every type of element which can be substituted must be of the same type as the *head* element type or is derived from the head type.

```
<element name="A" type="abc"/>
<element name="B"
         substitutionGroup="A" type="xyz"/>
```

Type xyz must be the same as type abc or be derived from abc. For example, abc could be a *decimal* type and xyz of type *integer* which is a derived type from decimal.

A Practical Example
Let us say that a database holds references to various topics where the source material for each topic can come from books, journals or newspapers.

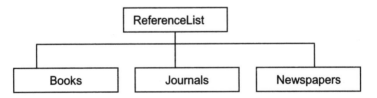

All three resources have at least a title, an author and a date. Both books and newspapers require a publisher, but it is only the book element which has an additional isbn attribute

Part of an XML document may look something like:

18: Element Substitution

```xml
<?xml version="1.0" encoding="utf-8"?>
<subjects
xmlns="http://www.currency.org"
xmlns:xsi="http://www.w3.org/2001/XMLSchema-instance"
xsi:schemaLocation="http://www.currency.org
                    schema18-1.xsd">
<refList topic="WildFlowers">
 <book>
  <title>Wild Flowers in Britain</title>
  <author>Fred Dibbley</author>
  <date>1997-02</date>
  <ISBN>0-440-34319-4</ISBN>
  <publisher>RINC Co.</publisher>
 </book>
 <journal>
  <title>Outdoor Pursuits</title>
  <author>Samatha Higgins</author>
  <date>1999-03</date>
  </journal>
 <newspaper>
  <title>Where have all the flowers
         gone?</title>
  <author>L. Vanodon</author>
  <date>1954-04</date>
  <publisher>Daily Trumpet</publisher>
 </newspaper>
</refList>
         <!-- more refLists follow -->
</subjects>
                <!-- Ex18-1.xml -->
```

We shall start with a user-defined base type which includes the three basic elements for all three resources:

```xml
<complexType name="basicInfo">
 <sequence>
  <element name="title"  type="string"/>
```

```
  <element name="author" type="string"/>
  <element name="date" type="gYearMonth"/>
 </sequence>
</complexType>
```

Next we declare our `refList` element to contain any number of `resource` elements and a `topic` attribute.

```
<element name="refList">
 <complexType>
  <sequence>
   <element ref="L:resource"
           maxOccurs="unbounded"/>
  </sequence>
   <attribute name="topic" type="string"/>
 </complexType>
</element>
```

Next, we need to make the `resource` element a type of `basicInfo`.

```
<element name="resource" type="L:basicInfo"/>
```

Now here is the clever bit. Since `refList` can contain any of our three types of resources: `book`, `journal` or `newspaper`, we need to be able to substitute any of these three for `resource`. Note the prefix `L:`.

```
<element name="resource" type="L:basicInfo"/>
<element name="book"
        substitutionGroup="L:resource"
        type="L:bookType"/>
<element name="newspaper"
        substitutionGroup="L:resource"
        type="L:newsType"/>
<element name="journal"
        substitutionGroup="L:resource"/>
```

18: Element Substitution

In other words, we should be able to use any one of the three where we could use `resource`. Notice that resource does not appear in the XML instance. It could but that is not our intention in this scenario.

Since `journal` is exactly the same type as `basicInfo`, we do not need to state its type.

Because `book` and `newspaper` extend the `basicInfo` type, we shall have to make them extended types. So, all that remains is to specify how `bookType` and `newsType` differ from the `basicInfo` type. In both cases we need to extend the base type (`basicInfo`) to include extra child elements, and that means using a complex type with complex content.

```
<complexType name="bookType">
 <complexContent>
  <extension base="L:basicInfo">
   <sequence>
    <element name="ISBN" type="string"/>
    <element name="publisher" type="string"/>
   </sequence>
  </extension>
 </complexContent>
</complexType>
<complexType name="newsType">
 <complexContent>
  <extension base="L:basicInfo">
   <sequence>
    <element name="publisher" type="string"/>
   </sequence>
  </extension>
 </complexContent>
</complexType>
```

Of course, we could go much further and specify patterns for the isbn. Here is the complete listing for our less ambitious version. It contains a root element subjects which can take one or more refLists.

```
<?xml version="1.0" encoding="UTF-8"?>
<schema
targetNamespace="http://www.currency.org"
xmlns="http://www.w3.org/2001/XMLSchema"
xmlns:L="http://www.currency.org"
elementFormDefault="qualified">
<element name="subjects">
 <complexType>
  <sequence>
   <element ref="L:refList"
            maxOccurs="unbounded"/>
  </sequence>
 </complexType>
</element>
<complexType name="basicInfo">
 <sequence>
  <element name="title"  type="string"/>
  <element name="author" type="string"/>
  <element name="date"   type="gYearMonth"/>
 </sequence>
</complexType>
<element name="refList">
 <complexType>
  <sequence>
   <element ref="L:resource"
            maxOccurs="unbounded"/>
  </sequence>
  <attribute name="topic" type="string"/>
 </complexType>
</element>
<element name="resource" type="L:basicInfo"/>
```

18: **Element Substitution**

```
<element name="book"
         substitutionGroup="L:resource"
         type="L:bookType"/>
<element name="newspaper"
         substitutionGroup="L:resource"
         type="L:newsType"/>
<element name="journal"
         substitutionGroup="L:resource"/>
<complexType name="bookType">
 <complexContent>
  <extension base="L:basicInfo">
   <sequence>
    <element name="ISBN" type="string"/>
    <element name="publisher" type="string"/>
   </sequence>
  </extension>
 </complexContent>
</complexType>
<complexType name="newsType">
 <complexContent>
  <extension base="L:basicInfo">
   <sequence>
    <element name="publisher" type="string"/>
   </sequence>
  </extension>
 </complexContent>
</complexType>
</schema>
              <!-- schema18-1.xsd -->
```

A W3C example

Here is an example from the W3C Schema Part 0: Primer. Notice that the two elements, shipComment and customerComment can be substituted for an element comment which has been declared elsewhere. Its use within an XML document is quite neat.

```
<element name="shipComment" type="string"
         substitutionGroup="ipo:comment"/>
<element name="customerComment" type="string"
         substitutionGroup="ipo:comment"/>

   <!-- ... In an XML instance ... -->
 <items>
  <item partNum="833-AA">
    <productName>Lapis necklace</productName>
    <quantity>1</quantity>
    <USPrice>99.95</USPrice>
    <ipo:shipComment>Use gold wrap if
           possible</ipo:shipComment>
    <ipo:customerComment>Want this for the
           holidays!</ipo:customerComment>
    <shipDate>1999-12-05</shipDate>
  </item>
 </items>
....
```

What is the ipo:? That is another long story which we shall leave until Chapter 20 where we discuss the art of namespaces.

Blocking Element Substitution
An element may wish to prevent other elements from substituting with it. This is achieved via:

```
block="substitution"
```

```
<element name="LU" type="string"
         block="substitution"/>
<element name="metro" substitutionGroup="LU"
         type="string"/>
<element name="subway" substitutionGroup="LU"
         type="string"/>
```

Now we could not replace LU with metro or subway.

18: Element Substitution

Global v. Local

We said earlier that substitutable elements and the *head* elements must be *global*. Global element declarations are the *immediate* children of <schema>. In other words, any declaration or definition which has <schema> as the parent. Whereas *local* element declarations are those which are nested within other element declarations or definition types.

A quick way to discover this is to give your schema document an .xml extension instead of, say, .xsd and then to open it in IE5 or higher. By collapsing the minus signs, you can tell which elements belong to schema. By expanding the plus sign, you can quickly tell which are local because they will appear within the global elements.

Attributes can also be local or global.

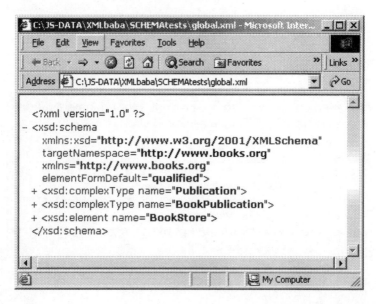

NINETEEN

Groups, Unions and Lists

Groups

Elements may be grouped together using the XML Schema group element. *(It cannot be used for grouping attributes, instead the* attributeGroup *element must be used.)* The one group can then be used by different elements. For example, suppose we have a list of journals and books. Both may require a title, author and date. So why not group these three together?

```
<group name="basicElements">
 <sequence>
  <element name="title" type="string"/>
  <element name="author" type="string"/>
  <element name="date" type="date"/>
 </sequence>
</group>
```

Now, the group can be used as follows:

```
<element name="journal">
 <complexType>
  <sequence>
   <group ref="basicElements"/>
  </sequence>
```

```
 </complexType>
</element>
<element name="book">
 <complexType>
  <sequence>
   <group ref="basicElements"/>
  </sequence>
 </complexType>
</element>
           <!-- in an XML instance -->
<book>
 <title>A Far Away Look</title>
 <author>Henry Smith</author>
 <date>1997-03-29</date>
</book>
<journal>
 <title>Henry Smith Looks Far Away</title>
 <author>A. Snipe</author>
 <date>1998-06-29</date>
</journal>
```

All group definitions must be global and referenced via a
ref attribute. Additional elements can be added to the
basic group, for example, our journals may require an
optional publication reference, whereas our books will
include an ISBN number and perhaps a reviewer. We
could add these to the basic group and, because we are
extending the base type with extra child element, we shall
have to use a complex type.

```
<element name="journal">
 <complexType>
  <sequence>
   <group ref="basicElements"/>
   <element name="publication"
            type="string" minOccurs="0"/>
  </sequence>
```

```
  </complexType>
</element>
<element name="book">
 <complexType>
  <sequence>
 <element name="isbn" type="string"/>
 <element name="reviewer" type="string"
          minOccurs="0"/>
 <group ref="basicElements"/>
  </sequence>
 </complexType>
</element>
```

Not a good ordering of elements for book, but just to show
that additional elements may precede a group reference.

Here is an example from the W3C Schema Part 1:
Structures. Note the use of the choice compositor.

```
<xs:group name="myModelGroup">
 <xs:sequence>
  <xs:element ref="someThing"/>
  . . .
 </xs:sequence>
</xs:group>
<xs:complexType name="trivial">
 <xs:group ref="myModelGroup"/>
 <xs:attribute .../>
</xs:complexType>
<xs:complexType name="moreSo">
 <xs:choice>
  <xs:element ref="anotherThing"/>
  <xs:group ref="myModelGroup"/>
 </xs:choice>
 <xs:attribute .../>
</xs:complexType>
```

19: Groups, Unions and Lists

The complexType named `trivial` will take the entire `myModelGroup`. The complex type `moreSo` has the `choice` compositor so that either `anotherThing` or `myModelGroup` can be chosen. Remember that `choice` is an exclusive-OR, so that one and only one may be chosen. (Note: the prefix `xs:` is explained in Chapter 20.)

`attributeGroup`

Let us give our book element two attributes, a `category` which can take one of the following: biography, fiction or non-fiction; and, an `instock` which can take either `true` or `false` Boolean values:

```
          <!-- in an XML instance -->
<publications>
<book category="fiction" instock="true">
 <title>A Far Away Look</title>
 <author>Henry Smith</author>
 <date>1997-03-29</date>
</book>
.....
</publications>
```

A DTD version would look like:

```
<!ELEMENT publications (book)+>
<!ELEMENT book (title, author, date)>
<!ATTLIST book
    category (biography|fiction|non-fiction)
                                #REQUIRED
    instock  (true|false) "false">
<!ELEMENT title  (#PCDATA)>
<!ELEMENT author (#PCDATA)>
<!ELEMENT date   (#PCDATA)>
```

Here is the corresponding XML Schema version. Note that there is a group of *elements* and a group of *attributes*.

```xml
<?xml version="1.0" encoding="UTF-8"?>
<schema
targetNamespace="http://www.currency.org"
xmlns:L="http://www.currency.org"
xmlns="http://www.w3.org/2001/XMLSchema"
elementFormDefault="qualified">
<element name="publications">
 <complexType>
  <sequence>
   <element name="book"
             maxOccurs="unbounded">
    <complexType>
     <sequence>
      <group ref="L:basicElements"/>
     </sequence>
     <attributeGroup
             ref="L:bookAttributes"/>
    </complexType>
   </element>
  </sequence>
 </complexType>
</element>
        <!-- global group definitions -->
<group name="basicElements">
 <sequence>
  <element name="title" type="string"/>
  <element name="author" type="string"/>
  <element name="date" type="date"/>
 </sequence>
</group>
<attributeGroup name="bookAttributes">
 <attribute name="category" use="required">
  <simpleType>
   <restriction base="string">
    <enumeration value="autobiography"/>
    <enumeration value="non-fiction"/>
    <enumeration value="fiction"/>
```

```
   </restriction>
  </simpleType>
 </attribute>
 <attribute name="instock"
            type="boolean" default="false"/>
 </attributeGroup>
</schema>   <!-- schema19-1.xsd -->
```

In the following, we have added an extra attribute, an
isbn for the book element which did not form part of the
attributeGroup.

```
<element name="publications">
 <complexType>
  <sequence>
   <element name="book"
            maxOccurs="unbounded">
    <complexType>
     <sequence>
      <group ref="basicElements"/>
     </sequence>
      <attributeGroup ref="bookAttributes"/>
      <attribute name="isbn" type="string"/>
    </complexType>
   </element>
  </sequence>
 </complexType>
</element>
```

In the following, we have a clientname and a
staffname element, each referencing the group
nameGroup. Note the simpler way of declaring each
element. We have added an attribute group to the
staffname element, but not to the clientname.

```
<?xml version="1.0" encoding="UTF-8"?>
<schema
targetNamespace="http://www.currency.org"
```

```
xmlns:L="http://www.currency.org"
xmlns="http://www.w3.org/2001/XMLSchema"
elementFormDefault="qualified">
          <!-- definition for namegroup -->
<group name="nameGroup">
 <sequence>
   <element name="firstname" type="string"/>
   <element name="lastname" type="string"/>
 </sequence>
 </group>  <!-- End of definition -->
<attributeGroup name="attRefs">
 <attribute name="staffid" type="ID"
            use="required"/>
 <attribute name="extension" type="string"/>
</attributeGroup>
<element name="staff">
 <complexType>
  <sequence>
   <element ref="L:clientname"/>
   <element ref="L:staffname"/>
  </sequence>
 </complexType>
</element>
<element name="clientname">
 <complexType>
  <group ref="L:nameGroup"/>
 </complexType>
</element>
<element name="staffname">
 <complexType>
  <group ref="L:nameGroup"/>
  <attributeGroup ref="L:attRefs"/>
 </complexType>
</element>
</schema>
          <!-- schema19-2.xsd -->
```

However, if we wanted to add extra elements or attributes to one of the elements, we would have to include a compositor. For example, should we need to add a `middlename` to the `clientname`, we would have to use the `sequence` compositor:

```
<element name="clientname">
<complexType>
 <sequence>
  <group ref="nameGroup"/>
  <element name="middlename" type="string"/>
 </sequence>
</complexType>
</element>
```

Creating data types
There are four ways to create your own data types. We have seen how a base type can be either *extended* or *restricted*. New types may also be created via the `list` and `union` elements.

Lists
On occasions, you may need to create a list of values, perhaps a list of weekly lottery numbers. To prevent incorrect entries, you will need to set up a data type with the following restrictions. The numbers must be positive integers, in the range 1 - 49; there must be six. The *list* element may prove useful in such a situation.

Here is the basic XML document:

```
<?xml version="1.0"?>
<lotteryDraws
xmlns="http://www.lottery.org"
xmlns:xsi="http://www.w3.org/2001/XMLSchema-instance"
xsi:schemaLocation="http://www.lottery.org
                    schema19-3.xsd">
<draw>
```

```
   <date>May 1</date>
    <numbers>21 3 37 8 9 12</numbers>
  </draw>
<draw>
   <date> May 8</date>
    <numbers>15 31 4 37 8 22</numbers>
  </draw>
<draw>
   <date> May 15</date>
    <numbers>48 17 19 35 44 11</numbers>
  </draw>
</lotteryDraws> <!-- Ex19-3.xml -->
```

There are three steps involved. First of all we have to create a data type of our own called `lottorange`. It has to be a simple type because it will not have child elements or attributes.

```
<simpleType name="lottorange">
 <restriction base="positiveInteger">
   <maxInclusive value="49"/>
 </restriction>
</simpleType>
```

Secondly, we need to convert our type to a `list`, since as the code stands we can have any positive integer in the range of 1 - 49, but just one. We use the `list` element. All `list` elements must be derived from a base data type. Our base element is our `lottorange`. Instead of the attribute `base`, however, the `list` element takes `itemType`, the type of item which can be used in our list.

```
<simpleType name="numsList">
 <list itemType="F:lottorange"/>
</simpleType>
```

Finally, we need to restrict the number of list items to six:

```
<simpleType name="lottoNums">
 <restriction base="F:numsList">
  <length value="6"/>
 </restriction>
</simpleType>
```

Here is the full schema, complete with our new list data type and the other declared elements:

```
<?xml version="1.0" encoding="UTF-8"?>
<schema
xmlns="http://www.w3.org/2001/XMLSchema"
targetNamespace="http://www.books.org"
xmlns:F="http://www.books.org" >
<simpleType name="lottorange">
 <restriction base="positiveInteger">
  <maxInclusive value="49"/>
 </restriction>
</simpleType>
<simpleType name="numsList">
 <list itemType="F:lottorange"/>
</simpleType>
<simpleType name="lottoNums">
 <restriction base="F:numsList">
  <length value="6"/>
 </restriction>
</simpleType>
<element name="lotteryDraws">
 <complexType>
  <sequence>
   <element name="draw"
            maxOccurs="unbounded">
    <complexType>
     <sequence>
      <element name="date" type="string"/>
      <element name="numbers"
               type="F:lottoNums"/>
```

```
     </sequence>
    </complexType>
   </element>
  </sequence>
 </complexType>
</element>
</schema>    <!-- schema19-3.xsd -->
```

Notes about the `list` type

1. You cannot create a list of complex types. Lists apply only to simple types.

2. In the XML instance document, each item in the list must be separated by whitespace. The value of whitespace is collapse (see page 195), so that a parser will remove extra spaces and any tabs or carriage returns.

3. `list` cannot be made up of other lists.

4. The only facets that you may use with a list type are:

length: to specify the length of the list

minLength: to specify the minimum length of the list

maxLength: to specify the maximum length of the list

enumeration: to specify the values that the list may have

pattern: to specify the values that the list may have

whitespace: to specify the values that the list may have

5. A list is really another way of creating a user-defined data type, just like restriction. In the case of `list`, it has to use a pre-existing data type, either built-in or user defined. The `itemType` attribute is used to refer to the base type the list will comprise.

Lists are not very useful for manipulating text values, such as paragraphs, sentences or word groups. Here is an example from the XML Schema: Part 2 Data types.

```
<simpleType name='listOfString'>
  <list itemType='string'/>
</simpleType>
<someElement xsi:type='listOfString'>
this is not list item 1
this is not list item 2
this is not list item 3
</someElement>
```

How many values are in the list? If you said three, you will be wrong and it shows why text and lists do not make good partners. There are in fact 18, each word is separated by white space, resulting in 18 values in total.

Union

The union element, like the list element, is yet another way of creating a data type. Let us suppose that we wish an element named <student> to contain either the student's *name* or the student's *id number*. There are several ways this could be accomplished, but we shall use the union approach.

```
<student>John Smith</student> or:
<student>123</student>
```

Since a union data type must be derived from other types, we shall have to create our two types. We shall then *enumerate* them because we need just one name or number in <student>.

```
<simpleType name="studentName">
 <restriction base="string">
  <enumeration value="John Smith"/>
  <enumeration value="Susan Hampshire"/>
  <enumeration value="Freddy Swot"/>
  <enumeration value="Aba Delwrinkle"/>
  <enumeration value="Francis Wight"/>
 </restriction> </simpleType>
```

```
<simpleType name="studentId">
 <restriction base="nonNegativeInteger">
  <enumeration value="123"/>
  <enumeration value="124"/>
  <enumeration value="125"/>
  <enumeration value="127"/>
  <enumeration value="129"/>
 </restriction>
</simpleType>
```

Now we need to create our derived data type using union:

```
<simpleType name="studentInfo">
 <union memberTypes="studentNameList
                     studentIdList"/>
</simpleType>
```

Note that we use the `memberTypes` attribute to list those types which can participate in the union, each one separated by white space.

Finally, we declare an element which will use our union type `studentInfo` and limit the class participants to ten.

```
<element name="XMLclass">
 <complexType>
  <sequence>
   <element name="student" type="studentInfo"
            minOccurs="0"  maxOccurs="10"/>
  </sequence>
 </complexType>
</element>
```

```
         <!-- in an XML instance -->
<?xml version="1.0"?>
<L:XMLclass
```

```
xmlns:L="http://www.books.org"
xmlns:xsi="http://www.w3.org/2001/XMLSchema-instance"
xsi:schemaLocation="http://www.books.org
                    schema19-4.xsd">
 <student>129</student>
 <student>Francis Wight</student>
 <student>123</student>
</L:XMLclass>
                  <!-- Ex19-4.xml -->
```

Creating a `union` by in-lining

In this method, we use two *anonymous* simple types, that is, they have no names.

```
<?xml version="1.0" encoding="UTF-8"?>
<schema
xmlns="http://www.w3.org/2001/XMLSchema"
targetNamespace="http://www.books.org"
xmlns:L="http://www.books.org" >

<!-- in-lining with anonymous simple types -->
<simpleType name="studentInfo">
 <union>
 <simpleType>
  <restriction base="string">
   <enumeration value="John Smith"/>
   <enumeration value="Susan Hampshire"/>
   <enumeration value="Freddy Swot"/>
   <enumeration value="Aba Delwrinkle"/>
   <enumeration value="Francis Wight"/>
  </restriction>
 </simpleType>

 <simpleType>
  <restriction base="nonNegativeInteger">
   <enumeration value="123"/>
   <enumeration value="124"/>
   <enumeration value="125"/>
   <enumeration value="127"/>
   <enumeration value="129"/>
```

```
  </restriction>
 </simpleType>
 </union>
</simpleType> <!-- end of in-lining -->
<element name="XMLclass">
 <complexType>
  <sequence>
   <element name="student"
            type="L:studentInfo"
            minOccurs="0" maxOccurs="10"/>
  </sequence>
 </complexType>
</element>
</schema>
            <!-- schema19-5.xsd -->
```

The disadvantage of the above method is that none of the anonymous simple types can be reused. Only global definitions can be reused and by in-lining we have made them children of studentInfo.

Using union and list together
Suppose we wanted to list all our students in a single element <students> either by names or by id numbers. This would involve the use of a list element. We would simply include the following in which we have created two list data types and amended our memberTypes to refer to these two new types in the union element. However, because list is not useful for manipulating text values with spaces, see page 260, we have to concatenate the names. I chose to use a colon.

```
<?xml version="1.0" encoding="UTF-8"?>
<schema
targetNamespace="http://www.books.org"
xmlns="http://www.w3.org/2001/XMLSchema"
xmlns:L="http://www.books.org">
```

19: Groups, Unions and Lists

```
<simpleType name="studentName">
 <restriction base="string">
  <enumeration value="John:Smith"/>
  <enumeration value="Susan:Hampshire"/>
  <enumeration value="Freddy:Swot"/>
  <enumeration value="Aba:Delwrinkle"/>
  <enumeration value="Francis:Wight"/>
 </restriction>
</simpleType>

<simpleType name="studentId">
 <restriction base="nonNegativeInteger">
  <enumeration value="123"/>
  <enumeration value="124"/>
  <enumeration value="125"/>
  <enumeration value="127"/>
  <enumeration value="129"/>
 </restriction>
</simpleType>

<simpleType name="studentNameList">
 <list itemType="L:studentName"/>
</simpleType>

<simpleType name="studentIdList">
 <list itemType="L:studentId"/>
</simpleType>

<simpleType name="studentInfo">
 <union memberTypes="L:studentNameList
L:studentIdList"/>
</simpleType>

<element name="XMLclass">
 <complexType>
  <sequence>
   <element name="student"
            type="L:studentInfo"
            minOccurs="0" maxOccurs="10"/>
  </sequence>
```

```
</complexType>
</element>
</schema>   <!-- schema19-6.xsd -->
```

```
<?xml version="1.0"?>
<L:XMLclass
xmlns:L="http://www.books.org"
xmlns:xsi="http://www.w3.org/2001/XMLSchema-instance"
xsi:schemaLocation="http://www.books.org
                    schema19-6.xsd">
<student>123 124 129 125</student>
 <student>Francis:Wight John:Smith</student>
</L:XMLclass>
              <!-- Ex19-6.xml -->
```

As the processor meets each value in the list of
<students>, it will check to see whether it is valid or not.

We can summarise how union may be used:

either:
```
<simpleType name="somename">
  <union memberTypes="a list of space
                      delimited simpleTypes">
</simpleType>
```

```
or: <simpleType name="somename">
    <union>
     <simpleType>
      ...
     </simpleType>
     <simpleType>
      ...
     </simpleType>
    </union>
   </simpleType>
```

maxOccurs

union can be applied to attributes as well as elements. Interestingly enough, maxOccurs is a union type. It can take either a nonNegativeInteger (cannot be zero) or it can take the string type enumerated to one word, namely, unbounded.

Here is some code from the XML Schema Part 2: Data types. It illustrates how union can be applied to an attributeGroup. Effectively, it sets minOccurs to any non negative integer with a default of 1 and maxOccurs to any non negative integer or the word unbounded.

```
<attributeGroup name="occurs">
 <attribute name="minOccurs"
            type="nonNegativeInteger"
            default="1"/>
 <attribute name="maxOccurs">
  <simpleType>
   <union>
    <simpleType>
     <restriction base='nonNegativeInteger'/>
    </simpleType>
    <simpleType>
     <restriction base='string'>
      <enumeration value='unbounded'/>
     </restriction>
    </simpleType>
   </union>
  </simpleType>
 </attribute>
</attributeGroup>
```

TWENTY:

Namespaces

In this Chapter, we shall examine namespaces. First of all, we shall see how and why namespaces were added to XML. Then we shall look at how, why and where to use namespaces in an XML Schema.

The Role of namespaces in XML

After XML 1.0 was released publicly, an entire family of XML based languages was developed. Take a male and a female rabbit and soon there will be many little bunnies hopping around. Remember that XML is a meta language, that is a language used to create other languages. Soon after its release, the Mathematical Markup Language (MathML), Scalable Vector Graphics (SVG), Synchronised Multimedia Integration Language (SMIL - pronounced smile), Chemical Markup Language (CML), as well as the Extensible Hypertext Markup Language (XHTML) and XML Schema appeared.

One of the aims of XML was to allow separate languages to be developed, each one concentrating on what it does best, yet being able to work together with any other member of the XML family. Thus, SVG is good with graphics, XHTML for rendering Web pages, MathML for describing mathematical equations. So instead of relying on one language to carry the entire burden of communicating over the Web, a developer could use several languages, each of which could work with the others. Thus, a web developer could use XHTML, XForms, SVG, SMIL and MathML to create an interactive web site.

So far so good. But each language has its own vocabulary, the valid set of words which can be used. Thus, XHTML includes, `<head>`, `<title>`, `<body>`, the `src` and `href` attributes, and so on. XML schema has `<element>`, `<sequence>`, `<attribute>`, `maxOccurs`, `string` and so on.

The problem now is, suppose two or more of the vocabularies use the same word? There is going to be some sort of conflict. Consequently, after the W3C released XML, they set out to resolve a few problems. One of these clearly being name conflicts. Take this classic example:

```
<html>
 <head>
  <title> Web Page title </title>
 </head>
 <body>
  <h3>List of publications,/h3>
   <publications>
    <book>
     <title>XML and namespaces</title>
     <isbn>1-234-34567-9</isbn>
    </book>
   </publications>
 </body>
</html>
```

There are two `title` elements, one clearly belongs to HTML, the other is a child element of `publications`. We are mixing two different vocabularies and we have a naming conflict. The solution is resolved by using namespaces. If the HTML could be given one namespace and publications another, then each title element would belong to a different namespace and the conflict becomes resolved.

```
<html xmlns="http://www.w3.org/1999/xhtml">
 <head>
  <title> Web Page title </title>
 </head>
 <body>
  <h3>List of publications,/h3>
   <publications
          xmlns="http://fred.ac.uk/pub">
    <book>
      <title>XML and namespaces</title>
     <isbn>1-234-34567-9</isbn>
    </book>
   </publications>
 </body>
</html>
```

As we shall see again and again in this Chapter, both of the root elements - <html> and <publications> - have been given a namespace via the XML namespace attribute – xmlns.

```
<html xmlns="http://www.w3.org/1999/xhtml">
```

The value of the xmlns attribute is a *name* (yes it *looks like* a URL but it is not). All the elements contained in the <html> root element belong to that odd looking namespace. Whereas:

```
<publications
          xmlns="http://fred.ac.uk/pub">
```

specifies that all the elements (and the attributes, if any) contained in the `publications` root element belong to another namespace. Now, `<title>` in the `<html>` part will no longer conflict with the same element in the `<publications>` part and a validating program will recognise each as a distinctly different element.

How this all works is explained below. Just for the moment, we simply need to be aware of the conflict and that by placing each one in its own namespace, the conflict becomes resolved. That is the concept behind namespaces in XML. So, let us now see how namespaces are implemented in XML Schemas.

Namespaces in XML Schema

Namespaces were added to XML, as we have just discussed. Their actual implementation, that is, how, when and where to use them, will vary according to which XML generated language is being used. Since DTDs are part of SGML, rather than XML, DTDs cannot implement namespaces. On the other hand, XML Schemas can and that is one of the reasons for their popularity.

The only reason for creating a schema, or a DTD, is to ensure that any data entered into an XML document can be validated against that schema or DTD. If we wanted to create just well-formed XML documents then, obviously, we would not need either of them.

An Example

Let us create a simple XML document, then an XML Schema, and see how to link them together for validation.

```
<?xml version="1.0" ?>
<book>
<isbn>1234567890</isbn>
<title>XHTML &amp; CSS explained</title>
</book>
```

Just one book, with an isbn number and a title. As it
stands, it is simply a well-formed XML document. But let
us add a schema which specifies that the isbn must be
numeric (we cannot do that in a DTD) and that the title
is a string.

```
<?xml version="1.0" encoding = "UTF-8"?>
<!-- Name1-Schema1.xsd -->
<schema
 xmlns = "http://www.w3.org/2001/XMLSchema">
<element name = "book">
 <complexType>
   <sequence>
    <element name = "isbn"
             type = "integer"/>
    <element name = "title"
             type = "string"/>
   </sequence>
 </complexType>
</element>
</schema>
```

Notice that the above schema has an xmlns (XML
namespace) attribute which has a value:

```
<schema
 xmlns = "http://www.w3.org/2001/XMLSchema">
```

Unlike DTDs, the XML Schema vocabulary has to be
associated with a namespace. What is the XML Schema
vocabulary? It comprises all the elements and attributes
which can be used when creating a specific schema. In
the above, we are using <schema>, <element>,
<complexType> and <sequence> as well as attributes
like xmlns, type, name and other features such as
maxOccurs, etc. All of these and, of course, all the other
elements such as <union>, <complexContent>,

`<simpleType>` and so on form the vocabulary of the XML Schema language.

This vocabulary must always associated with the following namespace: `"http://www.w3.org/2001/XMLSchema"`

What about *our* vocabulary, the one we are inventing in the same schema? We are inventing `<book>`, `<isbn>` and `<title>`. Furthermore, by using the `type` attribute, we specify the type of data which a corresponding XML document must adhere to in order to be valid. Thus, an `isbn` element can only contain an `integer`, the `title` element can contain `string` data.

targetNamespace

In a schema, the `targetNamespace` attribute is used to identify a namespace for the vocabulary we invent in that schema. Note that it is an attribute of the `schema` element. So, we have established *two* namespaces, one for the XML Schema and another for our own vocabulary.

```
<schema
 xmlns = "http://www.w3.org/2001/XMLSchema">
 targetNamespace="http://www.book.co.uk"
```

Because the `targetNamespace` is used, we are *also* required to include an `xmlns` reference to it within our schema, thus:

```
<schema
 xmlns = "http://www.w3.org/2001/XMLSchema">
 targetNamespace="http://www.book.co.uk"
 xmlns = "http://www.book.co.uk">
```

This second `xmlns` namespace is the one which is used to indicate our own vocabulary as opposed to the XML Schema vocabulary. In the above the second `xmlns` is the same as the target namespace. Is it redundant? No!

As we shall see later, we can have several additional namespaces listed (as well as the namespace for the XML Schema). When this occurs, one of them has to be chosen as the `targetNamespace`.

The target namespace is the one which must be 'quoted in' (used by) any XML document which wants to be validated against our schema vocabulary. A validator, will simply check each use of, say, `isbn`, in the XML document to see that it is being used correctly according to the definition laid down in our schema. But our schema has two sets of vocabularies, one for XML Schema and one for our own. The `targetNamespace` in our schema will identify `isbn` as belonging to our own vocabulary.

The following table lists the vocabulary which comes from the W3.org namespace and the vocabulary which come from our own namespace, `www.book.co.uk`

`http://www.w3.org/2001/` `XMLSchema`	`http://www.book.co.uk`
`<schema>`	`<book>`
`<element>`	`<isbn>`
`<complexType>`	`<title>`
`<sequence>`	
`xmlns,` `type` and `name` attributes	

Very shortly, we shall discuss in detail why all this is necessary. For the time being, just note that each element and/or attribute used in a schema belongs to one or other of the namespaces.

Here is the final version:

```
<?xml version="1.0" encoding = "UTF-8"?>
<schema
  xmlns = "http://www.w3.org/2001/XMLSchema">
```

```
 targetNamespace="http://www.book.co.uk"
 xmlns="http://www.book.co.uk">
<element name = "book">
 <complexType>
   <sequence>
    <element name = "isbn"
             type = "integer"/>
    <element name = "title"
             type = "string"/>
   </sequence>
 </complexType>
</element>
</schema><element name = "book">
 <complexType>
   <sequence>
    <element name = "isbn"
             type = "integer"/>
    <element name = "title"
             type = "string"/>
   </sequence>
 </complexType>
</element>
</schema>   <!-- Not yet valid -->
```

However, there is just one more adjustment to make before the above schema is valid.

Default namespace

In a schema, one of the namespaces can be designated as a *default* namespace. Briefly, what that means is that its vocabulary need not be *prefixed*. But the other one must be prefixed. Here is an example:

```
xmlns:L="http://www.book.co.uk"
```

The above has an extra :L after the xmlns attribute and before the equals sign. So our target namespace has become the prefixed namespace and the XML Schema namespace is the default (non-prefixed) namespace. The point is that there can only be *one* default namespace (in both a schema and an XML document). Note that it is the `xmlns` which specifies which is which, not the `targetNamespace`.

In the following, I reverse the two namespaces and make the XML Schema the prefixed namespace and the target namespace the default. It is conventional, but not obligatory, to use either `:xsd` or `:xs` as the prefix for the XML Schema namespace. You could use `:fred` if you wanted to.

```
<schema
xmlns:xsd="http://www.w3.org/2001/XMLSchema">
targetNamespace="http://www.book.co.uk"
xmlns="http://www.book.co.uk">
```

Which should we make the default, the XML Schema or the target namespace? You can make up your own mind when we discuss default namespaces a little later. We need to complete our discussion about namespaces before becoming side-tracked with default namespaces.

What is a namespace?
Not much, it is just a name. It looks like a URL, however, and that is where it becomes confusing when we see them for the first time. It is simply a name or label. The W3C thought long and hard about what type of name to use for a namespace. The crucial point they decided upon was that it had to be *unique*. No namespace could be the same as another. Now, the one thing which is guaranteed to be unique on the Internet is a URL. Every web server must and does have a unique address, rather like a telephone number, or a house address. Therefore, it was decided that in order to ensure that no namespace could be the same as another, they opted for a URL to act as the name

of a namespace. It does not have to be a real URL, but it must 'look like one'.

(In fact, they opted for a URI. A Uniform Resource Identifier is a short string which is used to refer to some resource. It can either be a URL or a URN. In the case of the URL, it can be http:, gopher:, mailto:, ftp:, etc. In the case of a URN it is also unique, for example:

`urn:publishing:book`

There is a serious discussion going on about whether a URN or a URL should become predominant in an XML Schema namespace. At present, either may be used.)

Although a URL namespace looks like a pointer to some resource, it is not used as one. Indeed, it need not point to anything and in most cases they do not point to anything. In other words, there is no end product out there which a browser using the URL could find. You are not meant to find a namespace on the Internet because it exists only as a means for naming a specific vocabulary. Hopefully, as we progress through this chapter and begin to give examples, this will become clearer.

Namespaces enable a parser to distinguish between the declaration for `<element>` in the XML Schema language vocabulary, and a declaration for `<element>` in, say, a hypothetical chemistry language vocabulary.

The first `<element>` is part of the XML Schema namespace:

`http://www.w3.org/2001/XMLSchema`

and the second would form part of another namespace as directed by the `targetNamespace` reference.

In the XML document
What do we need to do in an XML document in order to link it to a schema? In the following XML document, note

that we again have two namespaces referenced via the xmlns attributes.

```
<?xml version="1.0" ?>
<book
 xmlns="http://www.books.org"
 xmlns:xsi=
 "http://www.w3.org/2001/XMLSchema-instance"
 xsi:schemaLocation="http://www.books.org
                     name1-schema1.xsd">
<isbn>1234567890</isbn>
<title>XHTML &amp; CSS explained</title>
</book>
```

There are three attributes added to the root <book> element, actually they are formally called *declarations*.

1. The first declaration:

xmlns="http://www.books.org"

tells the validator that all of the elements used in this instance document come from the namespace:

"http://www.books.org".

Note that it is the same, and *must be the same*, as the target namespace used in the schema:

targetNamespace=*"http://www.books.org"*

2. Clearly, we need to tell the validator where to find the schema which uses that target namespace. We do this via a special attribute schemaLocation. However, this attribute is one of four special attributes found in the so-called *XMLSchema-instance* namespace and must be qualified with a prefix of xsi:

Do not confuse the XMLSchema-instance with the XML Schema namespace. They are two different references.

20: Namespaces

Because we are referring to another vocabulary, we need to provide an `xmlns` attribute naming the *XMLSchema-instance* namespace:

```
xmlns:xsi=
 "http://www.w3.org/2001/XMLSchema-instance"
```

In other words, the second namespace tells the schema validator that the attribute prefixed on the next line with `xsi`, is one which is defined in the *XMLSchema-instance* namespace. Like the XML Schema namespace name, the XMLSchema-instance namespace name is predefined and must be the one used when referring to it.

3. Now that we have declared the reserved XMLSchema-instance namespace, we can go ahead and give the location of the schema which specifies the target namespace.

```
xsi:schemaLocation="http://www.books.org
                    name1-schema1.xsd"
```

`schemaLocation` takes two values enclosed in double quotes. The first tells the schema validator that the namespace `http://www.books.org` is the target namespace to be found in the second value, `name1-schema1.xsd`.

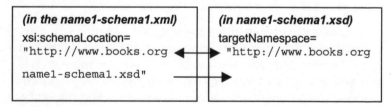

(in the name1-schema1.xml)
xsi:schemaLocation=
 "http://www.books.org
 name1-schema1.xsd"

(in name1-schema1.xsd)
targetNamespace=
 "http://www.books.org

4. A final recap:

```
xmlns="http://www.books.org"
xmlns:xsi=
 "http://www.w3.org/2001/XMLSchema-instance"
```

We have *two* xmlns attributes, the first has simply xmlns, the second has xmlns:xsi

The second one informs the validator that anything prefixed with xsi belongs to the XMLSchema-instance, as in the case of schemaLocation.

The first one is known as a *default* namespace which simply means that no prefix is used. We discuss this in more detail below. For the moment, bear in mind that there are two types of namespaces, those which require a prefix and those which do not.

XMLSchema-instance namespace
There are four attributes contained in XMLSchema-instance namespace:

xsi:schemaLocation: the location of a schema

xsi:noNamespaceSchemaLocation: the location of a schema which does not have a namespace (more of this later)

xsi:nil an element with this attribute may not have any element content, although it may contain attributes, see page 315

xsi:type yet another way to specify a derived type, see page 318

Default and Prefixed Namespaces
There are two different ways to declare a namespace in a schema, with a prefix or without a prefix. The latter is known as a *default* namespace. There can be only one default namespace, but its use is optional. Thus a schema author could decide to have no default namespace, preferring to have two prefixed namespaces.

In an XML document there must be at least two namespaces, one for the target namespace and one for the XMLSchema-instance namespace. It is conventional to use a prefix of xsi for the latter, leaving the target namespace the default. But like a schema, an XML author could decide to make both prefixed and not use a default.

Let us discuss the schema first. Every schema uses at least two namespaces, the XML Schema namespace and a target namespace. Should the XML Schema be the default namespace, or should the target namespace be the default namespace, or should neither be a default name space? There are advantages and disadvantages in each case. In practice, there is no best approach and what you choose to do is a matter of personal preference.

Example 1: Only the XML Schema namespace is prefixed
In the following example, we make the XML Schema namespace a prefixed namespace and the target namespace a default (with no prefix) namespace. When a prefix is used, xsd in our case (it happens to be conventional, but we could use any other prefix), all elements in that namespace must be prefixed. This is called *qualifying* the elements. Of course, it makes for extra typing.

xmlns:xsd="http://www.w3.org/2001/XMLSchema"

Now any vocabulary from the XML Schema namespace must be qualified with the xsd: prefix, including the <schema> element and the *values* for type attributes, such as string, gYear, decimal. Remember that these are derived built-in data types belonging to the XML Schema vocabulary.

```
<?xml version="1.0"?>
<xsd:schema
xmlns:xsd="http://www.w3.org/2001/XMLSchema"
targetNamespace="http://www.books.org"
xmlns="http://www.books.org">
```

```
<xsd:element name = "book">
 <xsd:complexType>
   <xsd:sequence>
    <xsd:element ref = "isbn"/>
    <xsd:element ref = "title"/>
   </xsd:sequence>
 </xsd:complexType>
</xsd:element>
 <xsd:element name="isbn"
              type="xsd:integer"/>
 <xsd:element name="title"
              type="xsd:string"/>
</xsd:schema>
            <!-- schema20-1.xsd -->
```

However, those elements and/or attributes which belong to the `http://www.books.org` namespace, via the `ref` attribute, are not qualified, because we have made it the default namespace.

Summary of above:
Because the XML Schema namespace has been prefixed, then anything which forms part of the XML Schema vocabulary must be qualified with the prefix specified in the declaration. Thus:
```
<prefix:element>, </prefix:element>,
<prefix:attribute>,</prefix:complexType>,
type="prefix:string", etc.
```

```
<xsd:attribute name="fred"
               type="xsd:string"/>
```

Because the target namespace is not prefixed, referred to as the *default* namespace, then the vocabulary within that namespace *must not* be qualified when referenced via a `ref` attribute or a `type` attribute:

```
<xsd:element name="isbn"  type="isbnType"/>
.....
<xsd:element ref="someDefinition"/>
```

Example 2: Only the target namespace is prefixed
In this example, we have made the XML Schema a default namespace, but have qualified the target namespace. So now, the XML Schema vocabulary is not qualified, that is there is no prefix, whereas the references to any global element in the target namespace vocabulary must be qualified. Consequently, the ref below needs to be qualified. If we had used something like:

type="prefix:myelementType" it would also need to be qualified.

```
<?xml version="1.0"?>
<schema
xmlns="http://www.w3.org/2001/XMLSchema"
 targetNamespace="http://www.books.org"
 xmlns:bk="http://www.books.org">
<element name = "book">
 <complexType>
   <sequence>
    <element ref = "bk:isbn"/>
    <element ref = "bk:title"/>
   </sequence>
 </complexType>
</element>
 <element name="isbn" type="integer"/>
 <element name="title" type="string"/>
</schema> <!-- schema20-2.xsd -->
```

Summary of above:
Now, the bk: prefix indicates what namespace isbn and title are in, namely, the http://www.books.org namespace. The prefix bk: is, in fact, a shorthand reference to the actual namespace. If we did not use the

shorthand, we would need to type in the full namespace name:

```
<?xml version="1.0"?>
<xsd:schema
 xmlns:xsd="http://www.w3.org/2001/XMLSchema"
 targetNamespace="http://www.books.org"
 xmlns:www.books.org="http://www.books.org">
<element ref = "www.books.org:isbn"/>
```

Did you notice that we said: " ... any global element in the target namespace must be qualified." ? That is discussed in the next Chapter under the `elementFormDefault` declaration. We are actually using the declaration but with a default value. But more of that later.

Example 3: Both are qualified

```
<?xml version="1.0"?>
<xsd:schema
 xmlns:xsd="http://www.w3.org/2001/XMLSchema"
 targetNamespace="http://www.books.org"
 xmlns:bk="http://www.books.org">
<xsd:element name = "book">
 <xsd:complexType>
   <xsd:sequence>
    <xsd:element ref = "bk:isbn"/>
    <xsd:element ref = "bk:title"/>
   </xsd:sequence>
 </xsd:complexType>
</xsd:element>
 <xsd:element name="isbn"
               type="xsd:integer"/>
 <xsd:element name="title"
               type="xsd:string"/>
</xsd:schema>
            <!-- schema20-3.xsd -->
```

20: Namespaces

Summary of above:
Now, because both namespaces are prefixed, we have to qualify the vocabularies of each namespace. This requires extra typing effort for the schema author, but under certain circumstances can be useful, see the next Chapter.

Conclusion
There can be only *one* default namespace. If we had two, then, a validator would not be able to determine which element, attribute, etc., belonged to which namespace. A namespace effectively allows a validator to check the 'correctness' of any given `element`, attribute, `type`, `ref` against a given schema.

What you cannot do is to have a default XML Schema namespace and *no* target namespace. Basically, you must choose one of the following:

- a default XML Schema in which case the target namespace must then be qualified
- a qualified (prefixed) XML Schema namespace (with or without a target namespace)

No targetNamespace
Target namespaces are not mandatory. Thus, you may wish to create a schema but not put any of your elements within a namespace. In which case, you will simply leave out the target namespace and as a consequence of that, you will no longer need an `xmlns` namespace for your target namespace.

Should you wish to do this, it would now be necessary to qualify the XML Schema namespace so that the validator can tell that the qualified elements belong to the XML Schema namespace and the un-qualified do not belong to any namespace.

If you are wondering why on earth anyone would want to do this, we need to cover the <include> element which is part of the next chapter. Until we do so, just note that the following is allowed.

Correct: Qualified XML Schema namespace but no target namespace:

```
<?xml version="1.0"?>
<F:schema
xmlns:F="http://www.w3.org/2001/XMLSchema">
<F:element name = "book">
 <F:complexType>
   <F:sequence>
    <F:element ref = "isbn"/>
    <F:element ref= "title"/>
   </F:sequence>
 </F:complexType>
</F:element>
 <F:element name="isbn"
               type="F:integer"/>
 <F:element name="title"
               type="F:string"/>
</F:schema>
               <!-- noname.xsd -->
```

An XML instance using the above schema

```
<?xml version="1.0"?>
<!-- noname.xml -->
<book
xmlns:xsi="http://www.w3.org/2001/XMLSchema-instance"
xsi:noNamespaceSchemaLocation=
                              "noname.xsd">
  <isbn>1234567890</isbn>
  <title>XHTML &amp; CSS explained</title>
</book>
               <!-- noname.xml -->
```

The above XML instance document is using the above `noname.xsd` schema. However, because that schema has no target namespace, the instance document has to use the `noNamespaceSchemaLocation` attribute rather than the `schemaLocation` attribute. Both are used to point the validator towards the schema but in this current scenario, we must tell the validator not to expect a target namespace. Hence we have just one value for the `noNamespaceSchemaLocation` attribute.

We still need the `xmlns:xsi` namespace since we are about to use one of the four attributes from the XML Schema instance namespace.

Finally, because the schema document has no namespace, none of the elements in this instance document are associated with a namespace. So we could do this:

```
<X:isbn>1234567890</X:isbn>
<title>XHTML &amp; CSS explained</title>
```

But, clearly, unless there is method in such madness, it could be potentially dangerous.

Until you become more familiar with XML Schema namespaces and all their varieties, follow one of these simple approaches.

If you want to reduce your typing effort in an XML document, then make the reference to the target namespace the default.

If you want to reduce your typing in an XML schema document, then make the XML Schema a default namespace. If you choose to have a target namespace then you must use a prefix with its associated `xmlns`. Then only `ref` or `type` attribute values which reference *global element declaration* or *a user defined data type* need to be qualified with the prefix. Only `ref` is shown below:

```
<?xml version="1.0"?>
<schema
xmlns="http://www.w3.org/2001/XMLSchema"
targetNamespace="http://www.books.org"
xmlns:J="http://www.books.org">
<element name = "book">
 <complexType>
   <sequence>
    <element ref = "J:isbn"/>
    <element ref = "J:title"/>
   </sequence>
 </complexType>
</element>
 <element name="isbn"
              type="integer"/>
 <element name="title"
              type="string"/>
</schema>
              <!-- schema20-4.xsd -->
```

Otherwise, make the XML Schema a qualified namespace and make the target and its `xmlns` unqualified. But there is now much more to type:

```
<?xml version="1.0"?>
<xs:schema
xmlns:xs="http://www.w3.org/2001/XMLSchema"
targetNamespace="http://www.books.org"
xmlns="http://www.books.org">
<xs:element name = "book">
 <xs:complexType>
   <xs:sequence>
    <xs:element ref = "isbn"/>
    <xs:element ref = "title"/>
```

```
   </xs:sequence>
 </xs:complexType>
</xs:element>
 <xs:element name="isbn"
              type="xs:integer"/>
 <xs:element name="title"
              type="xs:string"/>
</xs:schema>
            <!-- schema20-5.xsd -->
```

Here is an XML document for either of the above.

```
<?xml version="1.0" ?>
<book
xmlns="http://www.books.org"
xmlns:xsi="http://www.w3.org/2001/XMLSchema-instance"
xsi:schemaLocation="http://www.books.org
                    schema20-4.xsd">
<isbn>1234567890</isbn>
<title>XHTML &amp; CSS explained</title>
</book> <!-- Ex20-4.xml -->
```

In the above, we have a default `xmlns` reference to the target namespace in the schema, `schema20-4.xsd`.

In the following, we have a qualified `xmlns` reference to the target namespace in the schema, `schema20-4.xsd`.

```
<?xml version="1.0"?>
<P:book
xmlns:P="http://www.books.org"
xmlns:xsi="http://www.w3.org/2001/XMLSchema-instance"
xsi:schemaLocation="http://www.books.org
                    schema20-4.xsd.xsd">
<P:isbn>234567890</P:isbn>
<P:title>XHTML &amp; CSS explained
</P:title>
</P:book>
```

You should note that whether or not the target namespace in the *schema* is a default, that has no bearing on what an XML instance author decides to do. The target namespace in a schema could be made the default, but an XML author may decide to qualify it.

There is just one thing which we have not mentioned as yet, namely the `elementFormdefault` as used in schemas. This will have some bearing on what an XML document author *must* do. However, we have had enough for the time being and will leave that issue to the next chapter.

20: Namespaces

TWENTY-ONE

Working with Multiple Schemas

One schema can refer to other schemas. This is what we look at in this Chapter. We shall also look at the `elementFormDefault` declaration and see how it impacts on XML documents. This will help us to put the final nail into the coffin of namespaces.

Working with multiple schemas
We shall keep our examples very simple so that the syntax is easier to follow. First of all, here is a basic XML document which refers to a schema for validation.

```
<?xml version="1.0"?>
<book
xmlns="http://www.books.org"
xmlns:xsi="http://www.w3.org/2001/XMLSchema-instance"
xsi:schemaLocation="http://www.books.org
                    schema21-1a.xsd">

  <isbn>1234567890</isbn>
  <title>XHTML &amp; CSS explained</title>
</book>
            <!-- Ex21-1a.xml -->
```

21: <u>Multiple Schemas</u>

It is a very simple XML document which is validated against the `schema21-1a.xsd` below. It has two `xmlns` namespaces, a default namespace for the XML Schema and a prefixed namespace for the target namespace.

```
<?xml version="1.0"?>
<schema
 xmlns="http://www.w3.org/2001/XMLSchema"
 targetNamespace="http://www.books.org"
 xmlns:ipo="http://www.books.org"
 elementFormDefault="qualified">
<element name="book">
  <complexType>
   <sequence>
    <element name="isbn"    type="integer"/>
    <element name="title"   type="string"/>
   </sequence>
  </complexType>
</element>
</schema>
            <!-- schema21-1a.xsd -->
```

There is no requirement for the XML document to follow the exact qualification of namespaces used in a schema. If we would like to minimise the typing effort when creating the *schema*, then make the XML Schema the default namespace. The XML Schema vocabulary will not need to be prefixed. Since only one namespace can be the default, we must now qualify the target namespace `xmlns` reference with a prefix of, say, 'ipo'. All prefixed `ipo` elements and attributes in the schema belong to this qualified namespace.

```
xmlns:ipo="http://www.books.org"
elementFormDefault="qualified"
```

You can use any valid XML name as a prefix in the schema and it does not have to be the same as the prefix used in the actual XML instance. But we shall discuss this later.

Just in case you are using these exercises and trying to validate your work, you will need to include:

```
elementFormDefault="qualified"
```

We shall discuss exactly what `elementFormDefault` means below.

So far so good. But now, let us refer our XML document to a schema which includes another schema. The following XML document refers to a schema which is going to include another schema which defines the details for a book. Here is the XML document:

```
<?xml version="1.0"?>
<book
xmlns="http://www.books.org"
xmlns:xsi="http://www.w3.org/2001/XMLSchema-instance"
xsi:schemaLocation="http://www.books.org
                        schema21-1b.xsd">

  <isbn>1234567890</isbn>
  <title>XHTML &amp; CSS explained</title>
</book>
              <!-- Ex21-1b.xml -->
```

It is the same as the earlier one except that we have given a different file name to the XML document and to the schema which is to be used for the validation. Here is `schema21-1b.xsd`:

```
<?xml version="1.0"?>
<schema
      xmlns="http://www.w3.org/2001/XMLSchema"
      targetNamespace="http://www.books.org"
      xmlns:ipo="http://www.books.org"
      elementFormDefault="qualified">
```

21: Multiple Schemas

```
<include
      schemaLocation="bookDetails-1b.xsd"/>
 <element name="book"
          type="ipo:bookDetails"/>
</schema>
            <!-- schema21-1b.xsd -->
```

In the above, we declare an element named book whose type is that of bookDetails. But we have no defined type of bookDetails in this schema. So where is it and how can it be found? That is the purpose of:

```
<include
      schemaLocation="bookDetails-1b.xsd"/>
```

We have effectively said to a validator to include a schema called: bookDetails-1b.xsd. It is that schema which has defined the bookDetails. Here it is:

```
<?xml version="1.0"?>
<schema
 xmlns="http://www.w3.org/2001/XMLSchema"
 targetNamespace="http://www.books.org"
 xmlns:ipo="http://www.books.org"
 elementFormDefault="qualified">
<complexType name="bookDetails">
 <sequence>
  <element name="isbn" type="decimal"/>
  <element name="title" type="string"/>
 </sequence>
</complexType>
</schema>
            <!-- bookDetails-1b.xsd -->
```

The validator will search in the above schema to find a definition for bookDetails. Within the definition, it finds the declared elements for isbn and title. The net effect is the same as though we had simply typed those definitions straight into our `schema21-1b.xsd` schema.

Note that the `schemaLocation` in the `include` element takes only one value, unlike the `schemaLocation` attribute in an XML document which takes two.

But the important thing to bear in mind, is that *both* schemas, `schema21-1b` and `bookDetails-1b.xsd` must have the *same namespace*. Consequently, when the validator meets:

```
<element name="book"
         type="ipo:bookDetails"/>
```

it knows that `ipo:bookDetails` belongs to the same namespace as `schema21-1b.xsd` and would expect to find the *same target namespace* in `bookDetails-1b.xsd`.

If we had not included the `ipo:` prefix, (left it out altogether) where would the validator expect to find `bookDetails`? Because it would be a default type reference (no prefix) and because XML Schema happens to be the default namespace, it would look there and, of course, not find it.

We shall look at a few more examples later, after we have discussed the `elementFormDefault` attribute.

elementFormDefault

The `elementFormDefault` takes one of two possible values, either *qualified* or *unqualified*. When it is not present, as is the case throughout most of this book, it has a default value of `unqualified`. So, in most of our examples, we have been using:

```
elementFormDefault="unqualified"
```

without our realising it. So what does it do? It is present in schemas, not in XML documents. It specifies how the XML document must qualify the *element vocabulary* from the target schema, that is, all the element names we have made up. If the value is `qualified`, then all *global* and *local* elements in the XML document must be qualified. If the value `unqualified` is set, or the attribute omitted, then only global elements must be qualified.

`elementFormDefault="qualified"`

(What about global attributes, then? There is a separate mechanism for stating whether attributes must be qualified or unqualified, as discussed later.)

```
<?xml version="1.0"?>
<schema
 xmlns="http://www.w3.org/2001/XMLSchema"
 targetNamespace="http://www.books.org"
 xmlns:ipo="http://www.books.org"
 elementFormDefault="qualified">
 <element name="book">
  <complexType>
   <sequence>
   <element name="isbn" type="decimal"/>
   <element name="title" type="string"/>
   </sequence>
  </complexType>
 </element>
</schema>
            <!-- schema21-1a.xsd -->
```

Let us return to `schema21.1a.xsd`.

The `elementFormDefault` is set to `qualified`. Any XML document instance using the target namespace must, therefore, qualify *all* global and local elements.

```
<?xml version="1.0" ?>
- <schema
    xmlns="http://www.w3.org/2001/XMLSchema"
    targetNamespace="http://www.books.org"
    xmlns:ipo="http://www.books.org"
    elementFormDefault="qualified">
  - <element name="book">
    - <complexType>
      - <sequence>
          <element name="isbn"
            type="integer" />
          <element name="title"
            type="string" />
        </sequence>
      </complexType>
    </element>
  </schema>
  <!-- schema21-1a.xsd  -->
```

In the schema, book is global, that is, it is a direct child of schema, whereas isbn and title are local because they are children of book. To see which is which, simply give the schema file an xml extension and open it in IE5 or higher and it will be displayed as shown above.

Now we can easily see the relationship between the various elements. Thus, isbn and title are clearly children of book. They are local because they form part of <complexType>, whereas book can clearly be seen as a child of schema and is therefore global. However, because we have set elementFormDefault to qualified, all global and local elements must now be qualified in the XML document, as shown below:

21: **Multiple Schemas**

```
<?xml version="1.0"?>
<book
xmlns="http://www.books.org"
xmlns:xsi="http://www.w3.org/2001/XMLSchema-instance"
xsi:schemaLocation="http://www.books.org
                    bookx-1a.xsd"
<isbn>1234567890</isbn>
<title>XHTML &amp; CSS explained</title>
</book>        <-- Ex21-1a.xml -->
```

So, why are they not?

But they are! Look carefully at the xmlns which refers to the target schema namespace:

```
xmlns="http://www.books.org"
```

It happens to be a *default* namespace which means that all elements based on the schema have no prefix as their qualification. So, it is "*qualified*" after all, but without any prefix.

On the other hand, if we has done this in the XML document :

```
xmlns:fred="http://www.books.org"
```

and the schema had a *qualified* elementFormDefault, then we would have to qualify all the elements:

```
<?xml version="1.0"?>
<fred:book
xmlns:fred="http://www.books.org"
xmlns:xsi="http://www.w3.org/2001/XMLSchema-instance"
xsi:schemaLocation="http://www.books.org
                    schema21-1a.xsd"

<fred:isbn>1234567890</fred:isbn>
<fred:title>XHTML &amp; CSS
explained</fred:title>
</fred:book>
```

> ```
>          <!-- Ex21-1ab.xml
> ```
> *result when a qualified EFD is used in a schema* `-->`

elementFormDefault="unqualified"

If a schema specifies the `elementFormDefault` (EFD) to be *unqualified*, then only *global* elements from the schema are qualified in the XML document. Any local element in the schema *must not be qualified*.

> *In the schema:*
> ```
> xmlns:ipo="http://www.books.org"
> elementFormDefault="unqualified"
> ```

Now, our XML instance would have to look like this when a prefixed `xmlns` is used for the target namespace:

> ```
> <?xml version="1.0"?>
> <fred:book
> xmlns:fred="http://www.books.org"
> xmlns:xsi="http://www.w3.org/2001/XMLSchema-instance"
> xsi:schemaLocation="http://www.books.org
>                     schema21-1a.xsd">
>
>   <isbn>1234567890</isbn>
>   <title>XHTML &amp; CSS explained</title>
> </fred:book>
> ```
> ```
>               <!--Ex21-1ab.xml
> ```
> *result when an unqualified EFD is used in schema* `-->`

Now, just the global elements are qualified with the `fred:` prefix. All local elements must be unqualified.

> *Tip: If you wish to reduce the amount of typing:*
>
> *make the target namespace the default namespace in the XML document*
>
> *make the XML Schema namespace the default in the schema and set the value for the EFD to qualified*

21: Multiple Schemas

Prefixing in Schemas

In the following schema, we prefixed `bookDetails`:

`type="ipo:bookDetails"`

This is because the target namespace in the schema has been prefixed-qualified via its accompanying `xmlns`. Although the actual definition of `bookDetails` appears in another schema, and, because we are including a reference to it via the `include` element in this schema, they must both have the same namespace. Therefore, a validator must be told that `bookDetails` belongs to the namespace qualified with a prefix `ipo`.

```
<?xml version="1.0"?>
<schema
 xmlns="http://www.w3.org/2001/XMLSchema"
 targetNamespace="http://www.books.org"
 xmlns:ipo="http://www.books.org"
 elementFormDefault="qualified">
<include
     schemaLocation="bookDetails-1b.xsd"/>
 <element name="book"
          type="ipo:bookDetails"/>
</schema>
            <!-- schema21-1b.xsd -->
```

If `schema21-1b.xsd` had a default target namespace but the XML Schema has a prefixed namespace as follows:

```
xmlns:xs="http://www.w3.org/2001/XMLSchema"
targetNamespace="http://www.books.org"
xmlns="http://www.books.org"
```

would we still need to qualify `bookDetails`? The answer is no. Because, now `bookDetails` would belong to the default target namespace which has no prefix.

Let us look at the three files. The XML document remains unchanged. It has a default target namespace.

```
<?xml version="1.0"?>
<book
xmlns="http://www.books.org"
xmlns:xsi="http://www.w3.org/2001/XMLSchema-instance"
xsi:schemaLocation="http://www.books.org
                    schema21-2.xsd"
  <isbn>1234567890</isbn>
  <title>XHTML &amp; CSS explained</title>
</book>
             <!-- Ex21-2.xml  -->
```

The bookDetails-2.xsd **file looks like:**

```
<?xml version="1.0"?>
<xsd:schema
 xmlns:xsd="http://www.w3.org/2001/XMLSchema"
 targetNamespace="http://www.books.org"
 xmlns="http://www.books.org"
 elementFormDefault="qualified">

 <xsd:complexType name="bookDetails">
  <xsd:sequence>
   <xsd:element name="isbn"
                type="xsd:decimal"/>
   <xsd:element name="title"
                type="xsd:string"/>
  </xsd:sequence>
 </xsd:complexType>
</xsd:schema>
          <!--bookDetails-2.xsd -->
```

and the schema21-2.xsd **looks like:**

```
<?xml version="1.0"?>
<xsd:schema
 xmlns:xsd="http://www.w3.org/2001/XMLSchema"
 targetNamespace="http://www.books.org"
```

21: Multiple Schemas

```
 xmlns="http://www.books.org"
 elementFormDefault="qualified">
<xsd:include
     schemaLocation="bookDetails-2.xsd"/>
 <xsd:element name="book"
              type="bookDetails"/>
</xsd:schema>
           <!-- schema21-2.xsd -->
```

I trust this is all crystal clear! I did not get all of it the first time around, so, if necessary go back and revise it.

Import

Suppose an included file has a *different* namespace which, for some reason or other, we cannot change. We then need to use the import element:

Here is the XML document which this time has changed. It has a new element details which will contain isbn and title elements. Note the three xmlns and that each one is prefixed.

```
<?xml version="1.0"?>
<bk:book
xmlns:bk="http://www.books.org"
xmlns:D="http://www.details.org"
xmlns:xsi="http://www.w3.org/2001/XMLSchema-instance"
xsi:schemaLocation=
                "http://www.books.org
                 schema21-3.xsd
                 http://www.details.org
                 bookDetails-3.xsd">
 <bk:details>
  <D:isbn>1234567890</D:isbn>
  <D:title>XHTML &amp; CSS
                       explained</D:title>
 </bk:details>
</bk:book>  <!-- Ex21-3.xml  -->
```

- 302 -

Here is the schema to which it refers, `schema21-3.xsd`:

```
<?xml version="1.0"?>
<xsd:schema
 targetNamespace="http://www.books.org"
 xmlns:bk="http://www.books.org"
 xmlns:xsd="http://www.w3.org/2001/XMLSchema"
 xmlns:D="http://www.details.org"
 elementFormDefault="qualified">
<xsd:import
        namespace="http://www.details.org"
        schemaLocation="bookDetails-3.xsd"/>
 <xsd:element name="book">
  <xsd:complexType>
   <xsd:sequence>
    <xsd:element name="details"
                 type="D:bkDetailsType"/>
   </xsd:sequence>
  </xsd:complexType>
 </xsd:element>
</xsd:schema>
             <!-- schema21-3.xsd -->
```

Notice that the `import` element takes two attributes, a `namespace` *and* a `schemaLocation` with a *single* value. The element `book` contains a `details` element which will be of type `bkDetailsType`. The validator, having imported the `bookDetails-3.xsd` schema, will be able to locate the relevant definition for that type. How does the schema know that `bkDetailsType` belongs to the imported schema?

It is all done by namespaces, hence the popularity of schemas over DTDs. The `D:` prefix has been associated with the: `xmlns:D=http://www.details.org`

namespace, and the `import` element provides the location of this schema:

```
<xsd:import
        namespace="http://www.details.org"
        schemaLocation="bookDetails-3.xsd"/>
```

So anything with a D: belongs to www.details.org and cannot be confused with any other namespace.

Here is the imported schema:

```
<?xml version="1.0"?>
<xsd:schema
xmlns:xsd="http://www.w3.org/2001/XMLSchema"
targetNamespace="http://www.details.org"
xmlns="http://www.details.org"
elementFormDefault="qualified">

<xsd:complexType name="bkDetailsType">
 <xsd:sequence>
  <xsd:element name="isbn"
               type="xsd:decimal"/>
  <xsd:element name="title"
               type="xsd:string"/>
 </xsd:sequence>
</xsd:complexType>
</xsd:schema>
          <!-- bookDetails-3.xsd -->
```

Notice that it has its own target namespace:

```
targetNamespace="http://www.details.org"
xmlns="http://www.details.org"
```

As such it could be used directly by any XML document which references that target namespace. Because we have made bkDetailsType a type definition, we needed to create a new details element in schema21-3.xsd so that we could make it refer to this type.

The Chameleon Approach
We have seen how to handle schemas with the same
namespaces and how to handle those with different
namespaces. There is a third possibility, namely, when an
included schema has *no* namespace.

```
<?xml version="1.0"?>
<book
xmlns="http://www.books.org"
xmlns:xsi="http://www.w3.org/2001/XMLSchema-instance"
xsi:schemaLocation="http://www.books.org
                    schema21-4.xsd">

  <isbn>1234567890</isbn>
  <title>XHTML &amp; CSS explained</title>
</book>
          <!-- Ex21-4.xml -->
```

Here is the `schema21-4.xsd` schema and notice that the
`include` element is used again:

```
<?xml version="1.0"?>
<schema
 xmlns="http://www.w3.org/2001/XMLSchema"
 targetNamespace="http://www.books.org"
 xmlns:ipo="http://www.books.org"
 elementFormDefault="qualified">
<include
     schemaLocation="bookDetails-4.xsd"/>
<element name="book"
        type="ipo:bookDetails"/>
</schema>
          <!-- schema21-4.xsd -->
```

Next comes the included schema, the one which has no
namespace because the `targetNamespace` and its
accompanying `xmlns` have been omitted:

21: **Multiple Schemas**

```
<?xml version="1.0"?>
<xsd:schema
xmlns:xsd="http://www.w3.org/2001/XMLSchema"
elementFormDefault="qualified">

<xsd:complexType name="bookDetails">
 <xsd:sequence>
  <xsd:element name="isbn"
               type="xsd:decimal"/>
  <xsd:element name="title"
               type="xsd:string"/>
 </xsd:sequence>
</xsd:complexType>
</xsd:schema>
           <!-- bookDetails-4.xsd -->
```

The included schema, the one with no target namespace (and therefore no associated xmlns), is forced to adopt the namespace of the schema into which it is included. This is called a *coerced namespace*.

Important: *the schema with no target namespace must have a qualified XML Schema but not as a default!*

<include> v. <import>

The include element is used when schemas have the *same* namespaces or when the included schemas have *no* namespace. The import element is used when the schemas have *different* namespaces.

attributeFormDefault

The above attribute works in a similar way to the elementFormDefault but it is dealing with *attributes* rather than elements. The default (i.e. when it is not specified) is: attributeFormDefault="unqualified"

Let us add a couple of attributes to our example:

```
<?xml version="1.0"?>
<book
xmlns="http://www.books.org"
xmlns:xsi="http://www.w3.org/2001/XMLSchema-instance"
xsi:schemaLocation="http://www.books.org
                   schema21-5.xsd">
 <isbn>1234567890</isbn>
 <title language="English" date="2002-12">
    XHTML &amp; CSS explained
 </title>
</book>
             <!-- Ex21-5.xml -->
```

Here is `schema21-5.xsd`. Notice that it has an *unqualified* `attributeFormDefault`:

```
<?xml version="1.0"?>
<schema
 xmlns="http://www.w3.org/2001/XMLSchema"
  targetNamespace="http://www.books.org"
  xmlns:ipo="http://www.books.org"
  elementFormDefault="qualified"
  attributeFormDefault="unqualified">
 <element name="book">
   <complexType>
    <sequence>
     <element name="isbn" type="decimal"/>
     <element ref="ipo:title"/>
    </sequence>
   </complexType>
 </element>
 <!-- the global declaration for title -->
<element name="title" >
 <complexType>
  <simpleContent>
   <extension base="string">
    <attribute name="language"
               type="string"/>
```

```
    <attribute name="date"
                type="gYearMonth"/>
    </extension>
   </simpleContent>
 </complexType>
</element>
</schema>
             <!-- schema21-5.xsd -->
```

We chose to make the title element a global declaration. This makes it a complex type. But since we are adding attributes and no child elements we use the simple content model. We need to extend the title element with attributes, hence the use of <extension>.

However, we are really discussing the unqualified value for the attributeFormDefault. It is the default value when not given in the schema. It tells an XML author how to qualify attributes in the XML document. As you can see, it has no impact on Ex21-5.xml.

Let us now see its impact if the schema author had used the *qualified* value for the attributeFormDefault. The schema remains unchanged apart from the following two lines. We have *unqualified* the elementFormDefault:

```
elementFormDefault="unqualified"
attributeFormDefault="qualified"
```

Here is the valid version of the XML document:

```
<?xml version="1.0"?>
<L:book
xmlns:L="http://www.books.org"
xmlns:xsi="http://www.w3.org/2001/XMLSchema-instance"
xsi:schemaLocation="http://www.books.org
                    schema21-5a.xsd">
```

```
<isbn>1234567890</isbn>
  <L:title L:language="English"
           L:date="2002-12">
      XHTML &amp; CSS explained
</L:title>
</L:book>
                <!-- Ex21-5a.xml -->
```

Wow! All the attribute names have had to be qualified with the prefix used on the target namespace `xmlns`. One small change to a schema, many changes in the XML document! The rule is, that if the attribute form default is `qualified`, then the `xmlns` which references the target namespace *must use a prefix*. A default namespace is not tolerated. Because the namespace is now prefixed-qualified, element names also need to be prefixed depending on the value of the element form default in the schema. We chose `unqualified`, so only the global elements needed to be prefixed.

What are the global element declarations? `book` and `title`. `isbn` is a *local* element declaration, so it is not prefixed. But, if the `elementFormDefault` had been `qualified`, then that too would have to be prefixed. So if you are an XML author basing the structure on someone else's schema, you will need to look carefully at all these values.

Redefine

Suppose you would like to extend the book details to include a `cost` element.

```
<?xml version="1.0"?>
<book xmlns="http://www.books.org"
xmlns:xsi="http://www.w3.org/2001/XMLSchema-instance"
xsi:schemaLocation="http://www.books.org
                    schema21-6.xsd">
```

```
  <isbn>1234567890</isbn>
  <title>XHTML &amp; CSS explained</title>
  <cost>7.99</cost>
</book>
            <!-- Ex21-6.xml -->
```

The redefine element is useful in such situations, but it can only be used with schemas which have the same namespace or those with no target namespace. It is really an extension of the include element. What makes it different is that you can modify one of the 'included' components. Here is the bookDetails-6.xsd schema, it is identical to what we have looked at earlier. Note that it has no target namespace.

```
<?xml version="1.0"?>
<xsd:schema
 xmlns:xsd="http://www.w3.org/2001/XMLSchema"
 elementFormDefault="qualified">

<xsd:complexType name="bookDetails">
 <xsd:sequence>
  <xsd:element name="isbn"
               type="xsd:decimal"/>
  <xsd:element name="title"
               type="xsd:string"/>
 </xsd:sequence>
</xsd:complexType>
</xsd:schema>
         <!-- bookDetails-6.xsd -->
```

But here is our new target schema, the one used by the XML document instance:

```
<?xml version="1.0"?>
<xsd:schema
 xmlns:xsd="http://www.w3.org/2001/XMLSchema"
 targetNamespace="http://www.books.org"
```

```
  xmlns="http://www.books.org"
  elementFormDefault="qualified">
<!-- Like include, redefine must come before anything else.  -->
<xsd:redefine
          schemaLocation="bookDetails-6.xsd">

  <xsd:complexType name="bookDetails">
    <xsd:complexContent>
      <xsd:extension base="bookDetails">
        <xsd:sequence>
          <xsd:element name="cost"
                          type="xsd:decimal"/>
        </xsd:sequence>
      </xsd:extension>
    </xsd:complexContent>
  </xsd:complexType>
</xsd:redefine>
<xsd:element name="book"
                type="bookDetails"/>
</xsd:schema>
              <!-- schema21-6.xsd -->
```

Note, that like the *include* and the *import* elements, *redefine* must come *before* any element or attribute declaration or any type or attribute definition. We have also opted to make the target namespace the default namespace and have qualified the XML Schema namespace. We could have reversed the two to reduce the amount of extra typing involved in having to qualify all the XML Schema elements and primitive types.

Because we are effectively extending the bookDetails by creating a new definition, we have to use complexType with complexContent. The latter requires the extension element to extend the base type bookDetails.

21: **Multiple Schemas**

When the validator meets the `book` element, it will look up the details for this type from the `bookDetails-6.xsd` schema and extend it according to the definition specified in the `redefine` element.

```
<xsd:element name="book"
              type="bookDetails"/>
```

Let us add an attribute to `cost`:

```
<?xml version="1.0"?>
<book
xmlns="http://www.books.org"
xmlns:xsi="http://www.w3.org/2001/XMLSchema-instance"
xsi:schemaLocation="http://www.books.org
                    schema21-7.xsd">
  <isbn>1234567890</isbn>
  <title>XHTML &amp; CSS explained</title>
  <cost currencyType="Sterling">7.99</cost>
</book>
                <!-- Ex21-7.xml -->
```

`bookDetails-7.xsd` remains unchanged from the earlier version 6. But here is our new `schema21-7.xsd`:

```
<?xml version="1.0"?>
<xsd:schema
 xmlns:xsd="http://www.w3.org/2001/XMLSchema"
 targetNamespace="http://www.books.org"
 xmlns="http://www.books.org"
 elementFormDefault="qualified">
<!-- Like include, redefine must come before anything else.
-->
<xsd:redefine
     schemaLocation="bookDetails-7.xsd">
 <xsd:complexType name="bookDetails">
  <xsd:complexContent>
   <xsd:extension base="bookDetails">
```

```
    <xsd:sequence>
      <xsd:element name="cost">
       <xsd:complexType>
        <xsd:simpleContent>
         <xsd:extension base="xsd:decimal">
          <xsd:attribute name="currencyType"
                            type="xsd:string"/>
         </xsd:extension>
        </xsd:simpleContent>
       </xsd:complexType>
      </xsd:element>
    </xsd:sequence>
   </xsd:extension>
  </xsd:complexContent>
 </xsd:complexType>
</xsd:redefine>
<xsd:element name="book"
               type="bookDetails"/>
</xsd:schema>
             <!-- schema21-7.xsd -->
```

We are extending `bookDetails` via the `redefine` element to add another element `cost`. We have to use the `complexType` element with a `simpleContent` element. The latter is used because there are no child elements to be included in `cost`. The base type for `cost` is `decimal` and an attribute declaration is made for the type of currency.

An alternative way to achieve the same result is to use a `ref` attribute and hive off the definition for `cost` to some other place:

```
<xsd:redefine
        schemaLocation="bookDetails-7.xsd">
 <xsd:complexType name="bookDetails">
  <xsd:complexContent>
   <xsd:extension base="bookDetails">
```

```
   <xsd:sequence>
     <xsd:element ref="cost"/>
   </xsd:sequence>
  </xsd:extension>
 </xsd:complexContent>
</xsd:complexType>
</xsd:redefine>
<xsd:element name="book"
              type="bookDetails"/>
<!-- declaration for cost element -->
<xsd:element name="cost">
 <xsd:complexType>
  <xsd:simpleContent>
   <xsd:extension base="xsd:decimal">
    <xsd:attribute name="currencyType"
                    type="xsd:string"/>
   </xsd:extension>
  </xsd:simpleContent>
 </xsd:complexType>
</xsd:element>
```

We have covered many features in this Chapter, some of which need time to practise. It has so much information that it will probably be worth many revisits. Once you have grasped what we have covered, many of the mysteries vanish, such as why your documents never seem to be valid. A validator such as XML Spy will repay its purchase price time and again.

TWENTY-TWO:

Odds and Ends

Here are a few odds and ends to complete our study of XML Schema.

nil Content v. empty

You can indicate in a schema that an element is to have `nil` content. This is not the same as specifying that an element is *empty*. An empty element can *never* have any content. It is constrained by the schema.

```
<element name="special">
 <complexType/>
</element>

<!-- in an XML instance -->
<special/>
```

It does nothing, contains nothing, so what use is it? It could be used as some kind of placeholder or flag or marker which some other program could search for and react to accordingly. However, empty elements usually contain attributes:

```
<element name="staff">
 <complexType>
  <attribute name="staffID" type="int"/>
 </complexType>
</element>
```

```
<!-- in an XML instance -->
<staff staffID="123"/>
```

Because the above contains no content model for the `complexType`, the processor knows that it is empty, no text content, no child elements.

It could be used as follows:

```
<project>
The project team comprises: <staff
staffID="123"/>, <staff staffID="128"/> and
<staff staffID="145"/>. ...etc...
</project>
```

However, there may be occasions when you want an element sometimes to have no text content, but at other times to contain text content. The following shows an example:

```
<?xml version="1.0"?>
<staff xmlns="http://www.currency.org"
xmlns:xsi="http://www.w3.org/2001/XMLSchema-instance"
xsi:schemaLocation="http://www.currency.org
                    schema22-1.xsd">
 <PersonName>
  <forename>John</forename>
  <middle xsi:nil="true"/>
  <surname>Doe</surname>
 </PersonName>
 <PersonName>
  <forename>John</forename>
  <middle>Fred</middle>
  <surname>Doe</surname>
 </PersonName>
</staff>
            <!-- Ex22-1.xml -->
```

In the following:

```
<middle xsi:nil="true"/>
```

`middle` takes the `nil` attribute with a value of `true`. Since this is one of the four words from the XMLSchema-instance vocabulary, it is prefixed with `xsi`. This informs the validator that on this particular occasion the element will not contain any text content. The schema must make provision for this element to be variable. This is done via the `nillable` attribute. On this occasion it is valid for the `middle` element to be empty, but the element must still be present in the XML document instance.

In the following schema, we make this provision by using the `nillable` attribute:

```
<?xml version="1.0" encoding="UTF-8"?>
<xsd:schema
targetNamespace="http://www.currency.org"
xmlns="http://www.currency.org"
xmlns:xsd="http://www.w3.org/2001/XMLSchema"
elementFormDefault="qualified">

 <xsd:element name="staff">
  <xsd:complexType>
   <xsd:sequence>
    <xsd:element name="PersonName"
                 type="aPersonName"
                 maxOccurs="unbounded"/>
   </xsd:sequence>
  </xsd:complexType>
 </xsd:element>
 <xsd:complexType name="aPersonName">
  <xsd:sequence>
   <xsd:element name="forename"
                type="xsd:NMTOKEN"/>
```

```
   <xsd:element name="middle"
                type="xsd:NMTOKEN"
                nillable="true"/>
   <xsd:element name="surname"
                type="xsd:NMTOKEN"/>
  </xsd:sequence>
 </xsd:complexType>
</xsd:schema> <!-- schema22-1.xsd -->
```

Thus, schema authors can construct their schemas to allow XML document authors to use an element which can sometimes take content and sometimes not to contain content.

`xsi:type`

In Chapter 18, we discussed *element* substitution. That is, one element can be substituted for another element. But we can also substitute one *type* for another.

Any base type can be substituted by any derived type. In the following we have an element `staff` containing an unbounded number of `employee` elements. The latter is of type `permStaff`.

```
<?xml version="1.0" encoding="UTF-8"?>
<xsd:schema
targetNamespace="http://www.currency.org"
xmlns="http://www.currency.org"
xmlns:xsd="http://www.w3.org/2001/XMLSchema"
elementFormDefault="qualified">

 <xsd:element name="staff">
  <xsd:complexType>
   <xsd:sequence>
    <xsd:element name="employee"
                 type="permStaff"
                 maxOccurs="unbounded"/>
   </xsd:sequence>
  </xsd:complexType>
```

```
  </xsd:element>
 <xsd:complexType name="permStaff">
  <xsd:sequence>
   <xsd:element name="forename"
                type="xsd:NMTOKEN"/>
   <xsd:element name="surname"
                type="xsd:NMTOKEN"/>
   <xsd:element name="position"
                type="xsd:string"/>
  </xsd:sequence>
 </xsd:complexType>
<xsd:complexType name="tempStaff">
 <xsd:complexContent>
  <xsd:extension base="permStaff">
   <xsd:sequence>
    <xsd:element name="until"
                 type="xsd:date"/>
   </xsd:sequence>
  </xsd:extension>
 </xsd:complexContent>
</xsd:complexType>
</xsd:schema>      <!-- schema22-2.xsd -->
```

The permStaff element contains a sequence of single forename, surname and position elements.

Occasionally, temporary staff are taken on and when they are we wish to add an until element, stating when they will leave the company. We simply create a new type derived from the base type for permStaff. We have to use complexContent since we are extending the base type to include this child element - until. So far, this should be fairly obvious.

But what about the XML document? Somehow, we have to state when we want to use the basic permStaff type (called the *source type*) and when we want to use the derived type, the one with the extra element. That is where the `xsi:type` helps out.

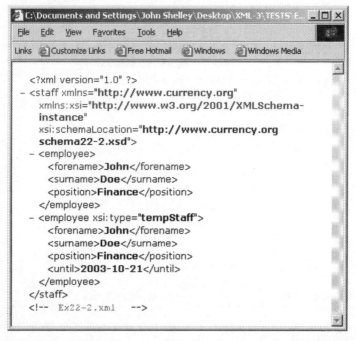

```
<?xml version="1.0" ?>
- <staff xmlns="http://www.currency.org"
    xmlns:xsi="http://www.w3.org/2001/XMLSchema-
    instance"
    xsi:schemaLocation="http://www.currency.org
    schema22-2.xsd">
  - <employee>
      <forename>John</forename>
      <surname>Doe</surname>
      <position>Finance</position>
    </employee>
  - <employee xsi:type="tempStaff">
      <forename>John</forename>
      <surname>Doe</surname>
      <position>Finance</position>
      <until>2003-10-21</until>
    </employee>
  </staff>
  <!-- Ex22-2.xml -->
```

The `xsi:type` is one of the four attributes in the XMLSchema-instance namespace, especially designed to cope with this situation. Hence, we have to include its namespace prefixed with the conventional `xsi`.

qualified v. unqualified

In `schema22-2.xsd` schema, we set EFD to qualified. In the XML document, the target namespace is set as the default. This means that we do not have to prefix-qualify the schema vocabulary: `staff`, `employee`, `forename`, `surname`, `position`, `until`.

But suppose we had set EFD to unqualified. Now the XML document on the previous page would be invalid, because we are using a default target namespace.

Remember that unqualified means that only global elements are qualified, local elements must not be. But because we have used a default namespace, all elements are non-prefixed. This means that there is no way for a validator to distinguish between global and local, so it gives up.

```
<?xml version="1.0" encoding="UTF-8" ?>
- <xsd:schema
    targetNamespace="http://www.currency.org"
    xmlns="http://www.currency.org"
    xmlns:xsd="http://www.w3.org/2001/XMLSchema"
    elementFormDefault="unqualified">
  - <xsd:element name="staff">
    + <xsd:complexType>
    </xsd:element>
  - <xsd:complexType name="permStaff">
    + <xsd:sequence>
    </xsd:complexType>
  - <xsd:complexType name="tempStaff">
    + <xsd:complexContent>
    </xsd:complexType>
  </xsd:schema>
  <!-- schema22-2.xsd EDF unqualified -->
```

I gave the schema an xml extension and opened it in IE6. It is now quite simple to check which are global components and which are local by clicking on the plus and minus signs. It is clear that schema has three child elements: staff, permStaff and tempStaff. These are the global components. Any components within the plus signs are local.

So what do we do? Either we must give EFD a *qualified* value in the schema and make the target namespace in the XML document a *default*. Or, we use an *unqualified* value in the schema, but then we must use a qualified prefixed target namespace in the XML document. Thus:

```
<?xml version="1.0"?>
<F:staff
xmlns:F="http://www.currency.org"
xmlns:xsi="http://www.w3.org/2001/XMLSchema-instance"
xsi:schemaLocation="http://www.currency.org
                    schema22-2a.xsd">
  <employee>
    <forename>John</forename>
    <surname>Doe</surname>
    <position>Finance</position>
  </employee>
  <employee xsi:type="F:tempStaff">
    <forename>John</forename>
    <surname>Doe</surname>
    <position>Finance</position>
    <until>2003-10-21</until>
  </employee>
</F:staff>
            <!-- Ex22-2a.xml -->
```

All we now have to do is to prefix-qualify all global elements and type definitions. This involves just the one global staff element. But can you work out why tempStaff must also be prefixed? It is because it is a global type definition in the schema. We are referring to it and must inform the validator that it belongs to the target namespace. We do this by prefixing it with the F prefix as used in that namespace.

It does require a bit of mental gymnastics.

Annotating your Schemas

The `<annotation>` element is used for documenting schemas. It is intended for two audiences, either a human reader or an application program. Both require the `annotation` element followed by the `documentation` element, if it is for human consumption, or the `appinfo` element when the annotation is for some application program.

Human reader - <documentation>

If you wish to provide comments to humans, including yourself, you can use the formal annotation approach:

```
<annotation>
<documentation>
Remember to modify this schema before August
2004.
</documentation>
</annotation>
```

This would be equivalent to the use of the standard XML comment, as used so far in this text:

```
<!--
Remember to modify this schema before August
2004. -->
```

For Application Programs

```
<annotation>
<appinfo>
Last modified: August 2004.
</appinfo>
</annotation>
```

It would now be possible for a program to read the element's content and do *something* with it. That sounds somewhat vague! Although the XML Schema defines these constructions, the specification does not define how the information should be interpreted, for either humans or programs. They are there should you need them, but what practical use is made of them will have to be written into a program.

They are frequently used to provide details about copyright and author.

Rules for using <annotation>
Annotations have no effect on validation provided that they appear in the right place. They cannot appear in any random place. They can go:

- before or after any global component
- at the beginning of any non-global component

```
<?xml version="1.0"?>
<schema
xmlns="http://www.w3.org/2001/XMLSchema"
targetNamespace="http://www.books.org"
xmlns:ipo="http://www.books.org"
elementFormDefault="unqualified">
<anno ... >.. </anno..>
 <element name="book">
<anno ... >.. </anno..>
  <complexType>
   <sequence>
    <element name="isbn"  type="integer"/>
    <element name="title" type="string"/>
   </sequence>
  </complexType>
 </element>
<anno ... >.. </anno..>
</schema>
```

Suppose you wanted to annotate the isbn element? You would have to do the following:

```
<element name="isbn" type="integer">
 <annotation ...>
 Your annotation
 </annotation>
</element>
<element name="title"  type="string"/>
```

\<documentation\>
This may take two attributes, `source` and `xml:lang`:

```
<annotation>
<documentation
   source="http://www.book.org/review.txt"
   xml:lang="FR"/>
</annotation>
```

If there is more detailed information in a file called, say
`review.txt`, the source attribute is used to point to it.
The `xml:lang` attribute specifies the language in which it
is written. Incidentally, the W3C recommends that an
`xml:lang` attribute *should* be included in all
documentation elements to indicate the language in which
it was written.

\<appinfo\>
This can take only the `source` attribute. It behaves as for
`documentation`:

```
<annotation>
<appinfo
   source="http://www.book.org/review.txt"/>
</annotation>
```

22: <u>Odds and Ends</u>

Useful Web Sites

XMLSchema resources
This is the site to visit for the main reference to XML Schema.

http://www.w3.org/XML/Schema

XML Schema Part 0: Primer & for name tokens

http://www.w3.org/TR/xmlschema-0/

XML Schema Part 1: Structures

http://www.w3.org/TR/xmlschema-1/

XML Schema Part 2: Datatypes

http://www.w3.org/TR/xmlschema-2/

Getting started with XML and DTDs.

http://www-106.ibm.com/developerworks/xml/library/xml-schema/#sidebar1

Provides a brief introduction to XML Schema

http://lucas.ucs.ed.ac.uk/xml-schema/

This site gives simple comparisons between XML Schemas and the technologies that have influenced it. It does not provide an exhaustive list of all XML Schemas features.

http://www.ascc.net/~ricko/XMLSchemaInContext.html

Another brief introduction to XML Schemas.

http://www.xml.com/pub/a/1999/07/schemas/index.html

Appendix A

W3C Schools - this site has a number of useful tutorials
http://www.w3schools.com/

This site is useful for validating XML documents against internal DTDs. You can upload a document from your local hard disc. However, external DTDs cannot be validated. The service is free and very fast. It comes from Brown University Scholarly Technology Group.
http://www.stg.brown.edu/service/xmlvalid/

This site is useful for validating schemas. You can upload a document from your local hard disc.
http://www.w3.org/2001/03/webdata/xsv

Although expensive, the XML Spy 4.4 Suite is ideal for those who need to do serious work with XML, DTDs and schemas. It locates any external DTDs and schema files referenced by an XML document. So you can do all your tests on your local PC. There is a free 30 day trial period for those who want to test it before purchasing a copy.
http://www.xmlspy.com/

This site is well worth a visit. It has a number of useful schemas as well as tutorials.
http://www.xfront.com/

For the Chemical markup language and MathML respectively:
http://www.xml-cml.org/ & http://www.w3.org/Math/

SGML and where it came from
http://www.w3.org/MarkUp/SGML/
http://www.sgmlsource.com/history/roots.htm

XML language codes
http://www.dsv.su.se/~jpalme/ietf/language-codes.html

Appendix B:

The ASCII Character Set

ASCII Character Set

In the following, the first 32 of the 128 characters are special and are used to control printing and communication lines. These are not printable characters and only a few are shown. No description is given when the meaning of the character is obvious. If a character has an *entity name* this is shown in the description. The name appears between an ampersand (&) and a semi-colon (;) for example, `&quot;`

Where names are not available, the ASCII code number is used preceded by a hash sign (#), thus, the tilde (~) would be entered as a character entity as follows: `&#126;`

Note that character entity names are lowercase sensitive!

Number	Character	Description
0	NUL	Null character
7	Bell	rings a bell
8	BS	backspace
9	HT	horizontal tab
10	LF	line feed

Appendix B

Number	Character	Description
13	CR	carriage return
32		space character
33	!	exclamation mark
34	"	"
35	#	hash sign
36	$	
37	%	
38	&	ampersand - &
39	'	apostrophe
40	(	
41	)	
42	*	
43	+	
44	,	comma
45	-	hyphen
46	.	full stop/period
47	/	solidus
48 - 57	0-9	digits 0 - 9
58	:	colon
59	;	semi-colon
60	<	<
61	=	equals
62	>	>
63	?	
64	@	commercial at
65-90	Letters A - Z	uppercase letters
91	[	
92	\	backslash
93	]	
94	^	caret
95	_	underscore
96	`	acute accent
97 - 122	letters a - z	lowercase letters
123	{	left curly bracket
124			vertical bar
125	}	right curly bracket
126	~	tilde
127	DEL	delete

Note: There is no sterling (£) pound symbol in the ASCII character set. It is actually number 163 in the Latin-1 set. That is why older e-mail messages had to contain the word *sterling* or *pounds*, for example:

```
Course Fee: 200.00 pounds
```

Most of our later e-mail programs can cope with many of the non-ASCII characters.

For those who are interested in the various character sets employed in computers, try this site. It is one of the most comprehensive (34 pages) articles I have found. Further references abound. Before I read the article I did not realise just how complex it is.

```
http://www.cs.tut.fi/%7Ejkorpela/chars/index.
html
```

For the rest of the Latin-1 character set, refer to the table on the next page. To find the decimal number for a character, use the first two digits in the left row and supply the third digit from the column headings. Thus, the yen symbol (¥) is read as 16 (row) & 5 (column), yielding the decimal number 165. Therefore, ¥ would give you a yen sign.

In general, XML authors can safely use the ASCII characters 32 – 126, with the exception of the *less than* and *greater than* symbols (< >) and the *ampersand* (&) since these three are regarded as mark-up characters by a parser. All the other characters from 128 – 255 should *always be given* as character entities.

Note the Euro symbol is decimal 128. As a character entity this would be typed as: € It works in IE5 but it does not work with Netscape 4.5. However, both Netscape 4.5 and IE5 accept the following character entity: € which is easier to remember.

Latin-1 Characters from 120 - 255

	0	1	2	3	4	5	6	7	8	9
12	x	y	z	{	|	}	~			
13	‚	ƒ	„	…	†	‡	ˆ	‰	Š	‹
14	Œ		Ž			‘	’	"	"	•
15	–	—	˜	™	š	›	œ		ž	Ÿ
16		¡	¢	£	¤	¥	¦	§	¨	©
17	ª	«	¬	-	®	¯	°	±	²	³
18	´	µ	¶	·	¸	¹	º	»	¼	½
19	¾	¿	À	Á	Â	Ã	Ä	Å	Æ	Ç
20	È	É	Ê	Ë	Ì	Í	Î	Ï	Ð	Ñ
21	Ò	Ó	Ô	Õ	Ö	×	Ø	Ù	Ú	Û
22	Ü	Ý	Þ	ß	à	á	â	ã	ä	å
23	æ	ç	è	é	ê	ë	ì	í	î	ï
24	ð	ñ	ò	ó	ô	õ	ö	÷	ø	ù
25	ú	û	ü	ý	þ	ÿ				

Appendix C

Regular Expressions

The `string` data type can take a *pattern* facet. The values of a pattern facet are *regular expressions*. The following table provides examples of regular expressions some taken from the W3C XML Schema Part 0: Primer, some from Roger Costello's PowerPoint slides, see Appendix A for reference, and some are my own. The second table explains some of the syntax.

There are many permutations and a validating parser such as XML Spy is more than useful for testing out your patterns.

Expression	Example Match(s)
`Chapter \d`	Chapter 0, Chapter 1, Chapter 2 .... *(note the space before the digit)*
`Chapter\s\d`	Chapter followed by a single space character, followed by a single digit
`chapter&#x020;\d`	chapter 1 *(hex 20 is the space character)*
`chapTer\s\w`	chapTer followed by a single space character, followed by a single digit, followed by a word character
`Espan&#xF1;ola`	Española
`\p{Lu}`	any uppercase character, the value of \p{} (e.g. "Lu")
`\p{IsGreek}`	any Greek character, the 'Is' construction may be applied to any block name (e.g. "Greek") as

Appendix C

Expression	Example Match(s)
	defined by Unicode
\P{IsGreek}	any non-Greek character, the 'Is' construction may be applied to any block name (e.g. "Greek") as defined by Unicode
a*x	x, ax, aax, aaax ....
a?x	ax, x
a+x	ax, aax, aaax ....
(a|b)+x	ax, bx, aax, abx, bax, bbx, aaax, aabx, abax, abbx, baax, babx, bbax, bbbx, aaaax ....
[abcde]x	ax, bx, cx, dx, ex
[a-e]x	ax, bx, cx, dx, ex
[-ae]x	-x, ax, ex
[ae-]x	ax, ex, -x
[^0-9]x	any non-digit character followed by the character x
\Dx	any non-digit character followed by the character x
.x	any character followed by the character x
.*abc.*	1x2abc, abc1x2, z3456abchooray ....
ab{2}x	abbx
ab{2,4}x	abbx, abbbx, abbbbx (note a can occur just once)
ab{2,}x	abbx, abbbx, abbbbx ....
(ab){2}x	ababx
[xyz]b	ax, bx, cx
[a-d]x	ax, bx, cx, dx
[-ac]x	-x, ax, cx
[ac-]x	ax, cx, -x
(ho){2} there	hoho there

Expression	Example Match(s)
`(ho\sho){2}there`	ho hoho hothere
`.abc`	any single character followed by abc; 5abc
`a{1,3}x`	ax, aax, aaax
`a{2,} x`	aa x, aaa x, aaaa x, ...
`[0-9]{1,10}`	any integer up to 10 digits
`\p{Sc}\d+(\.\d\d)`	£23.45
`[a-zA-Z-[Ol]]*`	a string comprised of any lower or uppercase character, except letter oh and letter el

Syntax	Example
`.` (period)	any character
`\.`	the period (without the slash, it would mean any character)
`\d`	any digit
`\D`	any non-digit character
`\s`	space
`\w`	any word *(comprising any of the alphanumeric characters including the hyphen)*
`\p{L}`	a letter from any language
`\p{Lu}`	an uppercase character from any language
`\p{Ll}`	a lowercase character from any language
`\p{Sc}`	a currency sign from any language
If you need any of the following characters as part of your pattern, they need to be preceded by a slash, otherwise they will have a syntactical meaning	
`\\`	backward slash
`\-`	the hyphen
`\^`	the caret
`\?`	the question mark
`\*`	the asterisk
`\+`	the plus sign

Appendix C

\{	open curly bracket
\}	closing curly bracket
\(	open round bracket
\)	closing round bracket
\[	open square bracket
\]	closing square bracket
\n	line feed
\r	carriage return
\t	tab

Symbols	Meaning
[abc]	only one character from the set allowed
[a-f]	one from the set range a to f, lowercase
(hofred)	the complete set hofred must be used
{1,4}	number of times, at least 1 and maximum 4
{2, }	at least twice and unbounded
*	none or unbounded
?	none or maximum once
+	at least once and unbounded
^	not
[^0-9]x or \Dx	any non-digit followed by x
.x	any character followed by x

More information can be found at the following site:

http://www.w3.org/TR/xmlschema-2/#regexs

Appendix D

Answers to tests

Test 1:
1. Where did XML come from?

It was derived from SGML. It has 80% of the functionality of SGML but only 20% of its complexity.

2. Which language was used to create HTML?
SGML.

3. Which language was used to create XHTML?
XML.

4. What does the term Extensible mean in XML?

It means that we can invent our own tag names.

5. When creating an XML document, what is the first thing you need to consider?

The full details of the data you are intending to supply.

Test 2:
1. What purpose does the root element serve in an XML document?

It will tell a parser program where the XML document begins and where it finishes. There can be only one root element.

2. How significant is case in XML?

Absolutely crucial. Unlike HTML, where case is not significant, an XML document must preserve case throughout. Thus: `fred FRED Fred` would be three totally different names within an XML document .

3. Every XML document is a new language. True or false?

True. Every time someone creates a document based on the XML syntax, it is a new language. It will contain a set of element and attribute names, called the vocabulary of the document, which has never been used in that way before. In English, it is akin to people writing letters. Each is unique.

4. Parent elements cannot contain grandchildren elements. True or false?

True. There are only parents and children. Only a parent can recognise its immediate child elements, but not any grandchildren.

Test 4:

1. How would you enter Suo Gân in an XML document?

Look up the ASCII character number for â – happens to be 226. Precede the decimal number with a #. (See page 109.) This would now be used as a character entity with a leading & and a trailing ; - thus: Suo Gân

2. Can any program open an XML file?

Yes, provided the program can read pure text. But it cannot check that the document is well-formed. That is what a parser program does.

3. What does a parser do to an XML document?

Checks that the document is well-formed. It can also check whether the document is valid, see page 98.

4. How does a parser recognise a character entity?

It begins with an & followed by one of the three valid forms for entering character entities and concludes with a semi-colon. The valid forms are either a name, if there is one, a decimal or hexadecimal ASCII code number.

5. Why do we need character entities?

Parsers have to parse textual content between element tags. Essentially, it has to look for opening angle brackets to find out where the closing tag or an opening child element may occur. Should we need an opening angle bracket as part of our textual content, then it must be represented as a character entity. But because character entities must begin with an ampersand, we cannot include an ampersand by itself. Thus < and & are known as mark-up characters. To distinguish between mark-up and textual characters we need character entities.

6. What two characters must not appear in parsed character data?

< and & as discussed above.

7. When an XML document is created, all the element and attribute names are known as a vocabulary. True or False?

True. Our XML documents will contain element and attribute names which we have invented. These names form the vocabulary for the XML document.

Test 5:
1. How is a well-formed XML document checked for validity?

A validating parser is required to check the XML document against a document type definition – a DTD.

2. If an XML document is not linked to an external DTD, it can still be validated. True or false?

True, provided that an internal DTD has been used within the XML document and a *validating* parser is used.

3. An XML document can be validated only against its DTD. True or false?

False. We shall see that either DTDs or XML schemas can be used.

4. How is the XML root element declared in an external DTD?

There is no specific declaration as such. It will be the one element which has no parent.

Appendix D

5. How is the XML root element declared in an internal DTD?

Via the DOCTYPE declaration. The root element name must follow immediately.

6. How is a text-only element declared as such in a DTD?

It must take #PCDATA.

7. A DTD is written in the XML language. True or false?

False. DTDs are associated with SGML. They are used to define the structure and content of XML documents.

8. What does the following declaration mean?
```
<!ELEMENT MOMMA (john, mary+, susan)>
```

MOMMA is the parent of three child elements. One `john`, one or any number of `mary`, followed by one `susan`. They must occur in that order.

9. Why is there a hash in front of #PCDATA?

So that it cannot be mistaken for an element name. Thus,

```
<!ELEMENT fred (PCDATA)>
```

would imply that PCDATA is a child of `fred`, whereas

```
<!ELEMENT fred (#PCDATA)>
```

means that `fred` can take parsed data as its content.

10. How is an XML document linked to an external DTD?

By using the SYSTEM keyword followed by the URL.

Test 6:

1. How is a mixed content element declared?
```
<!ELEMENT momma (#PCDATA |   fred)*>
```

A mixed content element can take both text and child elements. However, when declared as such, #PCDATA must come first, then the child elements each separated by the bar symbol. An asterisk must follow the enclosing round brackets. It cannot be absent when #PCDATA is used.

2. What is the problem with mixed content elements?

Any, none or all can be used and may occur in any order.

3. What must appear immediately after an element name in a declaration?

A space.

4. If no occurrence indicator is given, how many times can the element appear?

Once and only once.

5. How is an empty element declared?

Via the EMPTY keyword which must not be enclosed in round brackets.

6. How many and what are the connector symbols?

There are two connector symbols, the comma and the OR (bar symbol). The comma means that all elements must appear in the order given. The OR means that only one may appear, with the exception of Qu.1 above.

7. What is the difference between the following two declarations?

Note that one has the asterisk and the other does not.

```
<!ELEMENT flour (selfRaising | plain)*>
<!ELEMENT flour (selfRaising | plain)>
```

In the first, either or both elements may be contained in flour. I could even have two plain elements and two selfRaising followed by another plain. Horrendous!

In the second, just one or the other can be the child of any given instance of flour.

N.B: how even one little asterisk can be so important.

Appendix D

Test 7:
1. Where can CDATA and #PCDATA be used?

CDATA is used to specify the content for the value of an attribute.

#PCDATA is used to specify the content of an element.

2. How many types can an attribute take?

There are ten.

3. How many default values can an attribute take?

1 of 4. A string, `#IMPLIED`, `#REQUIRED`, `#FIXED`

4. If an attribute has been given a default value and an XML author omits the attribute, what action is taken by a parser?

The parser is bound to supply the default value for the attribute.

Test 9:
1. What are the five predefined entities built into an XML parser?

`&amp; &apos; &gt; &lt; &quot;`

2. What is the main purpose for using general entities?

To reduce the amount of typing in an XML document.
Some DTDs consist entirely of entities, say, for currency.
These are made available to the general public so that the wheel is not reinvented each time.

3. General entities are parsed, so what characters cannot appear as their content?

& and <

4. How is a general entity recognised by a parser?

It is enclosed between and & and a ; (semi-colon)

5. How is a general entity declared?

`<!ENTITY name "contents">`

6. How does a character entity differ from a general entity?

The character entity is used to supply individual characters from the ASCII character set, typically those not found on a keyboard, such as ½.

General entities are use to replace larger amounts of any text, typically those which are found on a standard keyboard.

7. How would you link an XML document to a DTD document which contains some entities you wish to use?

Via: `<!DOCTYPE bookList SYSTEM "books-2.dtd">`

8. Internal entities cannot appear in an external DTD. True or false?

False. Internal entities are those which are defined in a DTD, either an internal or external DTD.

9. In the text, `Ex9-3.dtd`, we had the following declaration?

`<!ELEMENT book (publisher | author| title)* >`

What is it saying? Is it a good way to declare element book?

It actually means that any of the three elements could appear. If the DTD wanted all three to appear in a given order, we would have to write it using the comma connector:

`<!ELEMENT book (publisher, author, title) >`

10. In the text, `EX9-3.xml` is shown in XML Spy. Why not use IE?

IE cannot locate external DTDs. The only way I could test my XML document was to use a program such as XML Spy.

Test 10:
1. In what document is a general entity used?

In an XML document.

2. In what document is a parameter entity used?

In a DTD.

Appendix D

3. What symbol is used to denote that a parameter entity is being declared and not a general entity?

The percentage symbol - % - which appears before the name of the entity.

4. What symbol is used to denote that a general entity is being declared and not a parameter entity?

None. The name of the entity appears immediately after `<!ENTITY name ...>`

5. How does a parser recognise that a parameter entity is being referenced rather than a general entity?

Parameter entities begin with a % whereas general entities begin with an &

6. What is the difference between a parameter entity used in an Internal DTD and one used in an external DTD?

Parameter entities can only be placed *between* declarations in an internal DTD. Likewise for those used in an external DTD but they can also be placed within (inside) declarations.

Test 13:
1. How could you say that an element can occur exactly 3 times?

```
minOccurs="3" maxOccurs="3"
```

2. What is the root element for an XML Schema?

<schema> ... </schema>

3. How is a simple type recognised by a parser?

Either by being empty, i.e. a forward slash at end of the start tag, or, by being surrounded by the <simpleType> declaration.

4. What is the equivalent of #PCDATA in an XML Schema?

The string data type, one of the primitive built-in data types of XML Schema.

5. What is the formal jargon term for `sequence, all` *and* `choice`*?*

Compositors.

6. What is the difference between `sequence` *and* `all`*?*

`sequence` means all elements must appear in the order given, whereas with the `all` compositor, again all elements must appear but in any order.

7. Can an empty simple type element contain any content?

Yes, text.

8. What is the difference between a simple type element and a complex type element?

Simple types cannot contain child elements or attributes.

Complex types can take child elements and/or attributes.

9. Where is an attribute declared in an XML Schema?

After the closing `sequence` compositor in a complex type.

10. How would you offer an XML author the choice between entering either a tel or email contact?

Use the `enumeration` facet.

Test 16:
1. Using XML Schema, how could you make certain that in a London telephone number, only 7 or 8 could appear after 020- in a valid XML document?

```
<pattern value="(020)-[78]\d{3}-\d{4}" />
```

2. If this was in a pattern:
`\d {3}` rather than `\d{3}` what difference would it make?

1 digit followed by three spaces, rather than 123. The space after \d is actually significant. Take great care! Also, you would need to use a string data type, not a decimal, since its character set is [0-9 + - & decimal point], no space allowed:

Appendix D

```
<simpleType name="dType">
 <restriction base="string">
   <pattern value="\d {3}"/>
  </restriction>
</simpleType>
```

3. How would you force a code number to have two leading uppercase characters in the range A-D followed by a three-digit number?

```
<pattern value="[A-D]{2}\d{3}" />
```

4. How would you force a code number to have two leading uppercase characters in the range A-D followed by a space and then by a three-digit number?

```
<pattern value="[A-D]{2} \d{3}" />
```

better still:

```
<pattern value="[A-D]{2}\s\d{3}" />
```

5. How would force a date to be in the range 1960 – 2006?
Here is a template you may like to use. The answer to Qu:5 is in bold:

```
<?xml version="1.0"?>
<schema
 xmlns="http://www.w3.org/2001/XMLSchema"
 targetNamespace="http://www.books.org"
 xmlns:L="http://www.books.org"
 elementFormDefault="qualified">
<simpleType name="fType">
  <restriction base="string">
    <pattern value="[A-D]{2} \d{3}" />
    <pattern value="\d\s{3}" />
    <pattern value="(020)-[78]\d{3}-\d{4}" />
  </restriction>
</simpleType>
```

```
<simpleType name="dType">
  <restriction base="decimal">
  <minInclusive value="1960"/>
  <maxInclusive value="2006"/>
  </restriction>
</simpleType>
<element name="book">
<complexType>
<sequence>
 <element name="fred" type="L:fType"
         maxOccurs="unbounded"/>
 <element name="DATE" type="L:dType"/>
</sequence>
</complexType>
</element>
</schema>
<!-- pattern tests -->
```

Here is the corresponding XML document:

```
<?xml version="1.0"?>
<book
xmlns="http://www.books.org"
xmlns:xsi="http://www.w3.org/2001/XMLSchema-
instance"
xsi:schemaLocation="http://www.books.org
                    pattern-tests.xsd">
         <fred>1   </fred>
         <fred>AD 123</fred>
         <fred>020-7345-1234</fred>
         <DATE>2007</DATE>
</book>
<!-- pattern-tests.xml -->
```

6. What is the difference between these three patterns:?
```
<pattern value="ab{3}"/>
<pattern value="(ab){3}"/>
<pattern value="[a|b]{3}"/>
```

- 347 -

The first is one **a** followed by three **b**s: `abbb`
The second is three sets of **ab**: `ababab`
The third is any combination of a and/or b:

`bbb  aaa  abb  bab`

Test 17:
1. When is a `simpleType` *used?*

When you wish to *restrict* any of the 44 simple data types.

2. When is a `complexType` *used?*

When an element requires attributes and/or child elements.

3. When is `ref` *used?*

When you need to reference an element which has been declared globally.

4. When is `type` *used?*

When you need to reference a user-defined data type.

5. When is `simpleContent` *used?*

When you need to extend or restrict a simple type.

6. When is `complexContent` *used?*

When you need to extend or restrict a complex type.

7. Given this: <enumeration value="Susan Smith" />
if I type <employee> Susan Smith </employee> into an XML
instance, will it be valid?

No, because there are no spaces before *Susan* and none after *Smith* in the enumeration's value.

Index

Notes:

**Notes:**